BECOMING PARTY POLITICIANS

CONTEMPORARY EUROPEAN POLITICS AND SOCIETY

Anthony Messina
series editor

BECOMING PARTY POLITICIANS

Eastern German State Legislators in the Decade following Democratization

Louise K. Davidson-Schmich

University of Notre Dame Press

Notre Dame, Indiana

Manufactured in the United States of America

Library of Congress Cataloging-in-Publication Data

Davidson-Schmich, Louise K., 1968–
Becoming party politicians : eastern German state legislators in the decade
following democratization / Louise K. Davidson-Schmich.
   p. cm. — (Contemporary European politics and society)
Includes bibliographical references and index.
ISBN-13: 978-0-268-02585-4 (pbk. : alk. paper)
ISBN-10: 0-268-02585-1 (pbk. : alk. paper)
1. Legislative bodies—Germany--States. 2. Legislators—Germany (East)—
Attitudes. 3. Legislators—Germany (West)—Attitudes. 4. Political parties—
Germany. 5. Democracy—Germany. I. Title. II. Series.
JN3971.A988D38   2006
328.43'1—dc22

                                                                    2006001549

für Klara

Contents

Tables and Figures

TABLES

FIGURES

Abbreviations and German Terms

ABBREVIATIONS FOR GERMAN STATES USED IN CODING PARLIAMENTARY TRANSCRIPTS

BAY	Bayern
BB	Brandenburg*
BLN	Berlin
BW	Baden-Württemberg
HB	Bremen
HESS	Hessen
HH	Hamburg
MVP	Mecklenburg-Vorpommern*
NRW	Nordrhein-Westfalen
NS	Niedersachsen
RLP	Rheinland-Pfalz
SA	Sachsen-Anhalt*
SAAR	Saarland
SAX	Sachsen*
SH	Schleswig-Holstein
TH	Thüringen*

* Designates an eastern state. Berlin is mixed.

OTHER ABBREVIATIONS

CDU   Christian Democratic Union

CSU   Christian Social Union

DVU   German People's Union

FDP   Free Democratic Party

GDR   German Democratic Republic

MdL   Member of a Landtag

PDS   Party of Democratic Socialism

SED   Socialist Unity Party

SPD   Social Democratic Party

SSW   South-Schleswig Voters Union

GERMAN TERMS AND THEIR ENGLISH TRANSLATIONS

Ausführungsgesetz	Implementation Law
Bescheinigung	Certification (for same-sex partnerships)
Bundesrat	Federal Council, states' representation at the national level
Bundestag	Germany's national parliament
Bundesregierung	Germany's federal government
Bürgerantrag	A nonbinding citizen petition (Bremen and Thüringen)
Bürgerbegehren	The first step in a process toward a local-level plebiscite
Bürgerentscheid	Referendum at the local level
eingetragene Lebenspartnerschaft	Legally registered life partnership
Familienbuch	Family book
Fraktion(en)	Party caucus(es)
Fraktionenparlament	A parliament dominated by party caucuses
fraktionslos	MdL without a Fraktion (an independent)

Frauen Union	The Christian Democratic women's organization
Junge Linke	The Party of Democratic Socialism's youth organization
Junge Union	The Christian Democratic youth organization
Jusos	The Social Democratic youth organization
Land/Länder	German state(s)
Landtag(e)	State parliament(s)
Lebenspartnerschaft	Life partnership
Lebenspartnerschaftsbuch (ẽer)	Life partnership book(s)
Lebenspartnerschaftsgesetz	Life Partnership Law
Lebenspartnerschaftsurkunde	Life partnership certificate
Mitglied des Landtages (MdL)	Member of a Landtag
Parlamentsreform	Parliamentary reform
Parteiverdrossenheit	Weariness or distrust of political parties
Standesamt	Registry Office
Urkunde	Certificate (as in a marriage certificate)
Vertriebenenverbände	Organizations representing ethnic Germans expelled from territories that Germans lost after World War II
Volksbegehren	The second step in the process toward a plebiscite
Volksentscheid	Referendum; the third step in a three-step process
Volkskammer	The national legislature in East Germany
Volksinitiative	The first step in a process toward a plebiscite
Volkspetition	A nonbinding citizen petition (Hamburg)

Acknowledgments

Much I have seen and known; cities of men
and manners, climates, councils, governments . . .
I am a part of all that I have met.
　　　　　　　　　—Alfred, Lord Tennyson, *Ulysses*

Like Tennyson's Ulysses, this book has been influenced by a range of factors, many of which I may not even recognize. The following acknowledgments are my attempt to explicitly thank those whose influences I do recognize, but these remarks extend to "all that this book has met." I would not have even come to write this book had it not been for Perry Rogers, who got me interested in political science, Volker Berghahn, who encouraged me to go to graduate school, and especially my parents, Alan J. and Louise C. Davidson, who instilled in me the importance of education. The idea of comparing eastern and western Germans' political behavior within identical political institutions originated in my dissertation completed at Duke University in 1999. Comments by a number of faculty members and peers at Duke, including Peter Lange, Herbert Kitschelt, Joe Grieco, Meg McKean, Diana Morlang, and Amy Poteete, helped make that project a success and inspired me to broaden the scope of my work after receiving my Ph.D.

I wish to thank the following individuals and institutions for their help in translating my initial ideas into a completed book manuscript during the intervening years. Without financial support for field research, data collection, and writing, this project would never have materialized. The University of Miami provided major sources of this funding, including two McLamore Summer Research Awards (in 2001 and 2002), a General Research Support Award in 2001, new faculty research funds, work-study students, and extensive opportunities to travel to conferences. This funding allowed me to hire excellent research assistants including Karin Hummel, Martin Kaiser, and Markus Thiel. Jason Niggley coped admirably with tedious data entry. Without their assistance, I would still be gathering and coding data.

Had members of German state parliaments not responded to my many queries, I never would have been able to come to an understanding of how political amateurs become partisan politicians. Fortunately, my experiences with parliamentarians and former parliamentarians in Berlin, Brandenburg, Mecklenburg-Vorpommern, Niedersachsen, Sachsen, Sachsen-Anhalt, and Schleswig-Holstein were all overwhelmingly positive. These politicians were extremely generous with their time and insights. They arrived at interviews on time and prepared, patiently explained to me their actions, dutifully answered what some considered strange questions, and gave me documents which proved quite valuable. All of the German state parliaments' public relations offices and archives, and their joint undertaking, *Parlamentsspiegel*, made my work much, much easier by making data on the Landtage easily available, even from thousands of miles away. I am unable to thank all of these actors by name here, but their importance for my work should be clear in the coming pages.

Living abroad for an extended period of time could become a lonely or difficult experience. I had the good fortune to have helpful friends and family accompany me for the entire time, however, making fieldwork for me an overwhelmingly positive experience. My husband, Michael, joined me as often as he could and supported my work during painful separations. Matthias and Antje Gutfleisch as well as Renée and Dirk Flibotte-Lüskow and their families all were gracious hosts when called upon, as was Ute Roericht. Lars Handrich, Karsten Grabow, and the Schmich family all made sure I did not want for company while abroad.

Perhaps the most difficult phase of this project involved making sense of the extensive data I gathered and writing up the results. My thoughts have been considerably refined by presentations at the American Political Science Association and the German Studies Association annual meetings. The University of Miami Latin American Political Economy Niche Group and the American Politics Research Workshop all went beyond the call of duty and listened to my work. Werner Patzelt and members of his *Lehrstuhl*, including Ute Roericht and Helmar Schöne, welcomed me at the Technical University of Dresden. The quality of the feedback I received at all of these talks was extraordinarily high, and I thank all who attended.

Furthermore, a number of individuals have read all or parts of this manuscript and I have benefited immensely from their comments. Comments from Pete Moore helped to broaden chapters 1 and 6. Feedback from Gerhard Lehmbruch helped to greatly improve chapter 2, as did comments by Diana Morlang and Ken Shadlen. Reuven Hazan and David Olson along with other members of the International Political Science Association's Research Committee of Legislative Specialists offered extensive advice on multiple drafts of chapter 3. Many thanks to Frank Rehmet of Mehr Demokratie e.V. for his data regarding direct democracy attempts in Germany and for his comments on chapter 4. Peter Finger provided valuable information for chapter 5, and members of the German Studies Association including Joyce Mushaben, Art Gunlicks, and David P. Conradt were helpful in responding to an earlier draft of this chapter. Peter Lange provided useful advice on the project as a whole. Comments from two anonymous reviewers on the first draft of the entire book improved the final version immensely, as did editorial assistance from Matt Dowd. The book would never have seen the light of day, however, if Tony Messina and Barbara Hanrahan from the University of Notre Dame had not put their faith in this project; I thank them for their support.

Last but certainly not least, I would like to thank my husband Michael and daughter Klara. Michael has stood by my side every step of my career, moving with me to the tropical heat of south Florida and to the depths of eastern Germany, giving me encouragement when my spirits were flagging, celebrating when things went well, and patiently waiting for me to return when I went abroad or to conferences. He helped me translate correspondence into German and plenary transcripts into English. Most of all he respected how important this project was to me and always let me know how important I was to him. Without his encouragement I would have never completed this book. It is, however, to Klara that I dedicate this book. Thank you for giving me an incentive to finish the manuscript, and for waiting to come until I had completed the first draft.

chapter 1

Eastern German State Legislators' Political Attitudes and the Party State

While the Berlin Wall and East-West German border clearly embodied the dividing line between western Europe and eastern Europe prior to 1989, post-unification eastern Germany is much more difficult for scholars to categorize.[1] Academics within the field of German studies, originally focused on West Germany, tend to view the eastern part of the united country and its inhabitants as being more politically unlike western Germans than alike. More broadly focused comparativists and eastern Europeanists, in contrast, often exclude eastern Germany from their analyses of post-communist Europe because the unification of Germany, with its concurrent adoption of the Federal Republic's established political system, is assumed to have made eastern German politics more closely resemble public life in western Europe than in a post-communist country.

These differing outlooks are likely a result of their proponents' contrasting vantage points. Viewing eastern Germany from the outside, eastern Europeanists focus on the presence of identical political *institutions*—including the Basic Law's parliamentary, electoral, and legal systems, as well as the existence of established political parties. Not only did eastern Germany enjoy the advantage of inheriting a "ready made state" (Rose et al. 1993), this institutional transfer was supported by extensive human and financial resources. Clearly, eastern Germany is unique among post-Soviet states in this regard and thus has been referred to as an "advanced post-communist society" (Padgett 2000, 25).

Because scholars in this camp assume united Germany's political institutions will shape political outcomes, eastern German political elites are expected to more closely resemble established western European politicians than elites in a post-communist polity.[2] From the vantage point of German area specialists, however, the eastern individuals who occupy these identical political institutions have very different *political attitudes and values* than their western counterparts. Given that they were socialized under extremely different political conditions, eastern and western Germans' different political values are not surprising. The school of thought stressing elites' socialization and their resulting political attitudes in turn assumes that differing political attitudes will lead to different political outcomes in the eastern and western parts of the Federal Republic.[3]

The eastern German case is unique across Europe in that it allows social scientists to empirically test these conflicting assumptions about the causes of elite political behavior and policy choice. In western Europe, established democratic political institutions are inhabited by elites whose political attitudes and values have been shaped by decades of experience with democracy. In eastern Europe, in contrast, democratic political institutions are only emerging, and political elites hold post-communist political attitudes and values. In these two settings, it is not possible for social scientists to determine whether elite behavior and political outcomes are a result of institutional constraints or elite values. United Germany, in contrast, offers researchers a "laboratory"-like setting (Rohrschneider 1994) with near experimental conditions to investigate these questions. There politicians with very different attitudes and values work within virtually identical political institutions—institutions whose incentives are often at odds with post-communist political elites' values. If elite political behavior and public policy converge across the united country, institutions would seem to override the influence of elite attitudes and values. Conversely, if eastern political elites' political behavior and resulting policy choices differ greatly from westerners', even though the two groups occupy identical political institutions, elite attitudes would seem to have a stronger influence.

This book focuses on state parliamentarians in eastern and western German Länder in the decade since unification and explores the conflicting implications for legislative behavior of the two perspectives outlined above. These state legislators' political attitudes and values have been extensively investigated by both English- and German-speaking social scientists. I draw on their well-established findings about the differences between eastern and western legislators' political attitudes and values, and ask whether these beliefs have actually influenced politicians' legislative behavior and policy choices. (See table 1.1.) Specifically, I investigate whether eastern parliamentarians' skepticism of political parties reduced their willingness to run on a party ticket, assume inner-party office, or join an interest group affiliated with their party; whether eastern deputies' widespread distrust of party discipline hindered the creation of disciplined parliamentary party groups; whether eastern elites' preferences for direct democracy and social equality led eastern states to create constitutions more conducive to referenda than western states' and to more enthusiastically embrace citizen initiatives designed to bring about greater economic equality; and whether eastern legislators' political intolerance led them to deny rights to a disliked group.

Why Study German State Parliaments?

In October 1990 the eastern German Democratic Republic (GDR) was dissolved and joined the western democracy, the Federal Republic of Germany. The latter provided a reservoir of experienced individuals to fill leadership positions in politics, public administration, law, business, and other fields. A 1995 study of German elites in various sectors found fewer than 12% to be of eastern German origin, although approximately 20% of the German population lived in the GDR prior to 1989; of all the sectors, politics had the highest representation of easterners at 32%. Nonetheless, the more important the political office, the less eastern Germans were represented. Only 9.5% of the federal executive and 16.7% of the Bundestag's party leadership were eastern Germans.[4] Ten years after unification, two of the five governors of eastern German states were westerners as were about 40% of the ministers in state governments (Hoffmann-Lange 1998, 153).

It is only when one reaches the level of state parliaments that virtually all politicians are eastern Germans: since 1990, 95.6% of the people elected to eastern state legislatures were easterners.[5] Thus in order to examine the interplay between eastern German political elites' attitudes

Table 1.1   Eastern state legislators' political attitudes, institutions, political behavior, and policy outcomes

Easterners' attitudes	Western institutions	Political behavior/ public policy examined	Result
Distrust of political parties	The party state including a ready-made party system and an electoral system conducive to a high level of party involvement	Do eastern candidates join political parties, hold inner-party office, or join party-affiliated interest groups at the same rate as westerners?	Convergence toward the western model over the course of a decade.
Distrust of party discipline	Parliamentary and electoral systems conducive to a high level of party voting	Once elected, do eastern legislators vote with their party group at the same rate as westerners?	Convergence on the western model over the course of a decade.
Support for direct democracy	Highly representative form of democracy with only limited provisions for direct democracy; increasing budget constraints	Did eastern state constitutions provide for more direct democracy than western ones? In practice, have eastern parliamentarians supported referenda attempts more often than westerners especially vis-à-vis direct democracy and economic equality?	Eastern constitutions were *slightly* more conducive to referenda than western ones, but the partisan composition of government best explains institutional choice; over the course of a decade majorities oppose referenda initiatives while opposition parties support them. The same is true in the west.
Support for a large government role in ensuring economic equality			
Political intolerance	EU and federal policies requiring a minimal level of rights for gays and lesbians; Basic Law sets upper bound on rights	Have eastern parliamentarians been less willing than westerners to extend rights to a disliked group, in this case gays and lesbians?	In both eastern and western states, the partisanship of government rather than east/ west origin of deputies predicts rights extended.

and united Germany's political institutions, I focus on these subnational parliaments. German unification created five new federal states out of what had been the German Democratic Republic; at the same time, eastern Berlin became part of the already-existing city-state Berlin. The five eastern Länder created at unification include Brandenburg, Mecklenburg-Vorpommern, Sachsen, Sachsen-Anhalt, and Thüringen. Each of these new states was to be governed by a democratically elected state legislature, or Landtag; each state modeled its legislature and electoral system on a western partner state's. Their western partners were, respectively, Niedersachsen, Schleswig-Holstein, Baden-Württemberg, Nordrhein-Westfalen, and Rheinland-Pfalz. There are five additional western German Länder: Bayern, Bremen, Hamburg, Hessen, and the Saarland. The parliamentarians serving in these sixteen state legislatures are usually called Mitglieder des Landtages (MdL).

The Landtage are politically important in Germany's federal system because they can address regional concerns not dealt with at the national level, influence national-level politics through their executive's representation in the Bundesrat, shape the implementation of federal laws, and control education, the police, and the media. Since the initial Landtag election in 1990 there have been three further rounds of state-level elections. The first was held in 1994, the second in 1998 (in Mecklenburg-Vorpommern and Sachsen-Anhalt) and 1999 (in Brandenburg, Sachsen, and Thüringen), and the third rounds in 2002 and 2004.[6] The following analysis is based on events in the eastern Landtage and their partners between the former's creation in 1990 and the year 2002.

I study the effects of eastern legislators' antiparty sentiment, their skepticism of party discipline, their support for referenda and economic equality, and their political intolerance because these are the main areas in which extensive empirical research has determined that eastern and western German elites differ. Because their attitudes diverge most sharply in these areas, my argument that institutions—rather than values—shape elite political outcomes is most difficult to prove in these cases. If attitudinal factors are found to have little impact in the areas where Germans differ the most, it is unlikely that they will be of import in shaping other facets of elite political behavior. What I do *not* seek to do here is explain where the causal origin of these different attitudes and values lies; as will become clear in the chapters ahead, this topic has been extensively researched by others. Instead, I am simply concerned with what effect—if any—differing attitudes and values have on German parliamentarians' political behavior.

The cases chosen here were also selected to minimize the influence of the west's superior resources. All were instances where eastern legislatures had the maximum possible leverage over their own affairs and were relatively independent of western pressure. For example, I deliberately did not investigate policy areas where states had to take a stance in the Bundesrat that would influence national-level politics, nor did I examine areas such as taxation and spending that would have an influence on other Länder through Germany's system of fiscal federalism. In these areas western actors may indeed have used their superior economic resources to pressure easterners into acting a certain way. This was decidedly not the case in the issues under study here, however.

In Germany, state-level parties serve as the selectorate for the Landtage and candidates are elected by eastern voters. Thus individual politicians deciding which affiliations to pursue to gain an eastern state legislative seat are not subject to the concerns of westerners. Similarly, unlike deputies in the Bundestag, who are in a setting dominated by westerners, members of state parliaments were in caucuses made up overwhelmingly of eastern politicians. Whether party discipline was practiced at the state level or not was of little interest to national-level party organizations or other western-dominated bodies. While there was a national-level debate over direct democracy at the federal level, eastern state constitutions' rules governing plebiscites did not apply beyond state borders and were thus not of pressing importance to western party leaders. In the subsequent decade, whether eastern parliaments supported referenda in areas delegated to the Länder (such as education or state-level direct democracy) was also of little interest at the national level. Finally, while the same-sex partnership law was indeed an initiative of the governing coalition at the federal level, it was not a priority of the Social Democrats; instead, they were pressured into adopting the law by their Green coalition partner. At the time the Landtage had to implement this law, however, the Greens were not represented in any eastern state parliament and the ambivalent national-level Social Democrats did not exert discernable pressure on state-level parties to implement the law in certain ways. In all of these cases, then, eastern German politicians faced little direct pressure from westerners to behave in a certain way and instead are likely to have been motivated by the incentives inherent in the party state's institutions.

GERMAN STATE LEGISLATORS'
POLITICAL ATTITUDES AND VALUES

The research done on eastern and western Germans' political attitudes and values has identified five main areas of difference between both mass publics and political elites in each part of the country. Here I only briefly summarize these findings; the coming chapters will more thoroughly review this literature. First, opinion research has found that eastern Germans' experiences with decades of dictatorship by an all encompassing political party led them to distrust political parties even more than an increasingly skeptical western German electorate. This is true both at the mass and elite levels. As a result of this skepticism, parties across eastern Germany have fewer members and less-active inner-party organizations than their western counterparts—despite the best efforts of the major parties to develop such organizations. In addition to these societal trends, a majority of individuals considered electable after unification spent the pre-unification period either avoiding political life or high profile roles within the communist party and its allies. Thus while western German state legislators are consummate party politicians, the easterners elected to state parliaments following unification distrusted political parties and had little partisan political experience.

Second, attitudinal research has found that eastern politicians and their voters are skeptical of strict party discipline and united in their belief that common interests should outweigh partisan concerns when legislation is made. Political life in East Germany revolved around the practice of democratic centralism, which called for unquestioning adherence to decisions made by communist party elites. Those politicians and individuals who dared criticize the Socialist Unity Party (SED) and went against its iron discipline suffered personal and career setbacks, imprisonment, exile, or worse. As a result of these experiences, easterners strongly mistrust decisions made along party lines. A majority of those who were elected to eastern German state legislatures in 1990 had previously been apolitical professionals including doctors, teachers, veterinarians, and engineers. Some other new parliamentarians had been involved in the Roundtables which spontaneously emerged as communism crumbled; these bodies were set up expressly to oppose hierarchical, party-oriented decision making. These legislators had been trained to seek consensual or pragmatic technical solutions to problems rather than to engage in partisan debates. Their attitudes differ sharply from western German legislators' views, which are far more supportive of partisan competition.

Third, public opinion surveys of both German elites and the mass public have discerned that, while both eastern and western Germans favor democracy as a form of government, they have very different understandings of the term. In studies of mass attitudes toward democracy in Germany, easterners were found to be much more in favor of holding referenda to decide issues than were westerners; the latter were more comfortable with representative democracy. Similarly, the main difference between German elites' conceptions of democracy lay in their assessment of plebiscitary elements. When asked whether the adoption of referenda was a necessary supplement to representative democracy, eastern elites were more than twice as likely as westerners to favor plebiscites. Easterners' abundant support for direct democracy has been attributed to their experiences during the peaceful revolution that brought down the GDR. New Forum and the citizens' movements that brought down the communist regime were strong supporters of direct democracy, and their success legitimized direct democracy, in the eyes of eastern Germans.

Fourth, opinion surveys at both the mass and elite levels in eastern and western Germany have consistently found that eastern Germans hold socialist or planned economic values, whereas their western counterparts are much more strongly in favor of a market or social market economy. When asked what role the government should play in reducing income differentials among citizens, easterners are much more strongly in favor of government action than their western counterparts. These attitudes are not limited to the eastern German mass public, however. In a study of Berlin parliamentarians, eastern deputies expressed more support for government intervention in the economy and less support for unlimited profit and large income differentials than western elites. In all party families, western parliamentarians were more supportive of a market economy than their eastern colleagues; furthermore, eastern Christian Democratic Union (CDU) and Free Democratic Party (FDP) deputies' views of a market economy were closer to western Social Democratic Party (SPD) members' views than to members of the western branches of their own parties. There is considerable debate within this literature as to the origins of these attitudinal differences. Some scholars have argued that these results occur despite individuals' personal economic situation given their socialization in the GDR, while others believe that pocketbook assessments condition—at least in part—easterners' support for economic equality; still others argue that these differences result primarily from easterners' experiences as an economically disadvantaged group in united Germany. Despite their disagreements, all authors agree that significant attitudinal differences vis-à-vis the desirability of economic equality exist among Germans.

The fifth and final east/west attitudinal difference discussed here has to do with the willingness of both mass publics and political elites in Germany to "put up with what they don't like" by extending rights to disliked groups. This willingness, also called political tolerance, is a key component of a democratic political culture. Competitive elections and respect for all citizens' democratic rights and liberties are unlikely in a context where people are not willing to extend freedoms to those they dislike. Political tolerance has been widely studied in established democracies, and the introduction of public opinion surveys to eastern Europe after the fall of communism led to a number of investigations of political tolerance there as well. Mass levels of tolerance in eastern Europe were consistently found to be lower than in established democracies. Multiple studies have found that this intolerance also extended to eastern German citizens and political elites. For example, eastern citizens and parliamentarians were less likely than their western counterparts to favor allowing disliked groups to exercise freedom of speech. Explanations for lower levels of political tolerance in post-communist settings include Stalinist era indoctrination, the communist party's encouragement of citizens to show intolerance toward regime opponents, citizens' lack of opportunity to exercise tolerance for most of the twentieth century, and low levels of post-materialism in this part of Europe.

Thus eastern and western German mass publics and, the focus here, political elites differ greatly in terms of their political attitudes and values. When compared to their western counterparts, eastern German politicians entered office more skeptical of political parties, party discipline, representative democracy, the desirability of economic inequality, and political tolerance.

United Germany's Political Institutions and Elite Political Behavior

These well-established findings on eastern German political elites' attitudes raise, but fail to answer, a significant question: do eastern and western German politicians' contrasting values actually matter in terms of their political behavior and substantive policy choices? While it seems plausible that easterners will act in accordance with their beliefs, each of the five sets of eastern attitudes discussed above are at odds with the incentives created by the political institutions that eastern Germans inherited with unification. As a result, easterners acting in accordance with antiparty or antidiscipline beliefs are likely to find themselves marginalized or even excluded from political life, while some MdL also face strong disincentives to support plebiscites or to deny rights to disliked groups. An examination of united Germany's political institutions shows how they clash with the attitudes and values eastern parliamentarians brought with them to office.

The Party State and Politicians' Affiliations

Political parties play such a strong role in the German form of democracy that Germany has often been called a "party state":

> The Federal Republic is a functioning, stable party state. . . . The West German political parties tend to interpret this sentence of the Constitution, "The parties are to take part in forming the political will of the people," as their exclusive party privilege. . . . In fact, all political decisions in the Federal Republic are made by the parties and their representatives. There are no political decisions of importance in the German democracy which have not been brought to the parties, prepared by them and finally taken by them. This does not mean that other social groups have no power but that they have to realize their power within the party state. (Sontheimer 1973, 95)

With unification, eastern Germans inherited not only the institutions of the party state but also a well-established, well-funded party system. Germany's dual electoral system is a key component of the party state and provides many incentives for state-level politicians not only to join but to take an active role in a political party. At least half of the candidates elected to state legislatures are elected via party lists;[7] the exact percentage varies from state to state. As a result, candidates not affiliated with a political party cannot easily receive seats vis-à-vis the "second vote." The rest of the candidates are elected via single member districts.

While it is possible to run as an independent candidate in an electoral district, such candidates face stiff competition from members running on established parties' tickets. The latter enjoy the "brand" recognition that the party label offers them along with public funding for campaigns, monies given in Germany only to political parties. Finally, independent legislators have fewer rights in parliament than do members of a party caucus. As a result, independent candidates are less able to translate constituent wishes into public policy, reducing their attractiveness to voters.

Thus in order to win a seat in one of united Germany's state legislatures, a politician generally must be affiliated with a political party. Those individuals whose antiparty sentiment is so strong that they refuse to join a party are quickly excluded from political life by these institutional mechanisms. In order to run on a party ticket, however, an individual must do more than simply decide to adopt a party label. In Germany, party organizations control the nominations for coveted district mandates and top spots on party lists. As a result, ambitious politicians must prove their loyalty to their party by taking on inner-party positions, holding local-level offices for their political parties, and possibly becoming active in an affiliated interest association if they are to be nominated and subsequently elected. It is this process that has produced loyal party politicians in western Germany since the founding of the Federal Republic and, I argue, has begun to produce a cadre of partisan politicians in the eastern German state legislatures as well. Those individuals who have not acted in accordance with these incentives, and instead followed their antiparty beliefs, have not been selected to run for state-level office.

To trace eastern legislators' growing involvement with political parties I rely on the biographical data that the nearly 2500 state legislators under study were required to publish about themselves in the Handbook of each state parliament. This discussion and all others in the book are supplemented with material drawn from thirty-seven personal interviews with legislators representing all parties in seven different eastern and western Landtage. During the summer of 2001, I interviewed caucus leaders from each party in the state legislatures of Schleswig-Holstein, Mecklenburg-Vorpommern, Niedersachsen, Brandenburg, Sachsen, and Sachsen-Anhalt. I also interviewed the Social Democratic whip in Berlin as well as newspaper reporters who covered state parliaments for the *Kieler Nachrichten, Nordkurier,* and the *Sächsische*

Zeitung. In the text I identify these interviewees using their state and party affiliation. See Appendix A for a complete list of individual interviews. The interviews took a semistructured format; the section of the interviews relevant here concerned relationships between parliamentary party groups and groups outside the Landtag, including the party outside parliament, local officials, and interest groups. Rather than tape-recording the interviews, a practice which in previous research distracted some eastern respondents, I took detailed interview notes. The quotes presented in the text are drawn from these records.

The Party State and Party Discipline

While eastern legislators may run for office on a party ticket and be personally involved with their political party, this is not a guarantee that they will always vote with their parliamentary party group once in office. In western German Landtage, however, the party state manifests itself in a very high rate of disciplined voting. Again, though, this type of elite political behavior is starkly at odds with eastern mass and elite preference for technically correct, nonpartisan decision making. Despite these attitudes, the institutions of the party state offer ambitious politicians strong incentives to vote with their party caucus once elected.

The first incentive, of course, is the fact that in a parliamentary system the governing party or parties in the legislature must stand behind their chief executive and cabinet, or the government can fall (Gallagher, Laver, and Mair 2001). In order for opposition parties to provide voters with clear-cut alternatives to a disciplined majority, they too must act coherently in the legislature. Even scholars studying presidential systems where such executive branch instability is not a problem find that in the absence of legislative parties, new majorities would have to be cobbled together to pass each piece of legislation—a highly inefficient practice (Aldrich 1995). By joining a parliamentary party, MdL can rely on the expertise of other caucus members to guide their voting on issues about which they know little and simultaneously find allies who will support their positions on issues of importance to them (Cox 1987). Without coherent legislative parties, then, parliamentary work would be inefficient and uncertain. Moreover, the German system contains a number of resources and rules of procedure that enable such efficiency to occur. If individual members of a German state parliament want to have access to the resources and opportunities needed to influence policy, they are best associated with a party caucus. Further, if a party group hopes to pass the legislation it drafts, it must stand together when votes are taken.

The German political system also includes electoral factors promoting united legislative parties. In all but one state, between 50% and 100% of parliamentarians are elected via the list form of the proportional representation electoral system. In all but one state, voters must vote for a party and cannot alter the rank ordering of candidates on the ballot. Party members nominate candidates for places on electoral lists and are unlikely to select people who have consistently gone against their own party. Further, voters have little incentive to vote for a party whose caucus does not stand together in the legislature because they cannot predict what that party will do. Thus even the legislators who win constituency seats may find their electoral chances dimmed if their caucus is divided amongst itself or at odds with other branches of the party. All MdL, then, have incentives to vote with their party. If they do not toe their party's line, and instead act in accordance with their preference for consensus or cross-party decision making, they will likely not be returned to office.

Empirical investigation finds that eastern state legislators have indeed learned this lesson over the course of the past decade. The rise of disciplined voting in eastern legislatures was established by coding over 10,000 floor votes taken in 1991, 1996, and 2000. These votes are recorded in the transcripts of Landtag plenary sessions; the latter are available for all western states dating back to the founding of the Federal Republic and for all eastern states since 1990 from the German Parliamentary Information System called *Parlamentsspiegel*. This analysis was also supplemented by personal interviews with parliamentary whips, interviews that revolved around decision making on the floor of parliament, within parliamentary committees, in party caucuses, between coalition partners, and between the executive and the legislative branches.

The Party State, Direct Democracy, and Economic Equality

The party state's power extends not just to the procedural—*how* legislative decisions are made—but also to the substantive—*what* decisions are made. Germany's well-funded political parties have many resources to devote to developing public policies, and branches of the same party work across state lines to coordinate their party's position on issues relating to the Länder. This practice was common in the west before unification and simply expanded to incorporate eastern branches of the same party after unification. Thus parliamentarians who have adopted roles within their parties, and who vote along party lines, are likely to select the same public policies across states, regardless of whether these states are located in eastern or western Germany. One way to empirically verify this assertion is to examine cases where, based on their initial attitudes, one would expect state legislators in the two parts of Germany—regardless of party—to adopt different issue stances. Given Germans' varying attitudes toward direct democracy, economic equality, and political tolerance, ideal test cases of this hypothesis would involve policy implementation in these areas.

One of the first tasks with which eastern state legislatures were charged was drafting state constitutions, which regulated, among other things, the laws governing direct democratic procedures in their Länder. The Federal Republic's political institutions are highly representative; at the national level in Germany there is no provision for referenda. At the time of unification, some western German state constitutions contained no provisions for plebiscites, while others had very restrictive procedures. Given easterners' pro–direct democracy attitudes and the fact that they had free reign to determine the rules governing referenda in their states, it might be expected that the five new states' constitutions were likely to be much more conducive to direct democracy than western states'. To a limited extent this was indeed the case. In contrast to the west, all eastern states adopted some form of direct democracy in their constitutions. Furthermore, although the procedures they chose were marginally more friendly to citizen initiatives than the western model, the overall form of direct democracy selected by easterners paralleled the western Länder's restrictive model.

The specific details of the adopted model—as would be expected in the party state—fell along partisan lines. Just as at the national level and in western states, Christian Democratic/Free Democratic coalitions favored the most restrictive possible rules governing referenda, whereas Social Democrats and especially the Greens and members of the Party of Democratic Socialism (PDS) advocated institutions more conducive to plebiscites. Thus the form of direct democracy ultimately adopted in state constitutions can be explained to a considerable degree by the partisanship of the coalition drafting the constitutions.

When confronted with citizen initiatives throughout the 1990s, governing parties in eastern Germany—just as their counterparts in western states—fought to keep political decision making in parliamentary, rather than citizen, hands. This allowed the majority party (or coalition) in the Landtag to retain the control over policy making that it otherwise would have enjoyed in the Federal Republic's highly representative party democracy. Across Germany only opposition parties—regardless of partisanship—came out in favor of citizen initiatives as a way to curry favor with voters and to critique the governing party or parties. Since strong party discipline limits the ability of the parliamentary opposition to influence public policy, supporting citizen initiatives is also one of the few ways the opposition might actually be able to affect policy change.

When the substantive content of direct democratic initiatives over the course of the past decade is examined, it becomes clear that these findings are especially relevant to the hypothesis that Germany's party state, rather than easterners' political attitudes and values, is the main determinant of political decision making in the new Landtage. Over half of citizen attempts at referenda involved demands that the government either allow greater direct democracy or become more involved in the economy. But rather than embracing such initiatives, as their initial attitudes and values would suggest, eastern state legislatures proved just as resistant to these initiatives as their western counterparts. Majority parties and coalitions—regardless of partisanship—routinely refused to adopt policies put forth by citizens, legally challenged the validity of petitions put toward them, and campaigned vigorously against citizen-sponsored referenda. Just as in the west, only opposition parties favored these citizen initiatives. Thus in terms of direct democracy and social equality, MdL's partisan affiliation and their status as government or opposition better explain their policy stances than do their eastern or western origin. Parliamentarians were consistently more swayed by their institutional position than their political attitudes and values.

The extent to which state constitutions embrace direct democracy is based on data collected by the University of Marburg and the pro-plebiscite organization Mehr Demokratie e.V. The political debates that led up to these choices are traced by examining parliamentary debates over the drafting of state constitutions in 1990. Eastern states' actual experience with direct democracy is based on Mehr Demokratie's archive of attempted citizen initiatives. These sources of data were supplemented with personal interviews with parliamentarians focusing on their attitudes toward direct democracy, economic equality, and various citizen initiatives.

The Party State and Political Tolerance

Given that easterners have been found to have politically less tolerant attitudes than westerners, that is, they say they are less willing to extend rights to disliked groups, a second ideal test of the above hypothesis would be one involving choices about whether to actually grant civil rights to an unpopular group. The issue of same-sex unions offers just such a case study.[8] In 2001, Germany's federal government passed a domestic partnership law that the Länder were required to implement, although each state enjoyed some leeway as to how many of the rights enjoyed by heterosexual couples would be granted to same-sex pairs in their Land. If easterners had acted on their intolerant beliefs, they would have extended homosexual couples fewer rights than their more politically tolerant western counterparts.

However, there is evidence from established democracies that the relationship between political (in)tolerance and (un)democratic public policy, assumed by those who document politically intolerant attitudes, may not always exist. There are several institutional reasons to expect that the low average level of political intolerance among post-communist citizens may not always translate directly into intolerant public policy. First, in representative democracies like Germany, policy is actually made by political elites, not mass publics. In established democracies learning within democratic political institutions has been shown to shape the political tolerance of elected officials over time; elites are often more tolerant than ordinary citizens. Rather than being homogeneously tolerant, however, elites within long-established democracies have exhibited a wide range of opinions, suggesting that eastern German parliamentarians too are far from uniformly intolerant. In long-term democracies, elite political tolerance is often closely related to ideology or party affiliation. Given the importance of political parties in Germany's party state, and given easterners' proven willingness to join political parties, to vote with their party's Fraktion, and to support policies put forth by their national-level party organization, government partisanship rather than the eastern or western origin of deputies determined policy outcomes. While leftist majorities across Germany extended the most rights to gays and lesbians, rightist coalitions in east and west had the most restrictive laws.

Furthermore, state legislators were constrained by their subordinate institutional position in Germany's federal system. Politically tolerant MdL complained that the national law did not go far enough in extending rights to homosexuals but were not in a position to change the laws promulgated at the federal level. Similarly, politically intolerant statelevel actors tried but failed to stop implementation of a national law of which they completely disapproved. Politically intolerant easterners *and* westerners were forced to accept EU and German Supreme Court decisions allowing same-sex partnerships to be registered in their states. In other words, political institutions were a vital intervening variable between levels of political tolerance and public policy.

The relationship between political tolerance and policy outcomes was assessed by consulting three sources. First, the public debate over the Life Partnership Law and its progress through German political institutions were traced by reading contemporary newspaper articles. Second, partisan positions were determined by reading the transcripts of parliamentary debates on the various laws. Third, resulting policies were categorized according to the texts of the laws ultimately passed.

PLAN OF THE BOOK

In all of the above cases, I find that although they had some impact in the immediate post-unification period, eastern and western German politicians' attitudinal differences became increasingly irrelevant in the following decade as easterners learned the incentives involved in the political system they inherited at unification. United Germany's political institutions—collectively known as the party state—have made eastern parliamentarians today virtually indistinguishable from their western counterparts in terms of their willingness to become involved with political parties, to vote in line with their party caucus, to favor representative democracy and legislative control over economic and other policy areas, and to extend rights to disliked groups. Despite their differing socialization, eastern and western German state legislators today are all party politicians, and their choice of policies can be predicted by the partisanship of the state parliament rather than its geographic location in eastern or western Germany. The following five chapters trace the party state's transformative effect on eastern state legislators.

Chapter 2 examines MdL's relationships to their political parties in the form of holding inner-party office, occupying partisan political office outside the Landtag, and being involved with affiliated interest groups. This chapter establishes the electoral incentives that state legislators have to become party politicians and shows how eastern German parliamentarians have acted on these incentives, despite their initial skepticism of political parties.

Chapter 3 goes on to ask whether the kinds of partisan affiliations described in the previous chapter have had an influence on legislators' decision making while in office. It finds that this is indeed the case, tracing the rise of disciplined party voting in eastern legislatures between 1991 and 2000, despite easterners' professed resistance to party discipline after decades of dictatorship by an all-encompassing political party.

Chapter 4 in turn asks whether party voting has had an impact on public policy. This was indeed the case as early as the drafting of the eastern state constitutions immediately following unification. In terms of provisions for direct democracy, eastern legislative parties paralleled the national branches of their respective parties' stances, despite their greater attitudinal support for the practice. In the subsequent decade, although they were more supportive of social equality and direct democracy, eastern governing majorities—like their western counterparts—have not been supportive of citizen initiatives, even those in favor of greater direct democracy or more state involvement in the economy.

Chapter 5 examines the implementation of Germany's same-sex partnership law across the German states. Both in the eastern and in the western parts of the country implementation laws varied along partisan—rather than east/west—lines, despite varying degrees of political tolerance in the two parts of Germany.

Chapter 6 concludes by discussing the mechanisms through which the party state has trumped MdL's attitudes and values. It also addresses the implications of these findings both for the discipline of political science and for German politics. Finally, it offers some thoughts on the possibility of successful institutional transfer in settings beyond Germany.

Becoming Party Politicians: Eastern German State Legislators' Ties to Political Parties

Political parties play such a strong role in Germany that its form of democracy has been dubbed the party state (Sontheimer 1973, 95). This chapter examines the party careers of state legislators (MdL) in eastern Germany since unification extended the western German party state eastward. Under the Federal Republic's electoral and parliamentary systems, western MdL have been recruited through three main channels: via party office, through other partisan public office, and via voluntary groups affiliated with political parties. I investigate whether, since they were elected in 1990, eastern German MdL have become involved with political parties and related interest groups to the same degree as westerners. I further study whether candidates subsequently elected to the Landtage have followed this pattern. Most of the literature on the party-political involvement of political elites in post-communist countries has focused on politicians' experiences prior to the fall of communism[1] or has studied their party political involvement at a fixed point in time during the 1990s—usually early in the decade.[2] This chapter offers a fresh perspective because it examines parliamentarians' party careers *after* the transition to democracy, and it does so *dynamically*, spanning the entire decade.

Whether a class of party politicians has emerged in a post-communist setting is of further interest because it taps into an overarching debate in comparative politics about the viability of traditional western European political institutions in contemporary society. Increased levels of education, the rise of Parteiverdrossenheit, the declining membership in political parties and voluntary associations, and the rise of "American style" media driven campaigns in western Germany in recent decades have led some observers to question whether the party state model is relevant to western German society any more. Strong grassroots party organizations tightly connected to voluntary associations seem anachronistic, in which case individual politicians may see little utility in cultivating ties to these groups. If this true in western Germany, it is even more so the case in eastern Germany. Decades of dictatorship by the SED heightened public distrust of political parties, and as a result party membership is low and inner-party organizations are weak. Similarly, after decades of coerced participation in "voluntary" organizations such as youth groups and unions, many eastern Germans view democracy as the chance *not* to get involved in interest groups; membership in such associations is low in eastern Germany. Further, many easterners are wary of close party–interest group ties after having experienced first-hand the repressive results of the SED's domination of the latter organizations. The societal conditions for the party state seem therefore not to exist in eastern Germany and may be disappearing in the west as well.

Nevertheless, John Aldrich's 1995 work on the origin of political parties in the United States—also a context quite inhospitable to "factions" at the time parties formed—provides many reasons to expect that despite the incompatibility of the party state with eastern German *society* as a whole, *politicians* interested in a political career may nevertheless find incentives to become active in party and interest groups. Aldrich observes of the twentieth century United States, "in this age of party decline and candidate-centered elections, politicians' affiliation with a major party . . . increased. . . . Why then are politicians affiliating with major parties more today, if they need them less? Presumably they do *not* need them less, regardless of party decline and candidate-centered elections" (52).

Parties, he argues, offer what Schlesinger (1975) calls office-seeking politicians a number of benefits to help improve their chances of (re)election. Thus once political parties form, they create self-perpetuating institutional equilibriums. Candidates affiliated with a party have a higher chance of (re)election than those who are not, so the number of candidates choosing to run on a party ticket will grow, rather than shrink. Aldrich's analysis of the American case closely fits the eastern German context. There ambitious politicians inherited an established party system, ready-made to help them get (re)elected. While these parties may not have attracted widespread *mass* membership in eastern Germany, Aldrich's logic suggests that eastern *politicians* will face the same incentives as their western counterparts to affiliate with political parties and related interest groups.

Indeed, I find that over the course of their careers in state parliaments, eastern MdL have come to look more and more like westerners. They are more likely to hold office within their political party than they were in 1990, more likely to have held partisan political office other than their seat in the state capital, and are more likely to have cultivated ties to a voluntary organization than they were initially. Although differences remain, there are increasing similarities between western and eastern German state legislators in terms of their ties to political parties and interest groups. I develop these conclusions as follows: First, I will elaborate how the logic of the party state aids politicians in their quest for (re)election, even in a societal context inhospitable to political parties. Second, using information from public documents, I will investigate German state parliamentarians' ties to parties and voluntary organizations in the decade since unification. Third, I will conclude by discussing the cause and significance of these findings.

THE PARTY STATE AND THE EASTERN GERMAN LÄNDER

Sociological Factors and Elite Recruitment

Under the Federal Republic's electoral and parliamentary institutions, western state parliamentarians have been recruited through three main channels: via party office, through other partisan public office, and via voluntary groups affiliated with political parties (Kaltefleiter 1976; von Beyme 1986; Patzelt 1995; Saalfeld 1997). These channels stem from the Social Democrats' and Christian Democrats' pasts as mass (Neumann 1990) or catch-all (Kirchheimer 1990) parties with large memberships, extensive inner-party organizations, and close ties to interest groups. As western German society has changed since the 1950s, however, political parties and voluntary organizations have become less central to individuals' lives. Furthermore, post-communist eastern Germany has proved inhospitable to grassroots parties closely tied to interest associations. When only these sociological factors are taken into consideration, the future of the above-mentioned recruitment channels looks uncertain at best.

In recent years, the mass/catch-all party has begun to disappear in established democracies; some observers have proclaimed that societies with high levels of education and pervasive media—societies like western and eastern Europe—are increasingly characterized by new types of political parties (Panebianco 1988; Katz and Mair 1995; Dalton and Wattenberg 2000). In eighteen OECD (Organisation for Economic Cooperation and Development) countries between the 1950s and the 1990s partisanship among voters declined (Dalton 2000; Gallagher, Laver, and Mair 2001, 258) and voters increasingly paid attention to individual candidates and issues rather than party labels (Dalton, McAllister, and Wattenberg 2000; Sjöblom 1983, 385; Van Biezen 2002, 16). As voter interest in parties declined, so did party membership, and, in the case of Germany, individual party members became less active in their party organizations (Scarrow 2000, 90, 96; see also Katz and Mair 1995, 18; Gallagher, Laver, and Mair 2001, 275). Rather than finding out about elections, candidates, and issues from personal contact with party members, voters can today rely on the media for these cues. As campaigning has become less labor- and more capital-intensive, some have argued that there is less and less need for large party organizations. As a result, the past five decades in western Europe have been characterized by increasing personnel and monetary resources for central (national-level) party organizations and a weakening of subnational party organizations (Farrell and Webb 2000; Van Biezen 2002, 2–3; see also Van Biezen 2003).

There are also features of post-communist society that are at odds with Germany's party state. Eastern Europeans' experiences with decades of dictatorship by an all encompassing political party has led them to distrust political parties even more than an increasingly skeptical western European electorate (Crawford and Lijphart 1995; Kopecky 1995; Mair 1996; Rose 1995; Rose and Mishler 1997; Wyman et al. 1995). The same is true for eastern Germans, both at the mass (Hoffmann-Lange, Gille, and Krüger 1994; Minkenberg 1993; Olivo 1999; "Das Böse aus Bonn" 1996; Linnemann 1994) and elite levels (Bürklin 1997a; Hager 1997; Osterland 1994; Yoder 1999; Rohrschneider 1999). Instead eastern Germans supported referenda and other aspects of direct democracy, suggesting they preferred to see political decision making taken out of the hands of political parties (Fuchs, Roller, and Wessels 1997; Rohrschneider 1999). Moreover, qualitative studies of eastern political elites during the collapse of the GDR indicated that many were reluctant to form political parties (Baukloh, Lippert, and Pfaff 2001; Naßmacher 1996, 188) and questioned why parties should play an important role (Kolinsky 1993; Hager 1997).

As a result of this skepticism, a pattern of low party membership and organization is repeated across eastern Europe (Mair 1996); in Russia, political parties have been slow to emerge at all (Hanson 2001). As one would expect from the above literature, parties across eastern Germany have fewer members than their western counterparts (Linnemann 1994), despite concerted efforts by the major parties to extend the traditional mass/catch-all party model to the new Länder (Grabow 2001a). Further, after being pressured into joining communist organizations such as the Young Pioneers and the Free German Youth, eastern Germans may be particularly reluctant to enroll in inner-party groups today. In addition to having far fewer members than do western parties, eastern German parties have less-active inner-party organizations, such as the Christian Democratic women's group, the Frauen Union, or the SPD's young socialist organization, the Jusos (Grabow 2000). Since eastern parties are smaller and have less inner-party activity than those in western Germany, ambitious politicians may have little incentive to adopt inner-party offices in their search for supporters. Against such a backdrop, inner-party offices—especially at the subnational level—may become scarce and/or lose their importance as a recruitment channel.

In addition to these societal trends, individuals considered electable after unification spent the pre-unification period either avoiding political life or high profile roles within the communist party and its allies. Some contemporary parliamentarians never joined any political party during the GDR era. These people resisted joining a party even though this decision may have harmed their careers or their access to scarce resources. Many public-minded individuals retreated to apolitical technical or scientific careers rather than getting involved with the communist regime. Other parliamentarians elected after unification had indeed joined the SED or one of the other parties in the National Front, but held only low-ranking party office or avoided holding public office before 1989. Some Christian members of today's CDU joined the GDR-era Christian Democrats only to escape pressure to join the atheist SED.

Most of these legislators never rose very far within their parties. These past experiences may make eastern elites quite reluctant to assume party leadership positions today.

Not only would developments in western Germany and post-communist sentiment in eastern Germany make the desire to hold an inner-party office seem unlikely, local elected offices would appear to be a similarly anachronistic recruitment path for state legislators. As mass membership and inner-party organizations have declined in importance in western Europe, central party organizations have begun to use their resources to run professionalized campaigns, often led by a party leader, pollsters, political consultants, and advertising agencies (West 1989; Negrine and Papathanassopoulos 1996; Swanson and Mancini 1996). Rather than stressing candidates with experience in local office, parties running "Americanized" campaigns try to market an image or "an appropriate product" (Farrell and Webb 2000, 102). Such campaigns may select candidates who were successful businesspeople, actors, or sports stars rather than low-level elected officials. Public campaign finance encourages parties to redirect resources from the local level into national media campaigns (Van Biezen 2002, 14). Additionally, rather than finding out about voter interests through those holding local political office or using such offices to communicate the party's platform to voters, well-endowed central party organizations can rely on polling and advertising to fulfill these functions. As they conduct media-driven campaigns, party leaders may not view local political offices as an important recruiting ground. Finally, the aforementioned showy candidates aside, western political elites have become increasingly professionalized. State- and national-level politicians pursue long-term careers in which elites are chosen for their jobs based on their managerial skills and efficiency (Katz and Mair 1995, 18, 23; Panebianco 1988). Holding part-time, voluntary local offices may no longer be a relevant qualification for state office, and thus may not prove to be a key recruiting ground for state officials. Instead, eastern MdL may be expected to concentrate their energies in increasing their competence at their state-level position rather than running for lower-level political offices.

Indeed, interviews with grassroots party leaders in eastern Germany report difficulties finding candidates for local public offices ("Alle Parteien" 1998; Davidson-Schmich 2000; "SPD" 1998). Widespread distrust of parties in eastern Germany, combined with the greater likelihood of nonpartisan lists winning local elections, means that many lower-level elected offices are filled with nonpartisan candidates in eastern Germany (Naßmacher 1996, Hager 2002).

Societal factors may lessen not only the importance of party and other elected office as recruitment channels but also the value to politicians of joining voluntary organizations. As voters have become better educated, politicians more professional, and the media more pervasive, traditional ties between societal groups and parties have weakened. Contemporary western parties often do not represent the demands of interest groups; instead these groups make demands on parties (Katz and Mair 1995, 18, 23). Professionally run single-issue groups do not ally with one particular party but place demands on all elected officials, often relying on the media to communicate their demands (Dalton and Wattenberg 2000). Against such a backdrop, the recruitment of politicians from affiliated interest groups may become less prevalent.

In eastern Germany recruitment of political elites from voluntary groups seems particularly unlikely given that such autonomous groups were decimated during the communist era and are not particularly strong today (Padgett 2000). After decades of coerced participation in "voluntary" organizations such as youth groups and unions, many eastern Germans interpret democracy to mean that they do not have to get involved in voluntary groups. As a result, membership in such associations has also been low in eastern Germany. Many observers in turn report that eastern European parties have less extensive ties to interest groups than their western predecessors (Mair 1996; Benzler 1995; Olk 1996; Rueschemeyer 1998; von Alemann 1996; Van Biezen 2002, 7; see also Van Biezen 2003). Furthermore, monopolistic ties between the SED and communist-dominated interest groups, such as the GDR's trade union (Freier Deutscher Gewerkschaftsbund) and women's organization (Demokratischer Frauenbund Deutschlands), have soured easterners' desire to see parties and interest groups form close affiliations as they traditionally have in the west. Thus the traditional western recruitment channels—party groups, low-level elected office, and affiliated interest groups—do not fit the realities of political life in post-communist eastern Germany and, increasingly, in western Germany.

Institutional Incentives and Elite Recruitment

Despite these societal factors, I nonetheless argue that from the perspective of the individual politician there are career advantages to being involved with inner-party office, lower-level elected office, and affiliated interest groups—regardless of how the mass public views these types of affiliations. Western state parliamentarians have formed these ties as a result of the incentives created by Germany's electoral and parliamentary institutions. Each channel offers, as Aldrich anticipates, electoral benefits to office-seeking politicians. I make the assumption that the MdL under study here do desire (re)election, first because they have already shown a willingness to assume public office and second because, in the case of eastern German parliamentarians, other career options are limited. Given the high rate of unemployment in eastern Germany and the lack of experience in a market economy of those who have been professional parliamentarians since 1990, veteran legislators may have no alternative career option open to them now (Interview SPD Sachsen-Anhalt). This stands in stark contrast to the situation of westerners, many of whom are public servants who are guaranteed a job if they should lose their seat. With a salary around four thousand euros per month plus benefits, the job of state legislator is also a well-paid one by eastern standards. Losing a seat in parliament is likely to have dire financial costs for a veteran eastern parliamentarian (Interview FDP Brandenburg; Scherzer 2000, 14–15).

Germany's party state gives political parties an enormous amount of power. Germany's dual electoral system is a key component of this party state, and it provides many incentives for office-seeking state level politicians to play leadership roles in their parties. At least half of the candidates elected to German state legislatures are elected via party lists; the exact percentage varies from state to state.[3] As a result, candidates not affiliated with a political party cannot easily receive seats vis-à-vis the "second vote."[4] The rest of the candidates for the Landtage are elected via single member districts. While it is possible to run as an independent candidate in an electoral district, such candidates face stiff competition from candidates with a party label. As Aldrich (1995) observes, the latter enjoy "brand" recognition (49). Further, Aldrich points out, parties can offer the individual candidate additional resources for campaigning (50). In the German case, parties receive public funding for campaigns—a certain sum for every vote they get—which allows parties to provide their candidates with financial support for posters, leaflets, campaign rallies, and so on. Further, these benefits are not single-shot advantages in a given election, but because parties are enduring coalitions, benefits accrue to politicians over their long-term careers (25, 52). Most importantly, in Germany's parliamentary system independent candidates are not usually included in the executive branch of government which in practice dominates policy making. Similarly, independent legislators have fewer rights in parliament than do members of a party caucus.[5] As a result, independent candidates are less able to translate constituent wishes into public policy, reducing their attractiveness to voters.

In sum, if individuals want to start or continue their political careers, the best way to do so is to be placed on the party list (preferably in a position near the top of the list) or nominated by their party to run for a direct mandate. In Germany's party state, local- and state-level party organizations control these coveted nominations. Playing a leadership role within their party organizations, therefore, is a way for office-seeking politicians to have an influential role in the placement of their names on the electoral list or in their nomination for direct mandates. Similarly, involvement with a group of like-minded party members, such as the Young Socialists or the Christian Democratic women's organization, allows a candidate to build contacts with sympathetic party members who in turn can support her nomination. Furthermore, when parties put together their electoral lists, they try to appeal to a broad spectrum of voters by balancing the list not only in terms of gender and region, but also in terms of expertise, for example, creating a list with candidates having experience with educational policy, the police, and union issues. Leadership in the appropriate inner-party organization or activity in a relevant interest group are excellent ways for politicians to establish their credentials as experts in a particular field, increasing the chances that they will be selected for the party list.

Discussions with eastern parliamentarians show that they see the institutional advantages in holding party offices. As a Christian Democrat in Sachsen-Anhalt put it in a personal interview, "He who ignores his party organization is severely punished." He argued, "Anyone who wants a long-term political career must be anchored in his party. Members of the local party organization want to know more about political decision making than they read in the paper. They want to have access to decision makers" and will therefore nominate members of their group for higher office. The Social Democratic whip in the Brandenburg state legislature maintained that he had won his party's nomination for his direct seat over alternative candidates by stressing his role within the party. He successfully argued that his challenger was less well-placed within the party to be an advocate for the interests of the district.

Holding elected office at the town, city, or county level is also a useful way for a politician to secure nomination on the state-level ballot. Holding such offices helps direct mandate candidates achieve name recognition and gain a reputation for experience that can increase the likelihood that they will be (re)nominated for the Landtag. Partisan public office at the substate level also provides politicians with an excellent opportunity to routinely interact with local party members and hence gain supporters in the inner-party nomination process for higher office. Furthermore, such office allows state legislators to be in a position to respond to the concerns of local citizens, giving them an advantage when running for higher office.

Eastern legislators have also learned that holding local party office gives them more credibility in the state capital. During a personal interview, a Social Democrat in Sachsen-Anhalt noted, "Western legislators have a lobby backing them. When they sit at the table with other members of their caucus they are not alone. They speak for their whole local party organization. . . . This was not true at first in the east, but it's now changing. We now have people in the caucus who have a lobby behind them," and it is more likely that these people will get their way when they make demands on behalf of their constituents. A PDS legislator from Sachsen reported that he served on the city council in his home town as well as being the head of the PDS caucus in his county parliament. He claimed that this allowed people in his home region not only "to get to know and like me" but also for him to influence policies favorable to the "volunteer fire department, sports clubs, and other associations" in hopes of getting their electoral support. He also boasted that his wife was the mayor of his home town, offering him further visibility. A Social Democrat in Sachsen agreed, pronouncing holding local political office a "very good" career move.

For politicians seeking to further their careers, involvement with voluntary organizations is also a useful way of achieving visibility at the local level or among sympathetic voters (Patzelt 1997). Additionally, close ties to a voluntary group help individual candidates set themselves apart from others who are competing for a slot on the party list. When making electoral lists, party leaders often try to balance people with different expertise in order to appeal to the broadest range of constituents possible and to facilitate committee work in parliament. By affiliating with voluntary organizations of a certain sort—for example multiple women's organizations—politicians can increase their chances of nomination. Such interest groups have traditionally occupied an important place in the recruitment of western German MdL and have a key role in public policy making (von Alemann 1996). As one scholar put it, "One might even argue that interest groups and social movements are the underpinning of the party system" in western Germany (Wessels 1998, 209). For example, unions have historical ties to the Social Democratic Party, church and employers groups have links to the Christian Democratic Union, and environmental organizations enjoy close relationships with the Greens (Conradt 2001; von Alemann 1996).

Interviews with eastern MdL reveal that they recognize the electoral advantages of building ties to interest groups. A Social Democrat from Mecklenburg-Vorpommern reported that while joining and working with voluntary associations did "not come naturally" to members of his caucus, "we are now forcing ourselves" to build up such contacts to improve their electoral odds. One western civil servant stationed in Sachsen-Anhalt, Jörg Mayer, observed that SPD state legislators were beginning to associate themselves with sports clubs. He noted, "After seven years in power, the SPD here finally 'got it.' [Legislator X] from the CDU has been a lot better at this—he's become the head of [a large soccer club]." Similarly, a Christian Democrat from Mecklenburg-Vorpommern reported that he had worked hard to cultivate ties to local sports organizations. In sum, even if the general population is uninterested in involvement with political parties or voluntary organizations, individual politicians depend on these groups for (re)election and can be expected to affiliate with them, regardless of their overall size and strength. Furthermore, those politicians who do not form these kinds of affiliations are unlikely to be elected and thus will not be represented in the eastern Landtage.

EMPIRICAL EVIDENCE:
STATE PARLIAMENTARIANS SINCE 1990

In this section I test the above hypotheses by empirically comparing eastern and western German state legislators' involvement with inner-party office, partisan elected offices other than the Landtag, and membership in voluntary groups affiliated with parties. To do so, I draw on bio-graphical data about the 1086 state legislators elected in eastern Berlin and the five eastern German states (Brandenburg, Mecklenburg-Vorpommern, Sachsen, Sachsen-Anhalt, Thüringen) during each of the first three legislative periods (1990–2000). I compare this informa-tion to data from this period about the 1,385 legislators representing these Länder's western partner states (western Berlin, Niedersachsen, Schleswig-Holstein, Baden-Württemberg, Nordrhein-Westfalen, and Rheinland-Pfalz). This data comes from the Handbooks (*Handbücher*) of each state legislature in which state parliamentarians are legally re-quired to publish their biographies. This source is the most comprehen-sive and systematic collection of data available about eastern and western state legislators throughout the 1990s. However, it is important to note the potential bias of this source. MdL are not legally required to dis-close inner-party offices and unpaid public offices held, nor must they report all voluntary group memberships (see appendix B for more de-tails as to which voluntary group affiliations must be disclosed). As a re-sult the Handbooks make my case more difficult to prove because they systematically *under*count inner-party office, other elected office, and voluntary group affiliations. In the text below, I note the few instances where this bias becomes particularly pronounced.

For the purposes of this analysis, I divide state legislators into three groups:[6]

- *The Elite of Breakthrough:* Eastern state parliamentarians who were elected to political life in the very first eastern Landtag elections (1990).
- *The Elite of Consolidation:* Eastern state legislators who were first elected to public office in the second (1994) or third (1998/9) eastern Land-tag elections.
- *Western Elites:* Western state legislators in easterners' partner Land-tage between 1990 and 2000 (data collected from the most recent year an MdL served).

In the year 2000, over one third of eastern parliamentarians belonged to the elite of breakthrough, serving in the Landtage since their cre-ation in 1990; almost half of eastern MdL had been in office since the second term and only 17% of the seats in eastern state legislatures were filled by newcomers to state politics. These latter two groups comprise the elite of consolidation. By the end of the third term, the average eastern MdL had served for 9.1 years, while the typical western state legislator had had 9.3 years of experience.[7]

The logic of Germany's parliamentary and electoral systems makes it likely that the elite of consolidation will be involved with party offices, other elected offices, and interest organizations. The elite of breakthrough was not selected using the candidate selection processes outlined above, however. When the first term electoral lists were drawn up, the process for doing so was by all accounts quite chaotic (Patzelt and Schirmer 1996, 21). Parties simply held a meeting in which all interested people stood up and declared their interest in running for state office and their qualifications for the job. After the speeches were held, members voted on the party's list. One participant in such a meeting of the Brandenburg FDP called his nomination "a coincidence," and a member of the CDU in Sachsen-Anhalt agreed, saying that those who were the best speakers that day got good positions on the list. The latter maintained that because his newly formed state combined two GDR-era administrative districts, many Christian Democrats did not know each other prior to this meeting and had no other information with which to assess the talents and qualifications of potential candidates. A Social Democrat from Brandenburg said he was last on his party's electoral list because he was the last to sign up. However, even if the elite of breakthrough did not have party leadership roles, other public offices, or ties to interest groups when they were initially elected, Germany's political institutions provide incentives to obtain such qualifications after assuming office. Thus, over time the elite of breakthrough is expected to assume party office, other elected offices, and interest group roles at similar rates as their western counterparts.

The first elections to the new Landtage were held in the fall of 1990. Virtually all observers noted that the elite of breakthrough were political outsiders who did not have the same experiences as westerners with political parties, public offices, or interest groups (Welsh 1994; Patzelt 1997; Lock 1998; Yoder 1999). Given the wide-ranging changes to eastern German political parties during 1989–90, these findings are not surprising. The ruling Socialist Unity Party was so discredited that it purged its top leadership and changed its name to the Party of Democratic Socialism. The SED's former partners in the communist-dominated "National Front" joined their western counterparts and replaced their most compromised leaders with very low ranking members or brand new recruits. The East German Christian Democrats and the Democratic Peasant's Party of Germany united with the western Christian Democrats, and the communist-era liberal party (the LDPD, or Liberal Democratic Party of Germany) merged with the western Free Democrats. As a result, their caucuses included at least some members with GDR-era party-political experience; the figure for the CDU was 45% and for the PDS and FDP 25%.[8] The parties that were newly established in eastern Germany—the Social Democrats and Alliance 90/ Greens—had no veteran members to draw on for elected office. Thus the candidates chosen to run for office in the recently formed state parliaments had generally not been career, or even amateur, politicians before entering state legislatures. Instead, these newly elected parliamentarians were by and large previously apolitical scientists, veterinarians, and teachers. Finally, given the SED's efforts to dominate civil society, few new state legislators had had the opportunity during the GDR era to play leading roles in truly voluntary organizations.

Recruitment Through Party Office

One of the most important things to note from the outset is that all politicians elected to the eastern state legislatures over the first decade won political office by campaigning on a party ticket.[9] The electoral advantages to running on a party ticket quickly became clear in eastern Germany, just as they had in the west.

The initially high percentage of people involved with parties stands in sharp contrast to the experiences of other parliaments elsewhere in eastern Europe (Karasimeonov 1996, 55; Norton and Olson 1996, 235; Reschova and Syllova 1996, 100; Sobyanin 1994) and is a testament both to the strength of the German party state and to Aldrich's observation that, once established, parties are likely to attract office seekers. While the men and women who initially pressed for democratization in East Germany had formed nonpartisan Roundtables and electoral lists, they were shunned by voters in the first free elections held in the spring of 1990; the latter preferred a quick unification and cast their ballots for candidates running with western party labels. Many interviewees stated that they, or people they knew, ran for the first state parliament elections in the fall of 1990 as candidates representing the established western parties because they believed they had better chances of being elected. One member of Alliance 90 in Sachsen reported that when he was elected to the Landtag in 1990 he found that many of the people he knew both from the GDR opposition group New Forum and from the nonpartisan civil rights movement had been elected as Christian Democrats. Thus from unification onward, the presence of established political parties encouraged office seekers to affiliate with political parties, and electoral mechanisms deselected those who remained so skeptical of parties that they did not join. The institutions of the party state, then, already biased the selection of parliamentarians toward those who were predisposed toward political parties.

Willingness to run on a party label, however, is not the same as playing a leadership role in a political party. Nonetheless, an analysis of eastern state parliamentarians' biographies indicates that they are now almost as likely as their western counterparts to hold leadership positions within their parties. (See table 2.1. Appendix B lists the various kinds of party offices legislators can hold beyond simple membership.) By the year 2000, 73% of eastern state legislators reported playing or having played some type of role in their political party, compared to 81% in the west.[10] Interestingly, there are some considerable differences across the eastern German states in terms of reported party activity. While 81.8% of Mecklenburg-Vorpommern's legislators report holding party office, only 34.1% of Brandenburg's legislators do. The averages in Sachsen (73.7%), Thüringen (72.7%), Sachsen-Anhalt (68.4%), and

Table 2.1   State legislators reporting party leadership roles

	% playing a party role
East, 1990 (N= 554)*	66.0%
Those easterners in 2000 (N = 176)	76.7%**
Easterners entering in 1994 (N = 204)	69.5%
Those easterners in 2000 (N = 131)	70.0%
Easterners entering in 1998/9 (N = 148)	70.0%
Eastern average, 2000 (N = 454)	73.0%
Western average, 1990–2000 (N = 1385)	81.0%**

* Legislators from Brandenburg not included in the table due to the reporting habits in their Handbook.

** Difference of means significant at t.025 level, 2-tailed test.

eastern Berlin (68.2%) are much closer to Mecklenburg's. Due to the layout of Brandenburg's Handbook, I believe that the norms regarding the reporting of party office may differ in this state. In the handbooks for states like Mecklenburg-Vorpommern and Thüringen, legislators are allotted an entire page (at least) for their biographies, and the pages are laid out to include a special section on party office. In Brandenburg, however, legislators receive only one-third of a page for their biography, with no special section for party office. Since there is no legal require-ment to report the latter information in the Handbook, it may simply be that Brandenburgers have developed a tradition of not mentioning party office in the biographical information they report. Hence the legis-lators from Brandenburg are not included in the analysis in table 2.1.

Examining the career paths of individual politicians also provides support for the hypothesis that party office is important for ambitious politicians in eastern Germany, even if grassroots parties are not strong there. Among the elite of breakthrough, 66% reported holding (or hav-ing held) a leadership position in their party. Of the members of this co-hort still holding office in 2000, 76.7% reported playing key party roles. The percentage of those who entered during the second legislative pe-riod holding party office was higher than the percentage in the first co-hort; 69.5% of this cohort entered the state legislature with a party leadership role and, among those still in office in 2000, the number had risen slightly. The third cohort of parliamentarians had the highest ini-tial percentage of party leadership positions: 70%. Thus while statisti-cally significant differences remain between the percentage of western and eastern legislators holding party office, more than seven in ten of both the elite of breakthrough and the elite of consolidation play roles in their parties; furthermore eastern politicians show an increasing pro-pensity to assume party office over the course of their parliamentary ca-reers. These findings indicate the importance of parties for political elites, even in a context where grassroots parties are quite weak and dis-trust of parties strong.

There are variations among political parties, however. The far-right German People's Union (DVU), which won a surprising near 13% in Sachsen-Anhalt and exceeded the 5% threshold in Brandenburg in 1998/9, is the brainchild of a wealthy extreme-right publisher, Gerhard Frey. He finances campaigns and is reported to make most of the deci-sions for the party himself. When DVU parliamentarians from Sachsen-Anhalt were asked how they were chosen for the party list, they stressed they had been handpicked by Frey. As a result of his single-handed control of the party, it has few inner-party organizations or offices which deputies could hold. While over 80% of eastern CDU legislators, over 60% of SPD parliamentarians, and 57.5% of PDS caucus members held party offices, only one-third of the legislators from the German People's Union had held a party office. Notably, however, the DVU has never won seats in any state in more than two elections.

The SPD and Green parliamentarians elected in the first term were usually among the founders of their state-level parties, and CDU, FDP, and PDS legislators were quickly promoted as the old leadership was moved out. Thus the elite of breakthrough have become today's party leaders, just as their western counterparts head their states' parties. One scholar who studied the internal organization of eastern parties remarked that a parliamentary caucus meeting today is virtually the same thing as a meeting of a party's state-level leadership (Grabow 2001b; see also Patzelt and Schirmer 1996, 24). Young people now entering politics in the new states are indeed beginning to arrive with more western-style party backgrounds, as illustrated by the Handbook biographies of the youngest politicians to enter in the third term illustrate. One, Marco Steckel, was born in Sachsen-Anhalt in 1972, joined the Social Democrats in 1995, rose to the leadership of the Young Socialists (Jusos) in 1997 and worked at the party's state headquarters that year. Christian Gräff, an eastern Berlin Christian Democrat born in 1978, followed a similar path. He joined the CDU in 1995 and became active in the party's Junge Union youth organization. He moved up to the state level leadership of this organization and was elected to the Berlin state legislature in 1999. The PDS is also producing a generation of people who grew up active in the party, as the biography of Benjamin Hoff, an eastern Berlin student born in 1976, illustrates. He joined the party's *Junge Linke* youth organization in 1992 and became a PDS member the following year. In 1994 he moved into the federal leadership of the Junge Linke, and in 1995 he was elected to the state legislature. Members of the elite of breakthrough, like a Social Democrat from Brandenburg, observe that there is now much more competition for party posts than there once was in eastern Germany (Personal Interview).

Comparing the party involvement of eastern candidates who won their seats from the top 20% of their parties' lists to the activities of candidates who made it into office from the bottom 20% of their parties' slates shows the importance of party involvement for a good position on the list.[11] Of the legislators elected from the top quintile, 68% held party office. The percentage was the same among politicians who won both their party's nomination for the direct mandate in their electoral district and then the seat itself. In contrast, the percentage of legislators holding party office fell steadily across each quintile of the electoral list, and only 52% of the parliamentarians from the bottom quintile reported holding a party office.[12] Those who occupy such office clearly are likely to be rewarded when parties select candidates for their ballots.

In sum, almost three-quarters of eastern state parliamentarians play leadership roles within their parties, and individual politicians show an increasing propensity to serve in party office as their tenure in the Landtag progresses. Young politicians are now beginning their careers by assuming inner-party office, and those who do are rewarded with slots at the top of their party's electoral list. These findings support the hypothesis that political parties will remain important at the elite level, despite their grassroots weakness. The next section investigates whether this is the case for other elected offices as well.

Recruitment Through Other Public Offices

Typical western German politicians are recruited for the state legislature not only because they have held office within their own political parties, but often also because they have held lower-level elected offices. Just as eastern state legislators' involvement within their parties has grown over the past decade, so too has their experience in elected office outside of their Landtag seat, although the figure remains significantly below western levels. (See appendix B for the kinds of posts that often serve as a stepping stone to a Landtag career and table 2.2 for overall results). In 2000, 82.5% of western parliamentarians reported holding or having held other elected office, while this figure was 70.3% among eastern state legislators.[13] While statistically significant east-west differences remain, the elite of breakthrough are more likely to hold other public offices than they were in 1990, and almost two-thirds of the elite of consolidation are recruited after having experience in public office, indicating the importance of office-holding to winning party nominations.

Of the elite of breakthrough, 58.8% had previously held public office before joining the newly created state legislatures in 1990. Among the

Table 2.2   State legislators holding other public office

	MdL holding other public office
East, 1990 (N =652)	58.8%
Those easterners in 2000 (N = 208)	*73.7%**
Easterners entering in 1994 (N=247)	65.9%
Those easterners in 2000 (N = 156)	*71.0%***
Easterners entering in 1998/9 (N=187)	64.1%
Eastern average, 2000 (N = 548)	70.3%
Western average, 1990–2000 (N=1385)	82.5% *

* Difference of means significant at t.025 level, 2-tailed test.

** Difference of means significant at t.05 level, 1-tailed test.

members of this cohort who were still in office in 2000, 73.7% reported holding or having held such office. Those easterners selected as first-time state legislators in 1994 entered the Landtag with more frequent previous experience in elected office: 65.9% had already been elected to another post. By 2000, 71% of these parliamentarians reported holding or having held an additional public office. Finally, 64.1% of the third cohort, those MdL elected for the first time in 1998/9, had held public office before joining the state legislature, a lower percentage than the second cohort, but more experienced than the first cohort initially was.

This low figure for the most recent elites of consolidation was driven in part by the surprise victory of the far-right German People's Union (DVU). This party had not held office at the local level in eastern Germany when it exceeded the 5% threshold in Brandenburg and Sachsen-Anhalt state elections in 1998/9. Only one of the twenty-one legislators elected (4.8%), however, had ever held local political office (as a member of the FDP).[14] This stands in stark contrast to the other parties represented in eastern legislatures in 2000: 80.3% of CDU members, 71.5% of SPD parliamentarians, and 60.8% of PDS legislators hold or had held other public office.

Having held previous local office seems to be particularly useful for those politicians who wish to receive their party's nomination for a direct mandate. A significantly higher percentage of direct mandate winners (76.3%) than list candidates (64.4%) have previously occupied a public office outside of their post in eastern state legislatures.[15] The visibility and contacts that local offices offer appear to be valuable resources in the pursuit of a direct seat.

Interviews and examples from the parliamentary Handbooks also provide evidence of this trend. A Christian Democrat in Sachsen-Anhalt noticed that there was a "strong personnel overlap" between those in his party group and those who lead CDU caucuses in county parliaments. In an extreme case, Egon Sommerfeld, a Christian Democrat from Sachsen-Anhalt had held not only his seat in the state parliament since the first term, he had simultaneously been the head of county government (*Landrat*) and had served on his town council (*Gemeinderat*) and in the county parliament (*Kreistag*).

In sum, although east-west differences remain, the elite of breakthrough were significantly more likely to hold more than one public office in 2000 than they were in 1990. The majority of the elite of consolidation are now recruited after serving in lower-ranking posts, just like their western counterparts.

Recruitment via Interest Organizations

The greatest difference between eastern and western state legislators' recruitment patterns is found in their involvement with voluntary interest organizations such as unions, business associations, and environmental groups. On average, over the decade since unification, 74.6% of western German state legislators reported some kind of relationship with a voluntary organization. While the percentage of eastern state legislators mentioning ties to interest groups has increased over time, there is still a statistically significant gap between westerners and easterners. In 2000 only 58.6% of legislators in the new states reported involvement with interest associations; however, this variable shows the most dramatic movement toward the western pattern of all aspects of the party state examined here. (See appendix B for information on how this variable was measured and table 2.3 for overall results).

In 1990 only 43.2% of the elite of breakthrough reported ties to an interest group. By the end of the decade, 62% of the remaining legislators from this cohort reported connections to interest associations. Similarly, the elite of consolidation also has been more likely to be involved

Table 2.3   State legislators reporting interest group involvement

	MdL with interest group involvement
East, 1990 (N = 652)	43.2%
Those easterners in 2000 (N = 208)	62.0%*
Easterners entering in 1994 (N=247)	45.5%
Those easterners in 2000 (N = 156)	62.1%*
Easterners entering in 1998/9 (N=187)	48.9%
Eastern average, 2000 (N = 548)	58.6%
Western average, 1990–2000 (N=1385)	74.6%*

* Difference of means significant at t.025 level, 2-tailed test.

with an interest group over time. Among those legislators entering the eastern parliaments for the first time in 1994, 45.5% reported voluntary group activity, and this number rose to 48.9% with the cohort of 1998/9. These contacts grow with tenure in office: 62.1% of the eastern Mdl elected in 1994/5 reported connections to interest associations in 2000. This growth provides support for the hypothesis that, despite the overall weakness of interest groups in eastern Germany, political elites will find it in their interest to affiliate with them.

Despite the growth in party–interest group ties, significant differences among eastern legislators do emerge when partisan differences in contacts to interest groups are examined. In the east, 65.6% of SPD members, 57.1% of Christian Democrats, and 53.4% of PDS members report involvement with interest associations. In stark contrast *none* of the DVU legislators indicated that they had contacts with voluntary groups. Again, however, this type of party is the exception rather than the rule and has only once been subsequently reelected to a Landtag.

While there was no meaningful variation in voluntary group membership across quintiles on western electoral lists, there were statistically significant differences across eastern quintiles. Interestingly, however, it was not the top quintiles that had the highest rates of interest group involvement, but those individuals lower on the lists. Among eastern candidates in the top two quintiles, an average of 38.4% of the candidates had ties to voluntary groups, whereas in the bottom two quintiles this average was 60.2%.[16] Once eastern parties fill their top spots with loyal party office holders they seem to turn to those with ties to interest organizations, again confirming the usefulness of such contacts for a political career (see also Patzelt and Schirmer 1996, 22, 24).

Interviews with state legislators indicate that their relationships with voluntary organizations have been increasing over the past decade. Rather than differing societal conditions making interest groups irrelevant for politicians, the latter have sought out contact with what organizations there are. The German system of policy making causes legislators and interest organizations to routinely interact, providing increased opportunities to build bridges between politicians and even interest groups with small grassroots memberships. This latter factor is one reason that individual legislators report increasing contacts with voluntary organizations over their tenure in office. A Social Democrat from Mecklenburg-Vorpommern reflected in 2001 that "things are now changing . . . [contacts with interest groups are] a little more concrete and tight" than they were before. He reported the parliament had recently passed a law favoring unions when awarding public contracts because SPD members with union ties had pushed for the law. Similarly, when discussing a proposed law about state universities, he claimed that many in his party pushed for the interests of the educators union with whom they had close contacts. A PDS legislator in Sachsen-Anhalt recalled that initially voluntary organizations were reluctant to even get involved with the successors to the SED. He remembered that in the first electoral period "we were really happy if anyone wanted to contact us." He admitted that at first members of his caucus had so few ties to interest groups that they could "promise something to everyone." Today, however, he feels they are just like a "typical *Volkspartei* (catch-all party)" that has to balance different interests of its caucus members. He said that his caucus contained people with ties to business as well as to environmentalists and that deciding on a united stance on the construction of a highway had been quite difficult. A former Alliance 90/Green legislator in Sachsen reported that over the past decade members of his party have worked to develop close ties to labor unions. So eastern MdL concur that relations between legislators and voluntary associations have begun to bloom, even though such groups are less prevalent than in western states.

Further, the Handbook biographies show that many state legislators have cultivated extensive ties to voluntary groups. For example, Dr. Detlef Eckert, a member of the PDS in Sachsen-Anhalt elected in the third term, himself physically disabled, was closely involved with a number of athletic organizations and voluntary groups of people with disabilities, including serving as the president of the German Disabled Veterans Sports Association, a leading member in the Association of German Dancers, head of the German General Association of the Handicapped, and the speaker of the amputees in the German Association of Handicapped Athletes. These voluntary involvements carried over into his party career where he served as the PDS's Handicapped Ombudsman at the federal level as well as a member of the party's working groups on sports and on the needs of the disabled. His position enabled him to speak on behalf of the handicapped and serve as an expert on athletics in the parliamentary committee on Health and Social issues. Similarly, during the GDR era a CDU member of the Brandenburg legislature headed the local organization of the Democratic Peasants' Party of Germany. After unification he joined the CDU and became active in the German farmer's association, the *Deutscher Bauernverband*, where he today heads the Brandenburg chapter and serves on the board of directors at the national level. He also headed a committee in the Association of German Farmers, Gardeners, and Vintners as well as serving as the chair of an association of rural adult education programs. This specialization in agricultural affairs earned him the twentieth spot on his party's electoral list and a seat on the parliamentary agricultural committee.

Thus, although grassroots voluntary groups are weak in eastern Germany, affiliation with such groups is quite attractive to office-seeking politicians. The same is true of inner-party offices and local elected offices. While the frequency with which eastern MdL hold such positions remains below the western level, the trend is clearly in the western direction.

An Alternative Hypothesis

Skeptics may argue that these results are due to some other variable than the institutions of the party state. Critics would point out that the transfer of western Germany's formal parliamentary and electoral systems did not occur in a vacuum but in a context in which West Germany had considerably more economic and political resources than East Germany did. It is true that aspects of this context certainly did influence the degree—and especially the speed—with which the party state was adopted in eastern Germany. However, once transferred, the party state perpetuated itself through its own internal institutional logic.

The context in which institutional transfer occurred certainly did matter in the German case. As John Aldrich concedes in his seminal work *Why Parties?*,

> Saying that politicians might find it in their interest to create or use a political party is not the same thing as saying that they will choose to do so. A political party is a collective enterprise, subject to significant collective action problems in forming and maintaining it. Moreover, there may be other means of achieving politicians' goals. . . . Since forming or even affiliating with a political party is a voluntary choice of a politician, it is critical to examine the particular setting to see if (1) there is an incentive for politicians to turn to parties, (2) if it is feasible . . . and (3) there are no superior solutions. . . . Political parties are "solutions" of a particular kind. They must be institutions that are enduring, or at least that politicians expect to endure, if they are to be successful in achieving their goals. (1995, 58)

In the eastern German case, it is clear from the above discussion that Aldrich's first condition is met: the formal institutions of the party state provide strong incentives for politicians to turn to parties. The context in which German unification occurred ensured that his next three criteria were also met. It was entirely feasible for eastern politicians to affiliate with political parties as eastern Germany inherited not only a functioning party system, but one that was well-known to eastern German citizens. Virtually all of the latter had access to western television and radio before the Berlin Wall fell, and the West German evening news was commonly watched in the GDR. Furthermore, the hegemonic Socialist Unity Party in East Germany allowed the presence of so-called bloc parties, including a Christian Democratic Union and a liberal party; as a result, eastern voters were already familiar with these party families. Similarly, the Social Democrats had existed prior to the founding of the GDR, so this party was a known quantity as well. Against this backdrop of popular familiarity with the Federal Republic's parties, the western branches of these parties expended considerable financial and human resources to extend their party organization to eastern Germany. Some of these resources came from the public funding of political parties in the Federal Republic.

Not only did eastern politicians have incentives and opportunities to become affiliated with political parties, given the speed of German unification, there was little opportunity for a superior solution to develop. The Berlin Wall fell unexpectedly in November 1989, and less than a year later the first eastern state parliament elections were held. The first free elections in the German Democratic Republic, held in March 1990, brought a clear victory for western political parties and a resounding defeat of the eastern citizens' movement.[17] Given the time constraints and the electoral advantages to being affiliated with an established political party, ambitious eastern politicians came to view the established parties as a superior solution to other potential forms of organization including nonpartisan lists. Given the long duration for which western parties had existed, Aldrich's final criterion was clearly fulfilled as well: aspiring politicians could count on parties to endure well beyond the first election. While the future of the SED's successor party, the PDS, was less clear, it too represented a long tradition.

Thus within a year of the fall of the Wall, legislators in the five new Länder had chosen to affiliate with political parties. These politicians, who owed their success to their party label, then had few incentives to try and radically change the political institutions of the party state in their Land.[18] In other words, as Aldrich predicted, once parties established themselves, they became institutional equilibriums (1995, 61). Had the party state's formal institutions been transferred to eastern Germany without the accompanying established party system, joining a party may not have been as feasible or as desirable as an option for ambitious politicians. One of Aldrich's "superior solutions" may have emerged instead, or legislators may have had more incentive to change the formal institutions of the party state after they were elected.

Once the party state, with its parliamentary and electoral systems, was accepted by eastern legislators, however, its incentives began to exert their influence on the politicians within the system. From this point onward, western Germany's hegemonic economic and political position in the united country is less salient to explaining easterners' legislative behavior. While the presence of western advisors, journalists, financial resources, and the normative cachet the west carried certainly helped speed easterners' learning about their new political system, this learning would likely have occurred even without western Germany's hegemonic position, albeit at a slower pace.[19]

For example, Jörg Mayer a western public servant transferred to Sachsen-Anhalt, stated that when western advisors came east, they found a different "culture of interaction. They [the deputies] did not know what caucuses were. They didn't think about 'who is from which party' but rather 'who is suited for a job.'" After the first election, when it was time to decide who the President (speaker) of the legislature should be, the head of the majority caucus proposed that a particular deputy from an opposition party should have the job because of his strong political skills. His western advisors quickly informed him that this politically important position, with agenda-setting powers over parliamentary procedure, should not be given to a member of the opposition who could use his powers to the detriment of the majority. Upon receiving this advice, the eastern caucus head agreed to choose a President from his own party. In contrast to this quick lesson, in the realm of party discipline where western advisors had less influence, eastern caucuses were initially quite undisciplined. But by the end of the first electoral period they had learned through their own experience with plenary sessions lasting late into the night that a lack of discipline was inefficient and that they would be better off if it were abandoned.[20] In both instances, easterners learned that political institutions did not reward the values they brought to office with them; what differed was simply the timing of this learning.

A further testament to logic of institutions comes from the responses of the Party of Democratic Socialism to the party state. Although the former communists had few western advisors and were not part of a national party organization dominated by westerners and their resources, members of this party have assumed inner-party office, other elected office, and interest group membership at rates similar to deputies from branches of western parties.

IMPLICATIONS

Thus the empirical evidence presented here supports the view that the western German party state has begun to take root in eastern Germany, despite the inhospitable soil into which it was transplanted. The elite of breakthrough in eastern Germany has come to resemble western elites more and more with each passing term. Further, the individual legislators recruited today (the elite of consolidation) more often hold party offices, other elected offices, and positions within interest organizations than the elite of breakthrough did in 1990. While easterners have not yet converged on western levels, this appears to be the trend on all fronts. The only exception to the above findings is the German People's Union, but this is a minor party in the German system and has not met with prolonged electoral success. The DVU's success is not a uniquely eastern phenomenon either. In Hamburg in 2001 the Partei Rechtsstaatlicher Offensive (otherwise known as the Schill Partei), won a surprising 19.4% of the vote. Of its deputies to the *Bürgerschaft*, only 36% held a party office, 16% a previous elected office,[21] and 40% an affiliation with an interest group—numbers far below the western averages for these categories (81%, 82.5%, and 74.6%, respectively). Like the DVU in Sachsen-Anhalt, however, the Partei Rechtsstaatlicher Offensive was not returned to office in Hamburg. In short, despite all of the differences between eastern and western German societies, the united country's party state is shaping a class of partisan politicians in the eastern Länder in much the same way it shaped legislators in the western states.

This suggests that Aldrich's view of political parties as institutions useful to office-seeking politicians— even in times of grassroots party decline—is correct, at least in the German case. Because holding party office, other public office, or voluntary group membership is a valuable asset for an aspiring politician in the German party state, eastern parliamentarians have formed affiliations with these groups even as citizens have stayed away in large numbers. Had no ready-made parties existed, another equilibrium may have been reached, but the advantages offered by inner-party office, other elected offices, and affiliated interest groups were simply too strong for easterners to resist.

The findings presented here also have implications for the study of political parties in western democracies. Many of the attitudinal trends observed in eastern Germany and eastern Europe are also characteristics of the western German and western European electorates of the twenty-first century in comparison to these electorates in the 1950s. The phenomenon of Parteiverdrossenheit, or dissatisfaction with political parties, in western societies is akin to eastern Europeans' distrust of parties. In western Europe as the mass parties began to disappear, partisanship among voters declined, and voters increasingly paid attention to individual candidates and issues rather than party labels. These developments make western European electorates more like their eastern counterparts. As western voter interest in parties declined, so has party membership, and, in the case of Germany, individual party members became less active in their party organizations; elsewhere in western Europe in the past five decades subnational party organizations have also weakened. As in eastern Europe, then, it would seem unlikely that inner-party office would remain an attractive recruiting ground for candidates. Rather than finding out about elections, candidates, and issues from personal contact with party members and officials in their communities, voters in both eastern and western Europe can today rely on the media for these cues. Parliamentary work in both regions has become more professionalized and specialized. Against this backdrop, the attractiveness of local office holding as a qualification for state-level office would seem to lose its luster. Finally, membership in voluntary organizations in western Europe has declined since the 1950s. Just as in eastern Europe, then, voluntary group membership would seem less and less relevant for ambitious politicians. Given these conditions, it would seem as if the Federal Republic's decades-old party state model is becoming increasingly anachronistic, and a new type of telegenic candidate for state office would seem to be preferable.

Despite these differences, both western and eastern German elites have continued to follow the professionalization and recruitment patterns developed in western Germany in the postwar period. The ability of the party state to make inroads in eastern Germany, however, where the weakness of parties and voluntary organizations are much more pronounced, suggests that the western party state has more staying power than is often acknowledged. Although parties and interest groups are less rooted in western European society today than they were in the 1950s, they are still much more strongly anchored than in eastern Europe; it seems doubtful that traditional professional and recruitment patterns would survive in the inhospitable eastern German environment but disappear in the west.[22] Established western European political institutions persist despite the widespread sociological changes which have occurred in the region since the 1960s.

This is true not only of elite recruitment, but also of the way in which MdL vote on the floor of parliament once they are elected. Many observers initially argued that eastern elites would be more technocratic or consensus-oriented in their decision making than their western counterparts given their apolitical backgrounds (Yoder 1999, 130–31). The Roundtables which emerged as communism crumbled took a nonpartisan, consensual approach to policy making, and a majority of eastern elites and citizens claim to prefer that political decisions be made not by representatives of political parties but by the citizens themselves (Rohrschneider 1999, 82). The adoption of the western party state by elites, however, has meant that rather than being technocratic and consensual, legislative decision making has come to be dominated by partisan debate and majority rule. Parties with parliamentary majorities now determine public policies. The following chapters trace these processes.

chapter 3

Becoming Disciplined: Eastern German State Legislators and Party Discipline

While the SPD doesn't discipline its members the way the SED did, "a democratic party isn't a chicken farm. And furthermore, I for example, am no longer a simple locksmith but a member of the state parliament. You also earn good money and can finally fulfill some of your wishes. For example, you start to build a house. My wife wanted me to build a house. But I didn't build one. Maybe that's why our marriage broke up. As a parliamentarian I was gone every night and I didn't even build her a house. Oh well. Other members of parliament build houses and take out big mortgages based on their salaries. But after the first four years of their five year term in office, they suddenly start brooding in a big way and finally break out in a sweat: What will happen if I don't get elected again and I have to make my mortgage payments on time? That's when you start pounding the pavement so you look good in your district. But the people usually don't elect you directly but rather they elect a party. And the party decides who it wants to return to parliament! If it puts you right at the top of its list of candidates, you're sure that you'll automatically be returned to parliament and you can continue to make those big mortgage payments. That's also a kind of party discipline. In that case, the voters don't have to like you—the main thing is that the party likes you." (Heiko Gentzel, SPD whip in Thüringen, quoted in Scherzer 2000, 14–15)

As mentioned in the previous chapter, eastern German politicians and their voters joined the Federal Republic with skeptical attitudes toward political parties and representative democracy. We have seen that despite this skepticism, easterners have become increasingly active in their political parties, in terms of holding inner-party office, prior partisan office, and membership in affiliated interest groups. This chapter and the two that follow examine whether the reach of the party state extends beyond individual legislators' personal involvement in their party and actually influences their behavior while on the floor of parliament. Specifically, I ask whether MdL have become disciplined members of party caucuses or whether nonpartisan legislative decision making predominates.

This question is of interest because, like the question of whether partisan recruitment patterns could be transferred to eastern Germany, it addresses a long-standing debate within the study of western European politics. While students of western European politics have consistently observed that deputies from the same party caucus generally take the identical positions when votes are cast in legislatures there, the explanation for this commonly occurring party voting is more controversial. Scholars taking a sociological approach have argued that MdL hold together for normative reasons including party solidarity, socialization in proper behavior by caucus leaders, or simply because members of the same party families hold the same ideological convictions (Jewell 1970; Hix and Lord 1997, 142, 153).[1] In contrast, scholars from the rational choice institutionalist tradition have argued that discipline emerges as rational actors discover self-interested reasons to vote *en bloc* (Aldrich 1995; Cox 1987; Patzelt 1998b; Laver and Shepsle 1999).[2] The study of well-established western European legislatures has not enabled political scientists to resolve this debate.

The creation of the eastern Landtage after the fall of the GDR, however, provides a unique opportunity to investigate the origins of party voting. In this setting, established political institutions that produced highly disciplined legislatures in the past were extended to an area of the world where political elites did not share norms conducive to party voting. If sociological factors are indeed responsible for legislative discipline, it would follow that these new state legislatures would be very undisciplined, an outcome that has been observed elsewhere in eastern Europe.[3]

If, however, institutional factors shape legislators' voting behavior, it would follow that party discipline would be high in the new Landtage. Germany's parliamentary and electoral institutions create incentives for strong parliamentary parties that vote as united blocs around distinctly partisan platforms (Conradt 2001, 175; Patzelt 1998b). In fact, the Federal Republic's parliamentary system has been dubbed a Fraktionenparlament, a parliament of party groups (Fraktionen) (Schüttemeyer 1994). If incentives for partisan politics are indeed responsible for legislative discipline, it would follow that the new Landtage would be very disciplined; this result would be expected by those who take a rational choice institutionalist approach to the study of legislative behavior.

This chapter examines whether and how elite norms and political institutions influenced the development of party discipline in eastern Germany in the decade since unification. I argue that institutional incentives for partisan politics have created highly disciplined state legislatures akin to those in the west. I focus on the development of party discipline in the five eastern German states over the period 1990 to 2000 and compare legislative decision making in these states to their western partners.[4] I find that, while antiparty sentiment may have initially complicated the task of developing disciplined parliamentary parties in eastern Germany, over the past three legislative periods decision making in eastern states has come to resemble parliamentary processes in western Germany.

The results presented here also contribute to the growing body of literature on the development of post-communist legislatures. While some edited volumes have appeared on these newly democratized legislatures (Olson and Norton 1996; Remington 1994), and the eastern German Landtage have also been studied (e.g., Patzelt and Schirmer 1996), these works generally provide a snapshot of various parliaments at fixed points in time, usually in the early 1990s.[5] In contrast, this chapter traces the behavior of state legislators over the course of a decade, providing a much more dynamic account of the waning influence of elite attitudes and the increasing influence of democratic political institutions. In addition, the chapter is one of only a very few attempts to systematically analyze non–roll call voting in any of the German Landtage, likely due to the difficulty of compiling the necessary data.[6]

My findings are developed in four steps. First, I outline both the sociological characteristics of eastern elites and the institutional incentives present in the German political system for strong Fraktionen.

Second I examine legislative decision making over the three electoral periods that spanned the 1990s in order to empirically document the growing strength of parliamentary parties in eastern Germany. Third, I draw on interviews with MdL and transcripts of plenary sessions to show how institutional imperatives have led to increasing discipline over the past decade. I conclude by discussing the significance of these results.

SOCIOLOGICAL FACTORS AND INSTITUTIONAL INCENTIVES FOR PARTY DISCIPLINE

Sociological Factors Weakening Discipline

As established in the previous chapter, extensive mass and elite opinion studies have documented that, after decades of rule by an all-encompassing political party imposing iron discipline, eastern Europeans distrust political parties. Students of eastern Germany also found that—both at the mass and elite levels—a lack of trust in political parties was widespread. Instead, eastern Germans supported referenda and other aspects of direct democracy (Fuchs, Roller, and Wessels 1997; Rohrschneider 1999), suggesting they preferred to see political decision making taken out of the hands of political parties. Moreover, qualitative studies of the eastern political elites during the collapse of the GDR indicated that many were reluctant to form political parties (Baukloh, Lippert, and Pfaff 2001; Naßmacher 1996, 188). Instead, they questioned why parties should play an important role (Kolinsky 1993, Hager 1997), favoring consensus decision making rather than partisan competition (Yoder 1999, 130–31). Eastern German elites clearly joined the Federal Republic with skeptical attitudes toward political parties and representative democracy. Such norms are obviously not conducive to the creation of strong legislative parties.

Those elites who were elected to eastern German state legislatures in 1990, the elite of breakthrough, had generally been apolitical professionals including doctors, teachers, veterinarians, and engineers prior to 1989 (Yoder 1999, 116–17; Welsh 1994). These people were trained to seek pragmatic, technical solutions to problems rather than to engage in partisan debates. Those who had been politically involved had remained low-level party members or had joined parties other than the ruling Socialist Unity Party in order to escape pressure to join the communist party. Some other new parliamentarians had been involved in the Roundtables which spontaneously emerged as communism crumbled; these bodies were set up expressly to oppose hierarchical, party-oriented decision making. None of these backgrounds prepared eastern Germany's new politicians for western-style party politics or confrontations between government and opposition. As one observer noted, "Interviews with eastern parliamentarians revealed an overwhelming preference for consensus—not at the expense to the competition of ideas—but a general leaning toward a consensual style of politics. . . . [Elites believed that the] opposition should be taken . . . seriously and that many voices and ideas should be heard, rather than that of just the governing coalition" or party (Yoder 1999, 130–31). At the grassroots level, skepticism of political parties has translated into lower party membership in eastern Germany (Linnemann 1994) and less-developed inner-party organizations than in the west (Grabow 2001a). Because the elite of breakthrough were skeptical of party politics and unlikely to have had much experience in active party organizations, these eastern parliamentarians were unlikely to enter parliament with strong partisan identities or loyalties.

Moreover, eastern German party caucuses are much less ideologically cohesive than their western German counterparts (Linnemann 1994).[7] Because eastern parties either were established at the time of unification or were suddenly thrust into a completely different political environment, these parties did not have much time to establish clear stances on the issues confronting the new Länder. Since members joined parties before the organizations had had a chance to establish specific positions on issues only emerging as unification progressed, people with quite different political views entered the same party organizations. As a result politicians with extremely different ideological views and issue positions often found themselves in the same party group. This makes it unlikely that eastern Fraktionen will be highly disciplined due to the ideological cohesion of their members. Instead, in response to disagreements within caucuses, eastern German and European "political elites are less likely to be motivated by organizational loyalties and commitments, and are correspondingly more likely to resolve conflicts . . . by engaging in short-term mergers and alliances with other parties" (Mair 1996, 16) rather than holding fast when votes are taken.

In short, the sociological factors conducive to party discipline were not present in eastern Germany following unification. Elites distrusted strong political parties and favored consensual decision making; they initially had little if any grassroots experience with a party to develop strong partisan identities and loyalties; and MdL did not have strong ideological commonalities with their fellow caucus members. Nonetheless, as will be shown below, highly disciplined Fraktionen emerged in eastern Germany's new state parliaments. This discipline is a testament to Germany's strong institutional incentives for unified parliamentary parties.

Institutional Incentives for Discipline

The literature on parliamentary systems in general, and the German system in particular, clearly establishes many institutional incentives for disciplined legislative parties. The first, of course, is the fact that in a parliamentary system the governing party (or coalition) in the legislature must stand behind their chief executive and cabinet, or the government can fall. In order for opposition parties to provide voters with clear-cut alternatives to a disciplined governing party or coalition, they too must act coherently in the legislature. Were legislative parties not coherent, cycling majorities could lead to great political instability as governments rose and fell (Gallagher, Laver, and Mair 2001; Laver and Shepsle 1999).

Even scholars studying presidential systems where such executive branch instability is not a problem, however, find that in the absence of legislative parties, new majorities would have to be cobbled together to pass each piece of legislation, a highly inefficient practice (Aldrich 1995). Particularly in modern legislatures responsible for law-making in a wide range of complex and technical areas, it is difficult for an individual deputy to master or even understand all the pieces of legislation she is to vote on. By joining a parliamentary party she can rely on the expertise of other caucus members or executives from her party to guide her voting on an array of issues (Cox 1987). Being part of a parliamentary party and deferring to other party members in their area of expertise also provides an individual legislator with allies who will support his position on issues that are of importance to him. Without coherent legislative parties, then, parliamentary work would be inefficient and uncertain.

Moreover, the German system contains a number of resources that enable such efficiency to occur, in keeping with Article 21 of the Basic Law: "the parties shall take part in forming the political will of the people" (quoted in Conradt 2001, 288). Each state legislature has its own *Fraktionsgesetz* (legislative party law) which spells out the rights and duties of parliamentary parties. Each caucus is provided with public funding (a certain amount per member) to finance its parliamentary activities, including hiring administrative help to run the caucus office, funding a press office to do public relations work, and paying staffers to do policy-related research. In 1990 federal financing for Bundestag Fraktionen totaled ninety million deutsche marks. This spending means both that the party caucuses have considerable resources to devote to drafting legislation and that any bills which make it into committee and eventually to the floor of parliament have been approved by the majority Fraktion(en) (Schüttemeyer 1994, 38).

Independent members of state parliaments enjoy neither this influence on legislation nor access to these funds, although they are entitled to administrative and research help from the staff of the parliament as a whole. Seats on parliamentary committees, voting rights on these committees, a say in determining the parliamentary agenda, and the time allotted to legislators to speak in a plenary session are all allocated on the basis of Fraktion membership. The German Supreme Court has ruled that independent members are not guaranteed a seat with voting rights on any committee—although they may speak and make proposals—and they are not allowed a seat on the Council of Elders which sets the parliamentary agenda. Nor do they have a right to a minimum amount of time to speak on the floor of the parliament, as do party caucuses (Gesetzgebungs- und Beratungsdienst 1999). Thus if MdL want to have access to the resources and opportunities needed to influence policy, they are best associated with a party caucus. Further, if a party group hopes to pass the legislation it drafts, it must stand together when votes are taken.

Even if state representatives were willing to tolerate such legislative inefficiency, the German system includes electoral factors promoting united Fraktionen. Depending on the state, between 50% and 100% of parliamentarians are elected via the list proportional representation electoral system.[8] Voters must vote for parties and, outside of Bayern, they cannot alter the rank ordering of candidates on the ballot. Party members nominate candidates for places on electoral lists and are unlikely to give the nomination to someone who has consistently gone against his own party. Further, voters have little incentive to vote for a party whose caucus does not stand together in a united bloc when in government because they cannot predict what that party will do in office (Taagepera and Shugart 1989, 55–56). Studies of German voters indeed indicate that they are critical of internally divided parties, preferring to vote for united parties with clear goals (Patzelt 1998b). Thus even legislators who win a constituency seat may find their electoral chances dimmed if their caucus is divided amongst itself or at odds with other branches of the party. All MdL, then, have incentives to run on a party ticket and remain loyal to the party in legislative voting once they are elected to the Landtag.[9]

These institutional incentives for disciplined voting have been strong enough to withstand a number of challenges in western Germany over the years. For example, Article 38 of the Basic Law stands in sharp contrast to Article 21 cited above. Article 38 stipulates that deputies in the Bundestag are "not bound by orders and instructions, and shall be subject only to their conscience" (quoted in Conradt 2001, 291). In keeping with this Article, in 1984 over 150 members of the Bundestag called for reforms giving individual members of the legislature more independence from their parties (Schüttemeyer 1994, 40). Outside of the federal legislature, the rise in post-materialist values and education among western Germans in recent decades has led to the widely documented phenomenon of Parteiverdrossenheit, or dissatisfaction with political parties. The electoral success of the Greens, who promised to make deputies independent from the party's leadership, to hold public party caucus meetings, and to forgo party discipline, illustrates attempts even in western Germany to move away from powerful legislative parties. Opinion polls show both that a majority of German citizens would prefer to see parliamentary deputies vote their own opinion rather than the party line (Patzelt 1998a, 745) and that calls for the use of referenda have increased in recent years (Conradt 2001, 88). Despite mounting opposition to party discipline in western German society, parliamentary parties remain highly disciplined.

In sum, the logic of Germany's parliamentary, legislative, and electoral institutions have combined to create enduringly strong Fraktionen in western German Landtage and in the Bundestag. Because identical institutions were transferred to eastern Germany with unification, similarly high discipline is expected in the east despite the different sociological background of legislators there.

EMPIRICAL EVIDENCE:
PARLIAMENTARY VOTING IN THE NEW LANDTAGE

In the section below I draw on statements made by MdL on the floor of parliament and in personal interviews to trace the development of parliamentary parties in eastern Germany over the past decade. Studies of legislative discipline and party cohesion often rely on the use of roll call votes. Because party discipline in western Germany is so strong, however, roll call votes are generally not taken in German legislatures. In 2000, only 2% of the substantive[10] votes taken in the Landtage under examination were roll call votes. Such votes can only occur if a minimum number of deputies request a roll call; this usually happens when certain MdL or Fraktionen are expected to vote at odds with what they have been promising constituents, when the opposition wants to make the ruling party go on record as having voted for an unpopular measure, or when one party caucus wants to expose divisions in another (or force its opponent to discipline dissenters). For example, in Sachsen-Anhalt the Greens once requested a roll call vote explaining, "In this discussion we've experienced different positions within the FDP. And we've also discovered in the press that there are slightly different positions within the CDU as well. If some deputies are prepared to revise their opinions and agree upon a common position today, then we'd really like to hear what it is." The stenographer reported applause from the opposition and unrest among CDU and FDP deputies (SA-01-22-10).[11]

Thus, while I examine roll call votes below, I also draw on additional evidence gleaned by reading the transcripts of eastern plenary sessions from the second year of each of the electoral periods in the decade following unification: 1991, 1996, and 2000.[12] To see how eastern Landtage compare to those in the west, I also read the transcripts of plenary sessions from their western partner states' legislatures in 2000. Eighty percent of the time, legislative votes were prefaced with a statement from each Fraktion, declaring its position on the issue at hand. When votes were taken, the Landtag's stenographer noted the outcome of the vote and/or how each caucus voted; sometimes individuals or caucus leaders then gave statements justifying their votes. This information allowed me to categorize 92.9% of the 10,526 substantive votes taken in the years examined. Each vote taken was classified first according to who proposed it: the executive, the majority Fraktion(en), an opposition Fraktion, a Fraktion tolerating a minority government, an individual MdL, or a combination thereof. Second, I examined what kind of a measure was being voted on: a law (*Gesetz*), a motion (*Antrag*), an amendment (*Änderungsantrag*), a motion to send a proposal to a committee, or a procedural question. Third, I recorded whether a measure was accepted, rejected, or sent to a committee. Finally, I placed votes in the following categories:

- *No Opposition* (All deputies voted in favor OR the majority caucus voted *en bloc* in favor and the opposition abstained *en bloc*.)
- *Disciplined Majority* (The majority caucus voted *en bloc* in favor and at least one opposition party voted *en bloc* against, or vice versa.)
- *Undisciplined Majority: Individuals Dissent* (At least one individual did not vote with her party caucus.)
- *Undisciplined Majority: Coalition Splits* (The caucuses involved in the governing coalition, or members of these caucuses, voted in different ways so that one coalition partner was on the losing side.)
- *Unclear Lines of Division* (There was some opposition, but no further information about the nature of this opposition could be gleaned.)

While this method is less precise than using roll call votes, it clearly is a much more representative sample of votes taken and provides many more cases to examine.

The First Electoral Period: 1990–1994

The first elections to the newly formed eastern Landtage were held following unification in October 1990. Despite easterners' professed skepticism of parties, no candidates without a party affiliation were elected.[13] The parties winning seats included—as in western legislatures—the

Christian Democrats, the Social Democrats, the Free Democrats, and the Greens/Alliance 90.[14] In addition, the Party of Democratic Socialism, the successor to the communist party, won representation in all eastern legislatures. In the east, Sachsen's legislature contained a single-party majority, as did Niedersachsen in the west; all other states formed coalition governments.

In the east, the newly elected MdL faced several daunting tasks. A vast range of legislation needed to be passed immediately as there was a widespread absence of state laws in most areas. Almost overnight the new legislatures had to develop a body of law similar to that which had been developed in the western Länder over the course of four decades. Further, they had to complete this task under less-than-ideal logistical conditions. For example, because there was no parliament building in Sachsen's capital city of Dresden, the legislature first met in a church. Deputies in all states initially did not enjoy large offices or technical support; most Fraktionen did not have telephones, computers, or photocopiers.

It is likely that the high levels of education and pragmatic, problem-solving backgrounds of the new MdL enabled them to pass needed legislation with alacrity. A westerner who ultimately became the Sachsen CDU's whip observed that because most of his deputies had previously been technical experts, they approached parliamentary work as "a problem [that needed to be solved], they analyzed the situation and decided on a course of action." In an interview, a western spokesperson for the SPD caucus in the eastern state of Sachsen-Anhalt agreed that the "technicians and engineers" who joined his party caucus knew how to "deal with problems rationally," whereas western politicians, he claimed, "discuss and discuss again and then try to shed more light on the subject." As a result, he argued, westerners could not make decisions quickly but, at least in the first electoral period, eastern MdL were likely to say, "that's it, this is the way to go. There's no sense in perpetually discussing things." The Social Democratic whip in the northeastern state of Mecklenburg-Vorpommern, himself an engineer, concurred that initially he had approached parliamentary work like "research," looking for technically correct rather than political solutions. This stress on "policy not politics," as one western bureaucrat sent to work in the east called it, was in keeping with easterners' desire for consensus and a lack of partisan politics.

Rather than trying to put forth a distinctive party line at the expense of other caucuses' views, legislators entered the newly created Landtage with the goal of working together to make technically correct public policies. For example, in Sachsen-Anhalt the speaker of the Landtag opened a 1991 plenary session saying, "The citizens of this state who elected us desire constructive problem-solving and fewer party-political polemics" (SA-01-19-00). In Brandenburg a Christian Democrat warned, "dogmatic actions simply cannot be allowed to dominate something that has been arrived at through technical competence. This would remind us too much of the old days of 'holy' Politburo decisions. Waging political warfare against a law whose only deficiency is that it comes from the opposition is macabre" (BB-01-18-03, 1368).

One of the earliest assignments for the eastern legislatures was to develop rules for parliamentary procedure and party caucuses. As would be expected of deputies skeptical of parties, some of the parliaments in eastern Germany changed the rules used by their western counterparts to give more rights to independent deputies. In Brandenburg independents received a voting seat on one committee, and in Berlin, Thüringen, and Mecklenburg-Vorpommern independent MdL received a minimum amount of time to speak in plenary sessions (Gesetzgebungs- und Beratungsdienst 1999). Article 46 of the Sachsen state constitution stated that the Landtag should make rules governing the formation of Fraktionen but also that "the rights of independent parliamentary deputies may not be restricted," a clause not found in the Basic Law or its partner Baden-Württemberg's constitution (Sächsischer Landtag 2001, 104–5). Nonetheless, all deputies initially joined their party's caucus rather than remaining independents.

Between 1990 and 2000 in the western German states examined, only three of the 1,454 legislators left their party groups. In contrast, during the first electoral period, 20 of 654 eastern MdL left their caucuses. During the first decade after the founding of the Federal Republic, however, many members of the Bundestag did not immediately join or remain with a Fraktion, so the twenty initial eastern defections do not indicate a relatively high rate (Schüttemeyer 1994, 37). Moreover, many of the eastern deputies who left their caucuses did not do so voluntarily. Instead, they were forced out after it was revealed they had collaborated with the East German secret police, the *Stasi*. Of the twenty eastern MdL who left their original Fraktionen, only one (who joined another major

party) was reelected. In the term that followed, no legislators abandoned their parties, and in the third term only two MdL left their caucus to become independents.[15] Party groups, then, played a key role in
the five new Landtage from the start.

The initial strength of the Fraktionen is illustrated when the sixty-
eight roll call votes taken in eastern Germany in 1991 are compared
with the thirteen such votes taken in western legislatures in 2000. Figure 3.1 shows the average Rice Index of cohesion score for all party families. This index runs from 0.0 to 1.0. The former score indicates that a
Fraktion was split down the middle in every vote taken. Conversely, a 1.0
indicates that all members of the caucus voted exactly the same way in
every vote under consideration.[16] Western parties, as is the case in the
Bundestag, were highly disciplined. Both the Christian and Free Democrats had perfect cohesion (1.0) and the Social Democrats and Greens
were almost perfectly disciplined as well (indices of 0.99 and 0.98 respectively). The far-right Republicans were the least disciplined with a
Rice Score of 0.91. In the eastern Landtage in 1991, cohesion in roll call
voting was lower than in the west. The Christian Democrats were the
most disciplined with a score of 0.94; the PDS, Greens, and Social Democrats also scored at 0.90 or higher, with indices of 0.92, 0.91, and 0.90
respectively. These parties were followed by the Free Democrats with a
score of 0.87. All of these scores, however, are quite high and attest to
the strength of parliamentary parties in the eastern German legislatures, at least in terms of highly controversial roll call legislation. With
the exception of the Social Democrats, they are actually higher than the
rates of cohesion in the Bundestag during the first legislative session
(1949–1953). Then the Rice Scores were SPD 0.99, CDU 0.86, and FDP
0.84 (Schindler 1999, 1784). The above analysis of voting in the new
Landtage is based on only a very small sample of the overall votes taken
in 1991, however. The evidence from floor debates and the non–roll call
votes paints a more nuanced picture.

Of the 3,786 substantive votes taken in the eastern Landtage during
1991, only 18.3% of those with an identifiable pattern involved a disciplined majority outvoting a disciplined opposition, compared to 47.7%
of such votes taken in western state parliaments in the year 2000. (See
figure 3.2.) In the west 47.3% of the votes taken had no opposition while
this figure fell to only 33.9% in the east. In another 21.8% of the eastern
votes, individual deputies defected from their caucuses—compared to

Figure 3.1 Roll call voting in the Landtage, 1991–2000

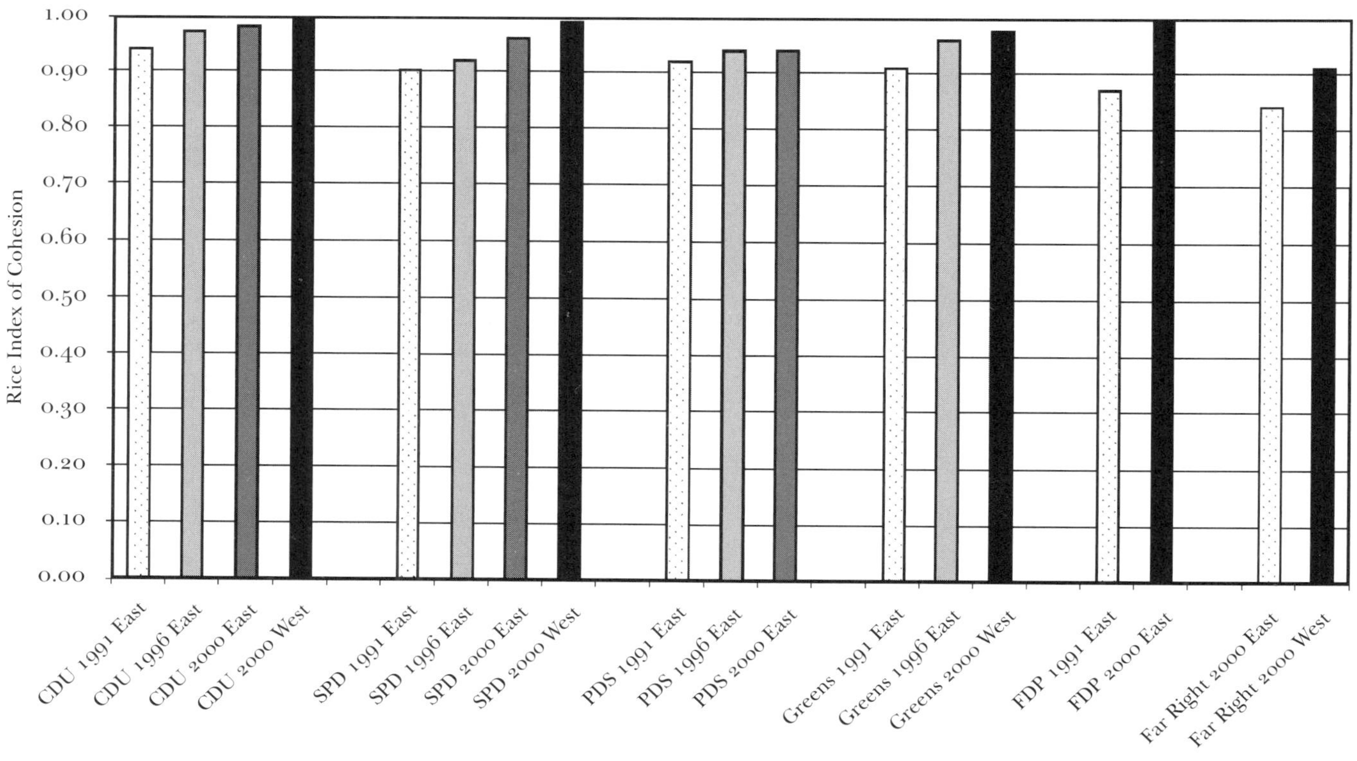

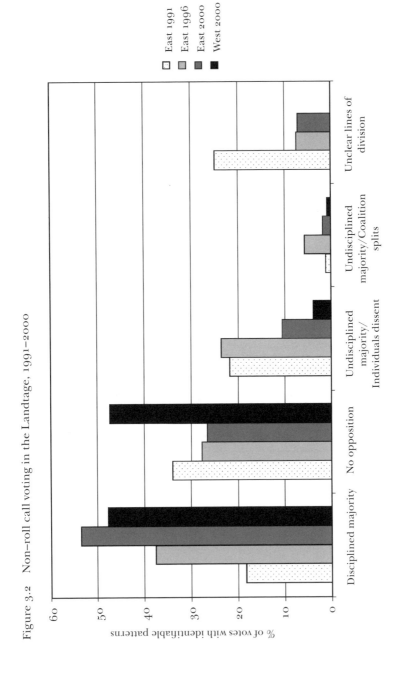

Figure 3.2   Non–roll call voting in the Landtage, 1991–2000

only 4% of the votes in the west. Similarly, in the eastern states with co-alition governments, the partners split 1.3% of the time while this hap-pened 0.9% of the time in the west. It is likely that the lapses in discipline in the new Länder were far greater than these figures indicate because the lines of division for one-quarter of the votes were not clear in the transcripts. The confusion in reporting results most probably was due to a lack of clear-cut party stances for the stenographers to record. In the west, only 0.4% of the votes had such ambiguous lines of division.

Many votes in the new Landtage were quite close, and sometimes an exact count of yeas and nays was required to determine the outcome of a vote. The following excerpts from plenary debates held in Sachsen and Sachsen-Anhalt during 1991 illustrate the difficulties that the Landtag Presidents had in determining the outcome of some early votes:

> Whoever would like to vote for this measure, please raise your hand.—Yes.—Who is opposed? . . . The voting must be repeated. Whoever would like to vote for motion 1/188, please stand up. . . . So, now we will count, very clearly—43. You may now sit down. Whoever is op-posed, please stand up now. Please count off! That's 46 votes. The motion is therefore rejected. (SX-01-16, 903)

> Whoever would like to vote in favor, please do so with a hand signal. All those opposed? Abstentions? I'm sorry, we're going to have to have an exact count. I'm requesting yet again the hand signals of those in favor [of the measure]. Please, can I have an exact count? Who is against this? 20 votes against. [The stenographer records un-rest.] This was the number signaled to me. Then we'll have to take this back again. Whoever is opposed, please give me a hand signal. 22 votes against. The abstentions again. Then it's clear that [this mea-sure] did not find a majority. [Unrest] I'm going to repeat myself again so that no misunderstandings crop up. (SA-01-13-02).

The following exchange is illustrative of the difficulties faced by party leaders trying to organize their Fraktionen. When informed that the whips of all parties had agreed to cancel a special session to debate the Sachsen hunting law, an opposition Free Democrat took the floor demanding, "if the whips are of the opinion that there's no need for [the special session], that's their opinion. It isn't necessarily the opinion of the deputies on the floor." The stenographer records members of the majority Christian Democrats applauding this statement and two calling out "jawohl!" and "quite right!" (SX-01-16, 825-26).

MdL at times showed overt pride in their lack of discipline and were defensive when voting along party lines. As the leader of the Sachsen PDS party group stated, "I want to explain the voting behavior of my caucus. The Fraktion voted against the law. There was no party discipline in doing so. All the deputies in our caucus voted this way as a free decision." Then the leader of the Greens took the floor and declared, "I, like all the members of my caucus, voted out of my free will against" the law (SX-01-30-11, 1939). A member of the Greens in Sachsen-Anhalt asked for a postponement of a floor vote saying, "Mr. President, we just got this motion on our desks two minutes ago. We haven't even had the chance . . . to check [what we're voting on]." When reminded that his party supported the measure and had agreed to the plenary agenda, the deputy argued, "This is in principle correct. But in my function as parliamentarian I have the opportunity to make up my own mind. I can't do that in two minutes" (SA-01-23-05).

Similar splits occurred in the first electoral period between members of the executive and their parties' Fraktionen in the Landtag. One of the most vehement examples occurred in Brandenburg where the Social Democratic President of the Landtag condemned a Social Democratic Minister in front of the parliament, saying "At this point I would like to make a further comment based on a similar incident in the last plenary session. The Finance Minister's portrayal did not correspond with the facts. . . . The data that were presented here were not correct. . . . I think that when a committee asks for a justification in regard to one of his decisions or motions, then the executive should give it. I see it as a breach of regulations to treat the parliament this way" (BB-01-30, 2255).

Coalition partners also attacked each other in plenary sessions. For example, after the FDP Minister of Science sent a draft Higher Education bill to the Brandenburg Landtag, his Green party coalition partner stated, "Ladies and Gentlemen, Colleagues, this law meets with our approval in many points but in many others it meets with our strict rejection. There's a lot of work that's going to be necessary before we can get a passable Higher Education bill that meets the quality standards we demand." He was cheered by members of the opposition (BB-01-15, 1198).

Despite this strong rhetoric, however, undisciplined MdL seem to have been kept at least somewhat in check. From the start, majority parties and coalitions were consistently able to pass their legislative agendas. (See figure 3.3.) In 1991, the average eastern legislature passed 78.3% of the laws proposed by the government or majority Fraktion(en), while only 0.6% of these laws were rejected by the parliament. The remaining laws, most of which were submitted to the Landtage late in the year, had not emerged from committee before December 1991. On average, eastern governing parties also were able to pass 80.4% of their motions and 79.9% of their amendments to bills on the floor. In contrast, on average only 2.4% of their motions and 2.0% of their amendments were rejected.[17] Again, the remaining proposals had not yet emerged from committees. While the governing Fraktion(en) enjoyed a great deal of success in the new Landtage, their failure rates were slightly higher than the average failure rates for western majority parties. In the west, majority caucuses saw none of their laws or amendments lose, and only 1.7% of their motions failed to pass.

In the German parliamentary system, committee seats are divided up in the same proportion as the legislature, so a united majority Fraktion or coalition has a majority in every committee and can shape legislation to its satisfaction. In the five eastern states in 1991, 99.1% of the decisions made by parliamentary committees were upheld in floor votes and only 0.6% were rejected. In the west no committee decisions were rejected on the floor and 95.8% were passed. The remainder in both parts of Germany were returned to committee for further discussion. It is important to note that because the partisan composition of the executive, the legislature, and committees does not vary in Germany's parliamentary system, German legislation is rarely "held hostage" in committee as a way of keeping it from a floor vote. Instead, virtually all proposals are processed by committees and returned to the floor as soon as feasible. To confirm this was indeed the case, I traced the fate of each type of proposal that had not emerged from committee in one state per year examined. The Länder investigated were chosen because their percentage of proposals failing to emerge from committee by December was closest to the five states' average that year.

An examination of the fate of laws remaining in committee in eastern Brandenburg in December 1991 found that all had been passed by

Figure 3.3   Success of majority proposals, 1991–2000

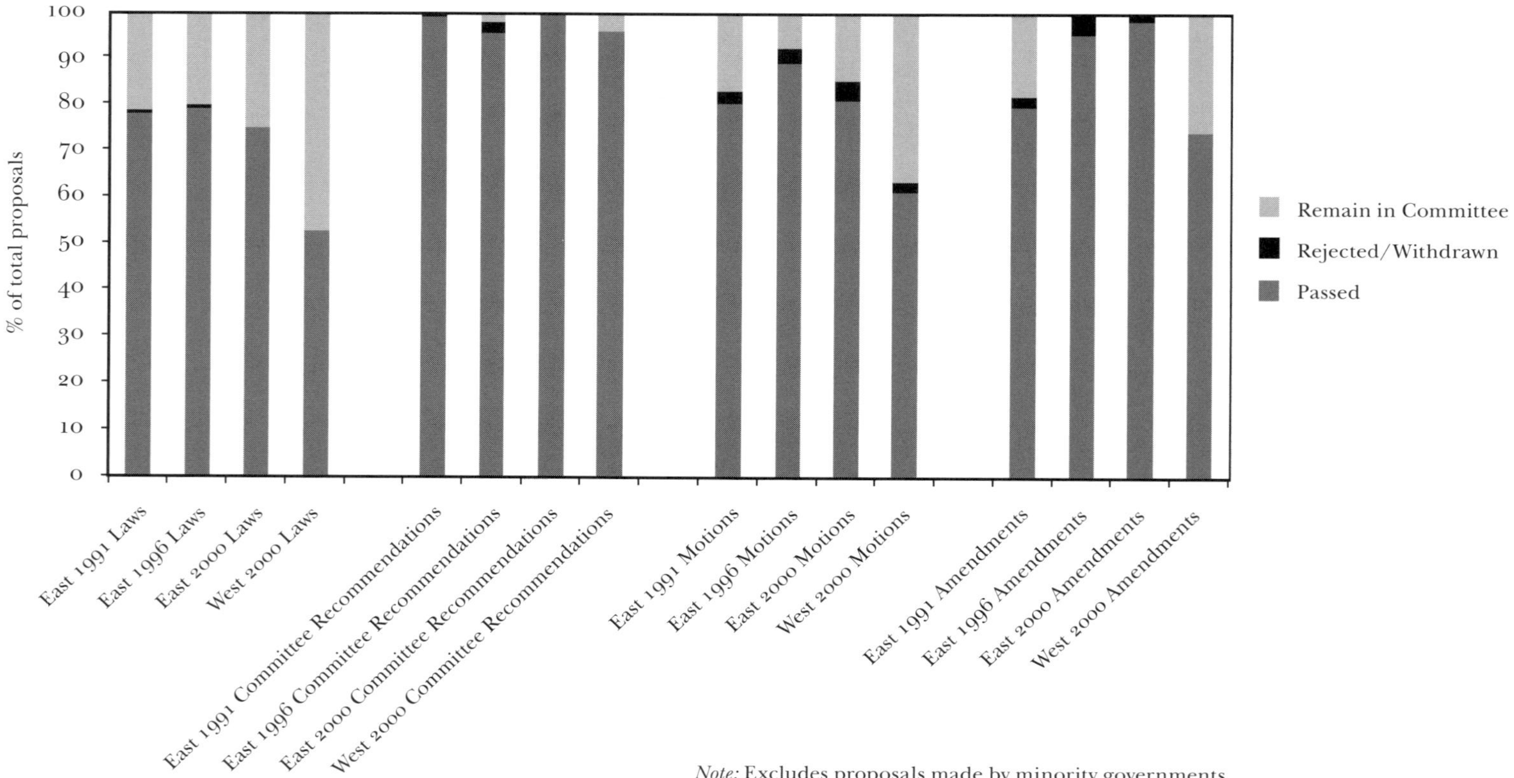

Legend:
- Remain in Committee
- Rejected/Withdrawn
- Passed

y-axis: % of total proposals (0, 10, 20, 30, 40, 50, 60, 70, 80, 90, 100)

Categories:
East 1991 Laws, East 1996 Laws, East 2000 Laws, West 2000 Laws, East 1991 Committee Recommendations, East 1996 Committee Recommendations, East 2000 Committee Recommendations, West 2000 Committee Recommendations, East 1991 Motions, East 1996 Motions, East 2000 Motions, West 2000 Motions, East 1991 Amendments, East 1996 Amendments, East 2000 Amendments, West 2000 Amendments

Note: Excludes proposals made by minority governments.

Table 3.1: Coalition discipline, 1991–2000

	East 1991 N = 4 states	East 1996 N = 3 states	East 2000 N = 3 states	West 2000 N = 4 states
Laws proposed by a coalition partner alone	2	1	0	1
Motions proposed by a coalition partner alone	30	0	1	13
Amendments proposed by a coalition partner alone	13	0	1	0

Note: Figures are totals for all states with coalition governments that year.
Source: Parliamentary transcripts

May 1992. This was quite similar to the western rate. In Schleswig-Holstein all the remaining laws were passed by February 2001. There one motion was withdrawn but all others were ultimately passed or considered settled. Some motions, such as a call on a particular Minister to appear before a certain committee and give a report, never returned to the floor of the Landtag and were considered settled when the appropriate action was taken (e.g., the Minister appeared before the committee). In eastern Brandenburg all remaining motions were passed by April 1992. Finally, in terms of amendments, the one amendment remaining unpassed in western Niedersachsen was returned to committee and incorporated in a new motion which was ultimately approved on the floor of parliament. In the eastern state of Sachsen the remaining amendment had also passed by early 1992.

Although coalition and party discipline generally held in the above instances, this was not always the case. While in western states individual coalition members rarely made proposals without their coalition partners, eastern coalition members did so much more often even though such proposals had lower success rates than ones put forward by the coalition as a whole. (See table 3.1.) In the eastern Landtage in 1991, there were thirteen amendments proposed by a coalition partner alone, whereas in the west there were no such amendments proposed anywhere. Similarly the eastern legislatures saw thirty motions proposed by a coalition partner alone compared with only thirteen in the west. Laws proposed by a coalition partner alone were rare in both halves of Germany; only one was proposed in all western states and two in all of the eastern Länder.

Open splits within eastern coalitions were the exception rather than the rule in 1991, however. Majority parties and coalitions were moreover able to use their numbers not only to pass proposals they favored, but to defeat most of the proposals put forth by opposition parties. (See figure 3.4.) The opposition proposed an average of sixteen laws in the eastern states during 1991; only 9.3% were passed that year. While this success rate was low, it was still higher than that in the average western Landtag. In the western Länder in 2000, the typical opposition proposed ten laws, but only 4.0% actually passed that year. The success rate of opposition motions and amendments was similarly low across Germany: 30.1% of eastern opposition motions passed in 1991, and 14.9% of the opposition's amendments were adopted that year. These figures, while low, were still higher than in the average western Landtag, where only 12% of opposition motions and 2% of opposition amendments passed in the year under investigation.

Eastern opposition Fraktionen's occasional successes inspired them to more frequently make proposals than western opposition caucuses did. (See figure 3.5.) The average eastern Landtag considered 122 opposition motions and 113 opposition amendments in 1991 compared to 74 and 43, respectively, in the average western legislature.

Weaker partisanship meant that on a number of occasions eastern majority and opposition Fraktionen—or individuals associated with each—worked together to propose and pass various measures. In the average eastern legislature in 1991, five laws were proposed by the government and the opposition together compared to only two in the average western parliament. (See figure 3.6.) Easterners were far more active when it came to making joint motions and amendments—the average eastern legislature saw 31.8 such proposals compared to only 8 in the west. Similarly, eastern majority and opposition parties sponsored an average of six joint amendments while the western figure was only one. Acceptance rates for such joint proposals were 80% or above per year in both parts of the country.

In sum, during the first electoral period, majorities were disciplined enough to hold together in key roll call votes and to pass most legislation. Government majorities remained stable throughout the first electoral period as well. Nonetheless, on a day-to-day basis parties were less disciplined than their western counterparts, eastern coalition partners were more likely to act on their own than western ones, opposition parties were more likely to get their way, and there was more cross-party cooperation than in the west. Clearly, sociological factors did exert a degree of influence on eastern MdL immediately following unification.[18]

Figure 3.4   Success of opppostion proposals, 1991–2000

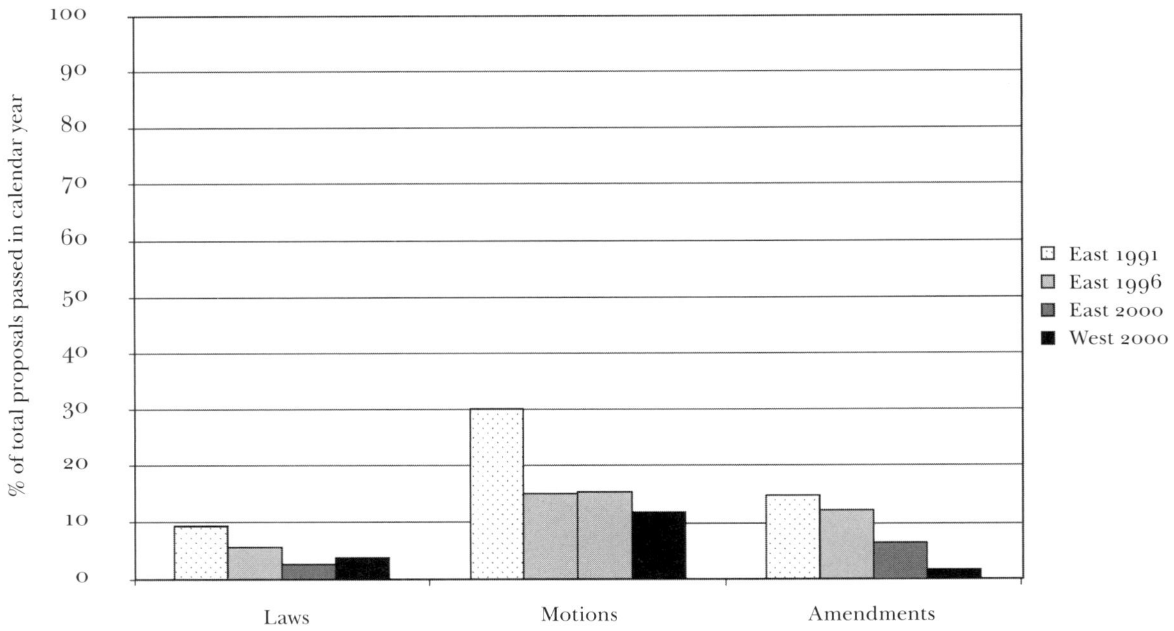

Legend:
- □ East 1991
- ▨ East 1996
- ▨ East 2000
- ■ West 2000

y-axis: % of total proposals passed in calendar year.
y-axis values: 0, 10, 20, 30, 40, 50, 60, 70, 80, 90, 100

x-axis categories: Laws, Motions, Amendments

Note: Excludes proposals made by "toleration" Fraktionen in minority governments.

Figure 3.5 Frequency of opppostion proposals, 1991–2000

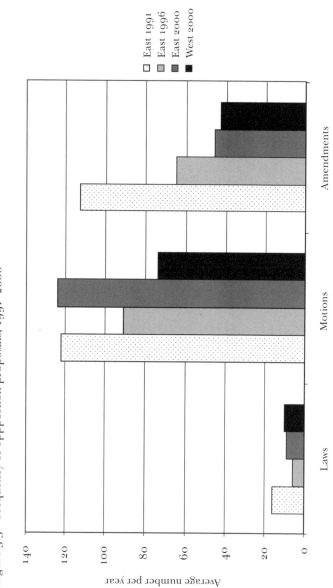

Note: Excludes proposals made by "toleration" Fraktionen in minority governments.

Figure 3.6 Frequency of joint government-opposition proposals, 1991–2000

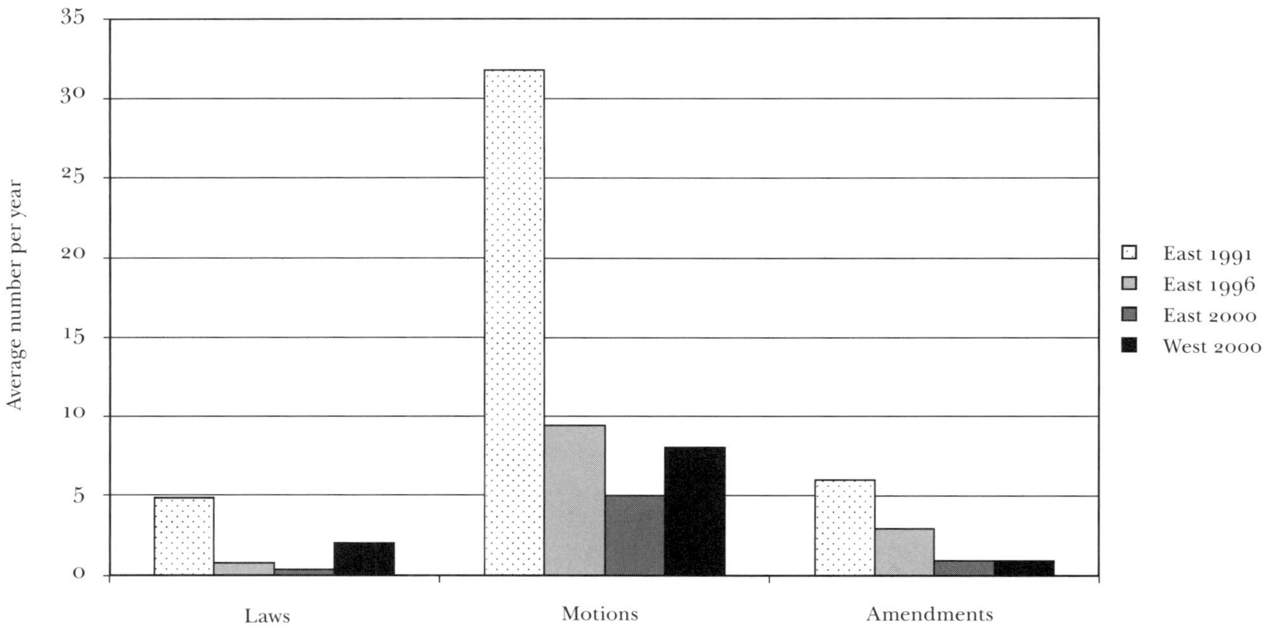

This influence has diminished steadily since then, however, suggesting that parliamentarians have come to appreciate institutional incentives for disciplined voting. This trend can be observed in the second electoral period.

The Second Electoral Period: 1995–1999

The 1994 elections returned the three major parties (CDU, SPD, PDS) to all of the eastern legislatures, the Greens only returned to the Sachsen-Anhalt Landtag, and the FDP failed to meet the 5% hurdle in all eastern states. Sachsen continued to have a single-party government, as did Niedersachsen in 2000. In Sachsen-Anhalt a minority SPD/Green government was tolerated by the PDS, a pattern not replicated anywhere else in Germany; coalitions formed in all other states under investigation.

In 1996, ninety-eight roll call votes were taken in the eastern Landtage, and the Rice Index for all parties represented increased, becoming more like western Fraktionen's indices. (See figure 3.1.) The CDU continued to score the highest, with a Rice Index of 0.97; the SPD's score increased to 0.92. These parties had similarly high scores in their second electoral period in the Bundestag; the SPD remained at 0.99 while the CDU increased to 0.90 (Schindler 1999, 1784). In the new Landtage in 1996, the former communists' cohesion score increased from 0.92 to 0.94 while the remaining Greens' jumped from 0.91 to 0.96.

Moreover, in terms of the more representative non–roll call votes, disciplined voting rose dramatically, from only 18.3% of the votes with identifiable patterns in 1991 to 37.6% in 1996. (See figure 3.2.) The occurrence of undisciplined individuals also increased slightly to 23.6% of these votes, however. Further, the number of votes in which coalition partners split also jumped to 5.8% from only 1.3%. Rather than indicating a decline in individual or coalition discipline, however, the above figures suggest their increase. As Fraktionen became more disciplined, the percentage of votes with unclear lines of division decreased considerably, dropping from 25% in 1991 to 7.6% in 1996. Because non–party line voting occurred more rarely in the second legislative session, it merited more comment on the floor of parliament. As a result, breaks in party or coalition discipline were easier to identify in 1996 than they were in 1991. For example, in Sachsen-Anhalt the opposition CDU once gleefully pointed out, "The encrusted relationship between the SPD [minority government] and PDS [the party that tolerated it]. . . has suddenly burst apart, showing visible splits that everyone can recognize" (SA-02-39, 2946).

Majority parties continued to be able to pass their legislative agendas in 1996, and the government of Sachsen-Anhalt survived a critical vote of no confidence. Of the laws proposed by eastern governments and majority caucuses, 78.7% passed and the failure rate was a mere 0.7%.[19] (See figure 3.3.) The remaining laws, most proposed late in the year, were not defeated but had not emerged from committee by December 1996. In the test case of Sachsen, all remaining laws were ultimately passed, most by April 1997, but one law not until March 1998. In addition, 97.4% of the decisions made by eastern parliamentary committees in 1996 were upheld in floor votes and a mere 0.6% rejected.[20] Eastern majority Fraktionen and coalitions also enjoyed overall success in passing their motions (89%) and amendments (95.6%), although a slightly higher percentage of their motions (3.2%) and amendments (4.4%) were either rejected or withdrawn than in 1991.[21] While all amendments were processed by the end of 1996, some motions remained in committee in December. In the test case of Sachsen-Anhalt, one motion was rejected but all others were passed by early 1997. Thus despite eastern MdL's initial skepticism of party discipline, eastern majorities remained able to pass their legislative agenda more often than not in the second electoral period. While they were still defeated slightly more often than western majorities—who saw none of their laws, amendments, or committee decisions rejected and only 1.7% of their motions—eastern majorities' failure rates were nonetheless quite low.

Moreover, in 1996 eastern coalition partners' cooperation actually exceeded western levels—only one law, and no motions or amendments, was proposed by a coalition partner on its own compared to one law and thirteen motions in the west.[22] (See table 3.1.) Majorities became more willing to use their weight not only to pass their own legislation but also to defeat an increasing percentage of the proposals made by opposition Fraktionen. (See figure 3.4.) The percentage of opposition laws passed in 1996 fell from 9.3% to 5.7%, while the share of their motions passed that year fell from 30.1% to only 15.1%; the success rate for amendments in 1996 fell from 14.9% to 12.3%. Eastern opposition parties found it ever more difficult to influence parliamentary decision making, making them ever more similar to their western counterparts. Furthermore, as in the west, the eastern opposition began to be more selective in the proposals it put forth. Their average number of draft laws fell from 16 to 6, the number of motions from 122 to 91, and the volume of amendments from 113 to 65. (See figure 3.5.) Members of the majority and the opposition Fraktionen also worked together much less frequently in the eastern Landtage in 1996. The average number of joint laws fell from 4.8 to 0.8, motions from 31.8 to 9.4, and amendments from 6 to 3. (See figure 3.6.) Finally, the number of unopposed votes decreased from 33.9% to 27.7% of the votes with identifiable patterns, in this case moving further away from the western figure of 47.3%. (See figure 3.2.)

With the exception of unopposed voting, then, all of these trends indicate that eastern Landtage were moving closer to the patterns exhibited in their western counterparts. Still, however, disciplined voting was less frequent than in the west, while opposition victories and cross-party cooperation were more frequent. All of these indicators, except unanimity, converged on western patterns during the third electoral period.

The Third Electoral Period: 1999–2003

The elections of 1998/9 again brought the CDU, SPD, and PDS to eastern state legislatures. The Greens were not returned to any eastern parliament, nor were the Free Democrats. The far-right German People's Union entered the Brandenburg and Sachsen-Anhalt Landtage. Eastern Sachsen retained a single-party government like western Niedersachsen. While Sachsen-Anhalt kept its unique minority government, all other states formed coalition governments. By 2000 these eastern Landtage had become highly disciplined parliaments, just like their western partners.

For the veteran eastern parties, the Rice Index of Cohesion for roll call votes inched ever closer to the 1.0 mark: the CDU scored 0.98, the SPD 0.96, and the PDS 0.94. (See figure 3.1.) The DVU's 0.84 score resembled that of the FDP when it first entered the eastern Landtage in 1991. The CDU's cohesion score was actually higher than the western Christian Democrats' ten years after the founding of the Bundestag (0.94) while the SPD's was close (0.99) (Schindler 1999, 1784).

Moreover, in contrast to the previous legislative periods, the disciplined roll call pattern was replicated in the rest of the votes taken in eastern state legislatures. (See figure 3.2.) In fact, the percentage of votes featuring a disciplined majority voting against a disciplined minority was higher in the eastern (53.4%) than in the western Landtage (47.7%). Votes in which individual MdL defected from their party caucus fell from 23.6% of eastern votes to 10.6%, and incidents in which eastern coalition partners split fell from 5.8% to 1.9%. Only 7.3% of the eastern votes had unclear lines of division. These figures remain higher than in the west (4%, 0.9%, and 0.4% respectively), but the ten-year trend is clearly toward greater discipline.

As a result of this discipline, the majority Fraktion(en) were very successful in realizing their legislative agendas in all states examined. In eastern Länder, just as in western ones, the government and majority caucus saw none of their laws defeated; 74.7% (east) and 52.5% (west) of laws were passed during the year.[23] (See figure 3.3.) The remaining laws were not defeated; they simply had not emerged from committee by December 2000. In the western test case of Schleswig-Holstein all the remaining laws were passed by February 2001, and in Sachsen-Anhalt all but one of the remaining laws had been promulgated by May 2001.[24]

Further, all of the decisions made by parliamentary committees in eastern legislatures, and 95.8% of those in western parliaments, were upheld in floor votes. Eastern majorities passed 81.2% of their motions and 98.2% of their amendments, while western majority Fraktion(en) passed 61.5% of their motions and 74.5% of their amendments.[25] Eastern majorities had a 4% failure rate for their motions, somewhat higher than the 1.7% rate in the west. Eastern majorities also continued to have a slightly higher failure rate for their amendments—0.9%—compared to 0.0% in the west. However, these failure rates are clearly minimal. All other proposals remained in committee in December 2000. In the eastern test case of Thüringen all of the remaining motions were eventually passed. In the western test case of Schleswig-Holstein all motions but one, which was withdrawn, were ultimately passed. No eastern amendments remained in committee in December 2000, and in the western test case of Niedersachsen the one that did was returned to committee and incorporated into a motion that ultimately was approved on the floor of the Landtag.

Coalition discipline continued to be strong. (See table 3.1.) No eastern coalition member proposed a law without its partner, and only one motion and amendment each were proposed by an eastern coalition partner acting on its own.[26] The figures for laws and motions were actually below the western figures that year (one and thirteen respectively). The number of amendments proposed by a coalition partner alone in 2000—one in the east and none in the west—barely differed across Germany. Overt clashes between coalition partners in plenary sessions all but disappeared.

Eastern majorities also showed a greater willingness than ever before to reject proposals made by the opposition. (See figure 3.4.) In the case of laws proposed by the opposition, only 2.7% became law in 2000, even lower than the 3.8% rate in the west. In terms of motions and amendments, eastern majorities passed opposition proposals only slightly more often than western ones. Eastern majorities approved only 15.4% of opposition motions in 2000, whereas western legislatures passed 11.8% that year. Similarly, opposition parties in the east saw their amendments accepted 6.6% of the time, while this figure fell to 1.8% in the west. Despite these differences, opposition Fraktionen's chances of passing legislation in either part of Germany is low and the chances in the east have decreased over time.

In spite of their decreasing chances of success, eastern caucuses do continue to remain more active than western ones in terms of proposing motions; they proposed 115 motions in eastern parliaments in 2000 and only 74 in western Landtage. (See figure 3.5.) The number of laws and amendments proposed by the opposition have converged across Germany, however. Only nine opposition laws were proposed in the east and ten in the west in 2000. Eastern Landtage saw forty-six opposition amendments and the western state legislatures forty-three.

Majority and opposition parties in eastern Germany also cooperated less frequently in 2000 than they had previously. (See figure 3.6.) The average eastern legislature saw less than one jointly proposed law compared to two in the typical western parliament. The same was true of cross-party motions, which averaged five in eastern and eight in western legislatures that year. Both sides of Germany saw on average only one amendment proposed by members of the government and opposition. In the east this represents a sharp rate of decline from 1991.

While the overall trend was convergence on the western model, eastern Landtage did continue to have lower rates of consensual voting.

(See figure 3.2.) Of identifiable votes taken in eastern legislatures, 26.6% featured no opposition in comparison to 47.3% in western state parliaments. Furthermore, eastern figures have been declining since unification, not rising in the western direction as has discipline. This stands in sharp contrast to the Bundestag, which saw unanimity steadily *increase* during its first decade (Schindler 1999, 1954). The lack of unopposed votes and low levels of cross-party cooperation in eastern Landtage may represent a backlash created when consensual individuals were confronted by partisan institutions. Because many eastern legislators entered parliament hoping to make nonpartisan, technically correct decisions, they may have been particularly frustrated by the growth of partisan decision making and become hostile toward their opponents, further reducing consensus. The few westerners present in eastern legislatures agreed with this assessment during personal interviews. The Christian Democratic whip in Sachsen noted that, compared to westerners, easterners were prone to taking differences of political opinion personally; rather than accepting the loss of a vote and going out for a beer together later, he said, politicians on opposing sides wouldn't look one another in the eye. A journalist in this state echoed his sentiments, observing that relations among Saxon MdL are either "quiet and harmonious" or "people are upset and emotional." He believed the deputies had failed to learn the "culture of disagreement" (*Streitkultur*) needed for parliamentary work. The eastern Social Democratic whip in the state of Mecklenburg-Vorpommern agreed that from his perspective westerners were "more willing to accept conflict" and knew better how to fit into a hierarchy. Easterners, he thought, tend to believe everyone is equal and should have an equal say in matters; opposition parties felt they had a right to be heard and were angry when ignored.

Incidents from plenary sessions also illustrate the tendency of opposition party groups to be frustrated if they are not accommodated. In Brandenburg in 1991, when the majority Fraktionen wanted to bring the law governing ministers to a vote without providing opposition parties additional time to raise arguments against the bill, the head of the CDU caucus declared, "it is absolutely unbearable parliamentary style to . . . deny the opposition the chance to express its opinion about the problems with ministerial pay. For this reason, we will no longer take part in the rest of today's plenary session, and we will take the liberty of describing this scandal to the public" (BB-01-15, 1233). Similarly, all Fraktionen in Sachsen-Anhalt agreed to stop the January 1991 plenary session in order to get together and draft a joint statement about the Gulf War. When the negotiations failed to yield a motion that all parties could agree to, the opposition PDS and Greens boycotted the rest of the session (SA-01-07-00).

In one final difference, eastern legislatures continued to move legislation through committees faster than their western counterparts. (See figure 3.3.) This efficiency may be a legacy of the early 1990s when eastern legislatures were required to develop a body of state law equal in size to their western partners' almost overnight, whereas their partners had had forty years to complete the task. In the first legislative period the average eastern legislature considered seventy-six brand new laws, while westerners only dealt with twenty-nine laws, mostly minor updates to existing legislation. To pass such voluminous legislation within a year, eastern committees were forced to quickly process proposals sent to them. In one extreme example, part of the 1991 Brandenburg budget law had its first reading in parliament before lunch, the budget committee debated it over lunch, and the second and third parliamentary readings of the bill took place in the afternoon (BB-01-27, 2005). Today, however, while they are still faster than western committees, the speed at which eastern committees consider laws has been steadily slowing, converging on the western pattern (Interview SPD Mecklenburg-Vorpommern).

In sum, Fraktionen in eastern Germany have become nearly as unified as those in their western partner legislatures; disciplined voting occurs not only in key roll call votes but also in most day-to-day decision making. Similarly, the use of cross-party decision making has been reduced, and eastern committees are beginning to slow their deliberations down. While the opposition gets its way more often than in the west, its success has declined significantly since the first electoral period. Only easterners' low level of unanimity remains considerably different from western decision-making patterns.

Causes of Convergence

The beginning of this chapter outlined a number of institutional incentives and argued that these were likely to lead the Fraktionenparlament to be recreated in eastern Germany. Personal interviews with deputies and excerpts from parliamentary transcripts suggest that eastern MdL do indeed recognize these incentives, which have played a key role in minimizing the influence of the consensual, antiparty attitudes that eastern deputies originally brought with them to parliament. Interviews show that eastern MdL clearly recognize the logic of a parliamentary form of government. The head of the Alliance 90/Green caucus in Sachsen observed in 2001 that when they entered the parliament, the Greens were "ur-democrats" and thought that decision making would resemble the Roundtables where each member could influence decisions through a true dialogue. He conceded, however, that this expectation was "completely naive and illusionary. We quickly became aware that we couldn't change what the majority wanted. There was no alternative to the usual parliamentary procedure in Saxony." Were his caucus not disciplined, the Social Democratic whip in Brandenburg mused, "we could just pack up and leave" the governing coalition. Similarly, the PDS whip in the eastern state of Sachsen-Anhalt observed the difference in his Fraktion's attitude toward party discipline between the time it was in the opposition and when it supported a minority government. He attributed his caucus's initial low discipline to "an attempt to distance itself" from the old SED; not voting along party lines "had a certain attraction [because it was] a little bit chic and very democratic." But he also knew it "didn't make much of a difference" the way his opposition caucus voted whereas the "difficult process" he had to go through to get his caucus to toe the line was "nerve wracking." In the next electoral period, however, when his party supported a minority government "it *did* make a difference" the way his Fraktion voted, and it had "a pistol at [its] breast" to unite around a party position.

In addition to discovering the logic of parliamentary government, plenary transcripts indicate that deputies quickly learned the efficiency incentives for disciplined party groups during the first year of parliamentary practice. The initial low degree of party cohesion made itself apparent in the lack of coordination between the Fraktionen and their representatives to given committees. Generally in German parliaments, caucuses discuss legislation *before* committee meetings so that their representatives can speak for the Fraktion in committee. These predetermined party lines hold both in committee and on the floor of parliament. This was certainly not the case in eastern Germany in 1991. Instead, the Fraktionen discussed legislation *after* committee meetings and often the party group as a whole had quite different opinions about bills than their representatives had expressed in committee. During committee discussions about Sachsen's police law, for example, CDU delegates agreed with the Greens to require that all policemen wear nametags while on duty. By the time the bill was debated on the floor, however, the CDU had added an amendment striking this provision (SX-01-23-05, 1405). Similarly, in a speech on the Sachsen wastewater law, the SPD speaker explained, "the representatives of the SPD in the Environment Committee voted in favor of the CDU's suggestion for a preamble to the law. After weighing all considerations one more time, we've changed our mind and are submitting an amendment to parliament" to revise the preamble (SX-01-19-10, 1104).

This lack of consistency in party positions and the willingness of deputies to vote against their caucus meant that, in contrast to established western legislatures, there was a much higher degree of uncertainty about the outcome of floor votes and much lower efficiency in decision making. The outcome of legislation was sometimes determined in a last-minute compromise forged on the floor of the parliament. A westerner who was the Christian Democratic whip in Sachsen agreed that, in the early years, plenary debates were more important there than they were in western Germany: "The discussion was significantly more intense; we made decisions during conversations, saying 'that's how we'll do it!' on the floor of the parliament." Examples of such last-minute compromises can be seen through separate incidents in Sachsen and Brandenburg. During the floor debate on the Sachsen police law, various amendments were proposed regarding the length of time police could detain a suspect. In committee, the CDU majority had passed a bill stipulating a week over a PDS proposal for twenty-four hours. When the PDS tried again on the floor to get this amendment passed, an FDP representative spontaneously moved, "Now then, there are two proposals in the room: on the one hand, 24 hours, and on the other hand, a week. For this reason the FDP suggests the following compromise: 4 days. If the police have to take someone into custody on Friday so that he won't cause any mischief over the weekend, he can be held until Monday." The CDU caucus split and the FDP's measure was passed (SX-01-23-09, 1414). In Brandenburg the opposition PDS and CDU Fraktionen made a motion regarding education policy. A lone member of the governing SPD suggested a compromise wording during the floor debate and the motion was passed without opposition (BB-01-16-02).

Furthermore, because party groups often changed their minds after committee meetings, specific parts of laws that in the west (and today in the east) are determined by committees were reopened for debate on the floor. Even if opposition parties maintained the same issue positions between committee and plenary sessions, there was always the chance that the governing party or parties might have changed their minds. During 1991 a number of plenary sessions lasted from ten in the morning to eleven at night; a review of parliamentary transcripts suggests that this duration was due to repeated attempts by the opposition to convince the sometimes-undisciplined majority to accept amendments that they had previously voted down in committee. For example, one opposition caucus head outlined the rationale behind these repeated amendment proposals: "It's true that the suggestions we're making here didn't receive a majority in the committee, but I don't believe that all deputies who are present here [on the floor] took part in the committee debate. Parliamentarians have a free mandate—they're beholden only to their conscience—and it could indeed be the case that the majority of the deputies are convinced that the suggestions are correct" (SX-01-22-06, 1330). In Sachsen-Anhalt a law governing localities had been rejected once on the floor and sent back to committee to be renegotiated. In committee, sixteen PDS amendments to the bill were rejected. During the third reading on the floor, the PDS tried (vainly) to get its amendments passed. The speaker for the party warned, "a voting marathon stands before us. . . . I think that this is necessary so that you, my esteemed colleagues, have a last chance to decide for the better" (SA-02-39, 2946).

The inefficiencies of these sessions taught the majority the importance of consistent discipline, and the opposition the bitter realities of majority rule and the need to be more selective in proposing amendments. After almost a year of "voting marathons," deputies clearly began to recognize the inefficiency of their prior actions. After a number of opposition amendments to the Sachsen hunting law were rejected, one MdL declared, "we cannot continue with the style of work we have cultivated so far." The stenographer recorded applause from all caucuses (SX-01-17-04, 945). In Sachsen-Anhalt, after a committee decision was rejected on the floor and returned to committee, a Christian Democrat concluded his remarks saying, "Incidentally, we should mutually agree to discipline ourselves to avoid taking this kind of discussion into plenary sessions. It's a real burden here" (SA-01-24-13). Members of the Brandenburg opposition were dissatisfied with a draft law and wanted to return it to a committee even though it had enough votes from the

coalition Fraktionen to pass. A speaker from the majority Social Democrats complained, "I simply reject having to go sit down in the interior
committee and chew through things we've already discussed" (BB-01-06,
1866).

As discipline rose, this on-the-floor style of decision making decreased and policy outcomes became more predictable.[27] The Christian
Democratic whip in Sachsen reported an increased role played by the
executive in policy making. His SPD counterpart mused that her party
had been successful in getting its proposals passed in earlier legislative
periods due to splits between the Christian Democratic Fraktion and its
executive; this happened less often as time went on. Interviews with
whips of caucuses in other eastern states similarly indicated that decision making had moved from the floor of parliament and committees
into the majority Fraktion's room and meetings with its executive or coalition partner (see also Patzelt and Schirmer 1996, 22).

In interviews with caucus leaders, however, the most frequently mentioned reason for increasingly unified Fraktionen had to do neither with
the logic of the parliamentary system nor with legislative efficiency but
instead with electoral incentives. The Christian Democratic whip in the
eastern state of Sachsen-Anhalt recalled that the members of his Fraktion elected in 1990 did not really know one another before the election
and had very different visions for the caucus; this led to fights among
CDU deputies and subsequently some members withdrew from the
party group. He argued that this led voters to question the CDU, asking
"what's wrong with your caucus that people want to leave it?" The Social
Democratic whip in Mecklenburg-Vorpommern agreed that while there
"needed to be" disagreements within the caucus and while such differences of opinion were "constructive, the voters don't like it." As a result,
his caucus tried to hide their differences behind closed doors; "it's not
open or honest, but that's the way this business works. I think this happens in other caucuses too."

Other politicians also saw electoral incentives to avoid consensus decision making and to transmit clear-cut partisan positions to potential
voters. The Social Democratic whip in Sachsen reminisced that at first
the SPD and CDU worked together to develop a state constitution and
the SPD did not play a strong opposition role. As a result, she believed,
it was not really clear to voters what her Fraktion stood for. In turn, she
argued, the party lost considerable ground in the next election. Based
on these experiences, she said, the Social Democrats today try to play a

"classic opposition role." They spend more effort trying to "develop a profile" by appointing a shadow government and criticizing the government's actions in many areas. Finally, other MdL noted that elections themselves served as a mechanism for caucuses to become more disciplined in the mid- to late-1990s. Christian Democratic whips in both Sachsen-Anhalt and Brandenburg noted that their parties sought to remove dissenting deputies by refusing to renominate them for the party list.

Interviewees did not mention sociological factors such as party solidarity or ideological cohesion as reasons why their party groups voted together. Whips did not view their jobs as socializing caucus members into appropriate norms of unity but rather as pointing out the hard logic of parliamentary realities to their compatriots. These realities included the need to keep the executive in power, to avoid grossly inefficient decision making, and to provide voters with clear-cut alternatives.

IMPLICATIONS

In other words, the institutional incentives outlined above—the logic of the German's parliamentary system and its electoral system—played a key role in building parliamentary parties in eastern Germany over the course of the 1990s. While some remnants of undisciplined voting and cooperation with the opposition remain in the eastern Landtage, the consensus-oriented opposition, frustrated when the majority party does not consult it, is now actually less likely than its western counterpart to vote with the governing majority and less likely to cooperate across government-opposition lines. Institutional incentives have created disciplined parliamentary party groups in a setting where politicians and their constituents held antiparty norms, where parties outside parliament were very weak, and where caucuses were ideologically divided.

Thus the emergence of disciplined eastern party groups in the decade after German unification provides strong support for the institutional, rather than the sociological, view of the origins of party discipline in democratic legislatures. In a setting where sociological factors—including antiparty norms and low ideological cohesion as well as weak party organization and identification—all suggest that party groups will not be united when votes are taken, the opposite occurs. The emergence of disciplined Fraktionen is consistent with the parliamentary and electoral institutions in place, and interviews with MdL suggest they are fully aware of the incentives built into these institutions. These findings suggest that causes of party voting in democratic legislatures can be found not by examining the sociology of deputies but rather by studying the nature of the arenas in which these individuals legislate. Even where ideological cohesion is low and party identification weak, discipline may still be high if electoral and parliamentary institutions are conducive to party voting agreement.

Party discipline also quickly emerged in post-war western Germany and has withstood the Federal Republic's change to a post-materialist society, increasingly skeptical of disciplined political parties. Spurred by this societal change, some western Landtage have undertaken reforms to try to move away from strict party discipline and strongly representative democracy. Schleswig-Holstein's 1990 constitution included the most liberal provisions for direct democracy to date in western Germany and introduced a measure of transparency in parliamentary decision making, including opening committee meetings to public scrutiny. In the latter half of the 1990s western states including Niedersachsen and Nordrhein-Westfalen also undertook a process of *Parlamentsreform* (parliamentary reform) to promote, among other things, more spontaneous debate on the floor of parliament, allowing backbenchers time to speak and raise issues for debate. To date, however, these changes have not significantly changed German parliamentary procedure. Open committee meetings have simply extended party line voting into committees, while deals among coalition partners now get hammered out before committees meet (Interview, SPD, Schleswig-Holstein). And while backbenchers may speak more often in plenary sessions, their disciplined voting remains unchanged. Future scholars may want to track these trends to see if they eventually produce more substantive results, although developments to date suggest that this is unlikely. Established western European political institutions persist despite the widespread sociological changes which have occurred in the region since the 1960s.

Studies of other areas of post-communist eastern Europe indicate that discipline is on the rise there as well. After experiencing the legislative incentives for party discipline, parliamentarians elsewhere in eastern Europe also began to see the advantages to party voting (Malova and Sivakova 1996, 122) and took steps to implement rules more conducive to disciplined decision making (Bach 1996, 213; Remington and Smith 1996, 174; Haspel 1998b; Sobyanin 1994, 191). This has also led to increased discipline in post-communist legislatures over the past decade (Fish 1995, 345). Future comparative studies pairing the eastern German case with other parliaments in eastern Europe with similar incentives for discipline will help assess the strength of the role played by contextual factors unique to Germany—such as the presence of an established party system and western personnel—on increasing discipline.

The results presented here, like those in the previous chapter, also help us assess the ramifications of opinion surveys that find contrasting attitudes and values on the part of Europeans socialized under communism and democracy. This research is often taken as an indication that eastern Europeans' political behavior will be at odds with western Europeans'. The rise of discipline in eastern German parliaments suggests that, despite their different pre-1989 experiences, eastern Europeans are just as capable of recognizing the incentives embodied in democratic political institutions as their western counterparts. In this vein, my findings can be interpreted as offering evidence that individual political actors are rational ones who respond strategically to their surroundings, whatever their prior socialization.

Finally, beyond simplifying parliamentarians' working day and avoiding government instability, disciplined legislative voting shapes the substantive content of the policies passed by the eastern Landtage. This is the focus of the next two chapters.

Becoming Representatives: Eastern German State Legislators, Direct Democracy, and Economic Equality

The previous chapter discussed how eastern and western MdL made decisions in Germany's state parliaments, documenting the rise of party discipline. This chapter focuses on the substantive policy implications of party discipline, specifically in terms of the direct democracy procedures written into eastern German constitutions and the Landtage's subsequent reactions to plebiscitary attempts. In western Germany prior to unification, the Greens repeatedly criticized the country's lack of national-level referenda, while the conservative CDU and Christian Social Union (CSU) defended the Federal Republic's highly representative political institutions. The FDP and the SPD were split on the issue of direct democracy. Following GDR citizen groups' success in bringing down the communist regime, eastern Germans in all political parties were more supportive of plebiscites than their western counterparts. Here I investigate whether or not easterners' attitudes led them to adopt more direct democratic procedures in their state constitutions than westerners had and whether or not their pro-plebiscite attitudes made eastern MdL supportive of actual direct democracy initiatives in the five new Länder. Many of these initiatives called for greater state involvement in the economy, providing an additional opportunity to investigate whether eastern MdL also acted on their oft-documented socialist economic values.

As was the case with the previous chapter, these questions are of interest because they tap into an overarching debate about the sources of legislator behavior. On the one hand, the sociological approach stresses the importance of parliamentarians' political attitudes and values in shaping their decision making on the floor of parliament. The institutional approach, on the other hand, underscores the power of the political rules of the game in molding deputies' behavior. Since eastern MdL's life experiences created in them a much stronger preference for direct democracy than western Germans' have, the sociological approach would expect the former to have created political institutions more conducive to referenda. Similarly, because eastern Germans are strongly in favor of economic equality and a large role for the state in achieving this goal, the sociological approach would expect them to be supportive of public policies designed to smooth out the inequalities created by capitalism. Given that such policies were proposed in direct democratic initiatives, this approach would predict that eastern MdL would be doubly supportive.

The political system that eastern MdL inherited at unification—the party state outlined in the previous chapters—is a highly partisan form of representative democracy. Because easterners joined parties and voted along party lines relatively quickly after unification, the institutional approach would expect the partisan debates over direct democracy to be repeated in the eastern states. Eastern branches of the Greens would be expected to promote greater direct democracy as they had in western states, whereas eastern CDU Fraktionen would be expected to be more skeptical of plebiscites and the like, just as this party family was in the west. Thus this approach would expect the partisanship of government, not attitudes toward direct democracy, to be the best predictor of eastern Länder's constitutional provisions for direct democracy

Furthermore, across western Germany incumbent parties have traditionally opposed citizen initiatives because referenda interfere with their prerogative to make public policy; in contrast, opposition parties, who have little ability to influence public policy in Germany's disciplined Landtage, generally favor such initiatives as they are one of their few means of shaping policy. If majority Fraktionen reject popular initiatives, supporting these citizen-sponsored proposals also offers opposition caucuses the opportunity to score points with dissatisfied voters. Thus the institutional approach would expect support for direct democratic initiatives to vary across eastern Fraktionen, depending on whether they were in the opposition or in the majority. Given that over half of these referenda called for either greater state involvement in the economy or for more direct democracy, this is a particularly difficult case for the institutionalist hypothesis.

I find that while eastern constitutions were slightly more friendly to referenda than western ones, the debate over direct democracy was, from the start, conducted mainly along partisan lines parallel to those at the national level. Furthermore, in the subsequent twelve years, legislative majorities, regardless of partisanship, were less receptive to direct democratic initiatives than were opposition parties in the Landtage—even when these initiatives called for greater direct democracy or economic equality. Easterners' party voting means that individual MdL's political positions can be predicted not by their east/west origin but by their partisan affiliation and whether their Fraktion is in the majority or opposition.

Before I develop this argument, an important clarification is in order. Ultimately, I wish to make two separate points in this chapter. First, although eastern German politicians have attitudes more strongly in favor of direct democracy than westerners, they did not create political institutions that were considerably more conducive to direct democracy than those in western Länder. MdL in governing Fraktionen have not been very supportive of most of the citizen initiatives which have been put forth since unification—even those calling for more direct democracy. Second, I use these plebiscite attempts to illustrate that although eastern German politicians have attitudes that strongly favor state involvement in the economy, in practice, MdL in governing Fraktionen have not been very supportive of direct democratic initiatives that seek just such state involvement. In both cases, elites have not acted in the way one would have expected by looking at their initial attitudes and values. My goal is to show the limited influence of two separate attitudes on elite behavior and highlight the role played by the German party state in limiting this influence, rather than to draw out some kind of relationship between support for direct democracy and for economic equality, causal or otherwise. In the eastern German case, extensive opinion research convincingly argues that MdL are in favor of both, but I do not mean to suggest that this is everywhere the case. Indeed, in the United States, proponents of direct democracy are often in favor of less government involvement in the economy and American states with citizen initiatives have significantly lower state spending than those with no citizen initiatives (Matsusaka 1995).

To show the limited influence of MdL's political attitudes on their legislative actions, I will look first at the literature on Germans' attitudes toward direct democracy and second at the institutionalization of this practice in western Germany. I then examine the parliamentary debates held when the five new states' constitutions were drafted and explore their provisions for direct democracy. After discussing the cause of state-to-state variance in these constitutions, I spend the rest of the chapter reviewing the eastern Länder's actual experiences with direct democracy between 1990 and 2002. I conclude by discussing the implications of my findings.

Eastern MdL's Attitudes toward Direct Democracy and the Federal Republic's Representative Institutions

Attitudes toward Direct Democracy

Shortly after unification, social scientists turned their attention toward eastern German mass and elite attitudes toward democracy, initially with the aim of assessing public support for this form of government. While support for democracy as a whole was high in the new Länder (Rohrschneider 1999, Weil 1993), closer investigations revealed that eastern and western Germans had very different conceptions of what democracy actually entailed. In a study of mass attitudes toward democracy in Germany, Dieter Fuchs identified two ideal types of democracy held by German citizens: a liberal-libertarian model and a democratic-socialist model (1997, 88). Both ideal types of democracy involve civil liberties, party competition, freely elected representatives, rule of law, private property, and a separation of powers. The democratic-socialist model, however, involves additional elements including a strong direct democratic component, a greater redistributive role for the state, some state-owned property, and greater government involvement in the market. Fuchs found that when queried about specific aspects of democracy, eastern Germans preferred his democratic-socialist model whereas westerners favored the liberal-libertarian model. For example, when asked if the use of referenda to decide important questions was a necessary part of democracy, 75% of eastern Germans compared to only 52% of western Germans agreed (98).[1]

These differences in democratic priorities can be observed not only among the mass publics in eastern and western Germany, however, but also within the ranks of elites. Wilhelm Bürklin's Potsdam Elite Study conducted in 1995 found that the main difference between German elites' conceptions of democracy lay in their assessment of plebiscitary elements (Bürklin 1997b, 243–45). When asked whether the adoption of referenda was a necessary supplement to representative democracy, eastern elites were more than twice as likely as westerners to favor plebiscites: 57% of eastern elites and only 27% of western elites agreed with the statement. Similarly, in a survey of Berlin state parliamentarians, Robert Rohrschneider found a higher degree of support for a range of direct democracy procedures among eastern deputies. (See figure 4.1.) Furthermore, when he asked state legislators an open-ended question as to what they believed was essential to democracy, eastern Berlin's parliamentarians were ten times more likely than their western counterparts to include direct democratic procedures in their list of essential components (Rohrschneider 1999, 87). Follow-up questions in these personal interviews also revealed eastern Berlin MPs to be much more supportive of direct democracy than their western Berlin counterparts and to express a higher degree of support for holding a hypothetical referendum on asylum seekers in Berlin. These results were consistent across two rounds of interviews held in 1992 and 1995.

Easterners' abundant support for direct democracy has been attributed to their experiences during the peaceful revolution that brought down the GDR. New Forum and the citizens' movements that toppled the communist regime were strong supporters of direct democracy (Sa'adah 1998, 65–66). Bürklin argued that the success of the Monday demonstrations against the government legitimized direct democracy in the eyes of eastern elites (1997b, 245). Rohrschneider reasoned, "apparently, the people's revolution in 1989 and socialism's aversion to representative ('bourgeois') institutions imbued eastern Germans with an appreciation for mass involvement in politics" (Rohrschneider 1999, 91–92).

More important for this chapter, those who observed such attitudinal differences predicted that they would have a substantive impact on public policy. Rohrschneider argues, "MP's plebiscitarian ideals are not simply abstract statements without relevance to the political process.

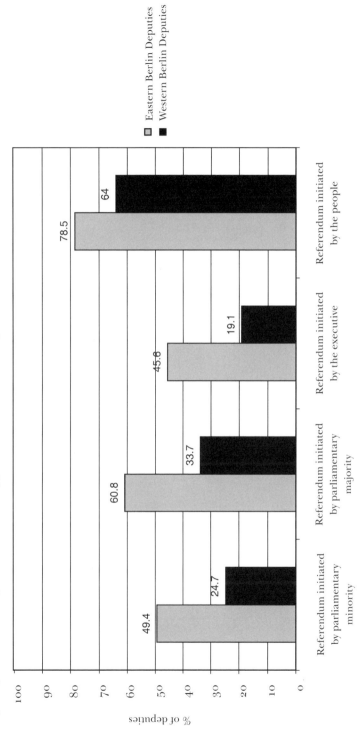

Figure 4.1   Berlin state parliamentarians' support for direct democratic procedures, 1992

Eastern Berlin Deputies
Western Berlin Deputies

% of deputies

Referendum initiated by the people — 78.5 / 64

Referendum initiated by the executive — 45.6 / 19.1

Referendum initiated by parliamentary majority — 60.8 / 33.7

Referendum initiated by parliamentary minority — 49.4 / 24.7

Procedure Type

Source: Rohrschneider (1991, 91).

Their ideals have practical consequences" (1999, 90). If political attitudes and values do shape elite political decision making, it would seem likely that easterners' support for direct democracy would have translated into a less representative form of democracy in the new Länder, creating both laws more conducive to plebiscites and a pattern of parliamentary support for actual direct democratic initiatives.

The Party State and Plebiscites

Direct Democracy at the National Level prior to Unification

A close look at the institutions that eastern MdL inherited at the time of unification, however, shows that the Federal Republic's party state was strongly at odds with direct citizen participation. Furthermore, the question of the appropriate extent of plebiscitary elements in the Federal Republic was a hotly debated topic at the national level when the Berlin Wall fall. Because eastern MdL became disciplined members of western political parties, it would seem highly likely that the Landtag debates surrounding direct democracy would parallel the discussion at the federal level and in western states. In order to investigate whether this was indeed the case, it is first necessary to trace the debates surrounding referenda at the federal level and in the western Länder.

When originally written, the Basic Law did not provide for the national-level use of referenda in Germany. This was primarily a result of Germany's negative experiences with plebiscites in the Weimar era. In the decades prior to unification, public support for direct democracy procedures grew, especially among members of the peace and environmental movements. In response, all major political parties in Germany began to form positions vis-à-vis direct democracy. Since their formation in the early 1980s, the Greens had consistently held plebiscitary elements as one of their foremost political goals and had introduced a law in the Bundestag calling for more direct democracy in Germany. The fact that this law was defeated did not deter 100% of Green MPs surveyed in 1989 from favoring national referenda (Klages and Paulus 1996, 30). At the other end of the political spectrum, most vigorously opposed to plebiscites were the CDU and CSU. Starting in 1978 their program included a statement declaring that direct democracy was not one of their political goals at the national level, although it was accepted by the CSU for the state level in Bayern. In 1989, a survey found 80% of CDU/CSU delegates to the Bundestag opposed direct democracy at the federal level (Klages and Paulus 1996, 28). When the Free Democrats were in the opposition, they at times called for the use of referenda at the national level. At the time of unification, however, the FDP was in coalition with the CDU and followed its senior partner's line on the issue. A 1989 survey of the FDP's Bundestag MPs found only one third in favor of referenda at the national level (Klages and Paulus 1996, 29). Caught in the middle were the Social Democrats. Some members of the party, including deputy SPD leader Herta Däubler-Gmelin, publicly called for the federal use of referenda, whereas the party's union wing tended to oppose the practice. This division was evident in a 1989 survey that found 48% of the SPD's Bundestag caucus against the use of national-level referendum and 52% in favor (Klages and Paulus 1996, 29). Finally, the PDS Volkskammer deputies were also strongly in support of referenda; 96% were in favor of direct democracy at the federal level (Klages and Paulus 1996, 31).

This issue became politically salient when a joint Bundestag-Bundesrat constitutional commission was planned for the 1989 fortieth anniversary of the Federal Republic. Its job was to consider—among other issues—changing the Basic Law to include some form of direct democracy at the national level. As the GDR fell and plans for unification emerged, this constitutional commission was also seen as a forum for considering changes to the Basic Law as a result of unification. The success of citizen demonstrations and Roundtables in eastern Germany, combined with strong public support for referenda there, moved plebiscitary elements to the forefront of the commission's agenda. In 1991 the constitutional commission was formed and included 32 members of the Bundesrat and 32 Bundestag deputies, chosen to reflect the partisan composition of both houses. Of these 64 commission members, only five Bundestag representatives were from eastern Germany, and of the ten people representing the eastern Länder in the Bundesrat, only four were originally from eastern Germany (Klages and Paulus 1996, 83).

The commission met between November 1991 and February 1993 and discussed a number of proposals regarding amending the Basic Law to include more direct democracy.[2] While the PDS, drawing on demands developed by the eastern German citizen movement, frequently called for the extensive use of plebiscitary elements, it did not make any formal proposals in the commission. The Greens began by submitting

proposals calling for the extensive use of direct democracy at the federal level, and the SPD by submitting more restrictive guidelines. The
two parties eventually split the difference and submitted similar plans to
the commission. However, neither of these recommendations was passed
due to strong opposition of the majority CDU and FDP Fraktionen and
the marginalization of easterners in both the commission and the Bundestag. As a result, the commission did not recommend to the Bundestag and Bundesrat that any direct democratic elements be incorporated
into a revised Basic Law (Klages and Paulus 1996, 100–105, 123).

The subsequently elected Social Democratic/Green federal government called for the national use of referenda in their coalition agreement, and a majority of Bundestag deputies supported an SPD/Green
initiative to this end in 2002; however, due to the opposition of the
Christian Democrats, Christian Social Union, and Free Democrats, the
bill did not receive the required two-thirds majority needed to change
the Basic Law. Thus over a decade after unification, plebiscites were still
not held at the national level in Germany.

Direct Democracy at the State Level in Western Länder prior to Unification

For the Land level, Articles 29 and 118 of the Basic Law required that,
after Baden-Württemberg was formed, any new delineation of state
boundaries needed to be approved by voters of all states involved.[3] Other
than that, however, the Basic Law makes no provisions regarding the
use of direct democracy procedures at the state level. Some western German state constitutions, including those of Hessen and Bayern, require
citizens to approve any changes that the government proposes to the
Land's constitution. These rules, however, represent more of an opportunity for citizens to react to elite initiatives than a way for grassroots interests to set the political agenda.

Prior to unification, eight of the eleven western states did allow bottom-up direct democracy, albeit in a rather limited form. (See table
4.1.) These states included Bayern, Baden-Württemberg, Bremen, Hessen, Nordrhein-Westfalen, and Rheinland-Pfalz, which allowed direct
democratic procedures following their creation after World War II, as
well as the Saarland, which adopted such rules in 1979, and Schleswig-
Holstein, which approved procedures leading to referenda the same
year Germany reunified. All of these western German Länder require a
multiple-step process for citizen initiatives to come to a popular vote.[4]

Table 4.1 Western state laws regarding direct democracy prior to unification

State (Year adopted direct democracy)	Referendum required for constitutional change?	Can referendum be used to change constitution?	% of voters who must sign to approve Volksbegehren	How long to collect signatures?	Where can signatures be collected?	Requirements for a Volksentscheid to pass
Baden-Württemberg (1947)	No	Yes, if 50% of eligible voters approve	16.6%	14 days	Public office	33% of eligible voters must approve
Bayern (1946)	Yes	Yes, if 25% of eligible voters approve	10%	14 days	Public office	No quorum
Bremen (1947)	No (Yes, if parliament does not pass unanimously)*	Yes, if 50% of eligible voters turn out and 2/3 approve	10% (20% if constitution change)	3 months	Anywhere	25% of eligible voters must approve
Hessen (1946)	Yes	No	20%	14 days	Public office	No quorum
Nordrhein-Westfalen (1950)	No	Yes, if 50% of eligible voters turn out and 2/3 approve	20% (8% starting 2002)	14 days (8 weeks starting 2002)	Public office	15% of eligible voters must approve
Rheinland-Pfalz (1947)	No	Yes, if 50% of eligible voters approve	20% (10% starting 2000) (2 months starting 2002)	14 days	Public office	25% of eligible voters must turn out
Saarland (1979)	No	No	20%	14 days	Public office	50% of eligible voters must approve
Schleswig-Holstein (1990)	No	Yes, if 50% of eligible voters turn out and 2/3 approve	5%	6 months	Public office with possibility of additional locations	25% of eligible voters must approve

Note: Shaded aspects are the state laws most conducive to direct democracy.
Note: Niedersachsen, Berlin, and Hamburg had no provisions for direct democracy prior to 1990.
Source: Mehr Demokratie e.V. (2003a).
* Klages and Paulus (1996, 150).

The first step (not present in every state) is called a Volks*initiative,* or a proposal to the state parliament that it either adopt a certain measure or that a referenda be held to d ecide the matter. Relatively few signatures are needed to begin a Volksinitiative, but western German state laws placed strict limits as to the content of such proposals. Initiatives were allowed as long as they did not affect the distribution of funds in the state budget or the pay of public officials, tasks reserved for the state legislatures. This requirement—a tradition in Germany since the Weimar era (Klages and Paulus 1996, 229)—essentially excludes any proposal that will have more than a token financial cost to the state; since the founding of the Federal Republic one quarter of citizen initiatives have been found to violate this clause (Mehr Demokratie e.V. 2002, 4). As a result, citizen initiatives were few and far between in the pre-unification period. If a citizen initiative is found to be on an acceptable topic, the Landtag must either address the issue or, if it refuses, citizens have the right to begin working toward a referendum on the issue. In five of every six cases, however, German Landtage have not adopted the measures proposed by citizens (Mehr Demokratie e.V. 2002, 6), and the subsequent road to the ballot box is arduous.

The next step in this process is called a Volks*begehren* and involves collecting, within a certain period of time, a particular number of signatures in favor of holding a referendum. Prior to unification, the number of signatures required varied from state to state, ranging from 5% to 20% of eligible voters. Such requirements are considerably higher than in places where direct democracy is more widespread, including Switzerland (2%) and U.S. states like California (2%) (Mehr Demokratie e.V. 2003a). Furthermore, these high numbers of signatures have to be gathered in a very short amount of time, ranging from 14 days in CDU/CSU-dominated states including Bayern and Baden-Württemberg to six months in SPD-dominated Schleswig-Holstein. To make matters more complicated for citizen initiatives, many states required that signatures be gathered not by grassroots activists going door to door or otherwise holding petition drives, but rather by interested citizens signing such petitions in a designated public office during business hours in order to have their identification verified and their signature witnessed.

Only if referenda initiators can mobilize a large segment of the electorate to sign petitions at public offices during a very short period of time can the third step—a referendum or Volks*entscheid*—be held. Only one third of signature gathering attempts in Germany have ever succeeded (Mehr Demokratie, eV. 2002, 5), and many of these initiatives have subsequently been disqualified due to their intervention in state spending. If a Volksbegehren is successful, the state parliament can decide to accede to citizens' wishes without holding a referendum. Alternatively, the state also has the right to place a counter-proposal of its own on the ballot with the citizen-sponsored proposal. As a result of these hurdles, the only citizen-initiated Volksentscheid to actually be held prior to German unification occurred in Bayern in 1968 regarding religious schools.[5]

Even if a grassroots-sponsored question finally appears on a ballot in Germany, however, further obstacles to its passage remain. Not only must a citizen proposal receive a majority of the votes cast in a referendum, some states require that a certain percentage of eligible voters approve the measure for it to pass. This means that if there is low turnout, a ballot initiative receiving an overwhelming majority of votes cast may still be declared invalid. While Bayern and Hessen had no such quota on eligible voters' approval, quotas elsewhere ranged from 15% in Nordrhein-Westfalen to 50% in the Saarland. Additionally, in most western states this percentage was usually 50% if the measure required a change to the state constitution Thus while direct democracy existed on paper in the western German Länder prior to unification, its practice at the state level was far from routine anywhere in the west.

Direct Democracy at the Local Level in Western Länder prior to Unification

While referenda were not held nationally, and rarely held at the state level, they were also scarce at the local level prior to unification. The first German Land to adopt local-level referenda[6] was Baden-Württemberg, and its use of plebiscites is usually attributed to its location on the Swiss border. The form of local-level direct democracy used in that Land, however, was quite limited. It contained relatively high signature and turnout requirements and a long list of topics citizen initiatives were forbidden from addressing (Geitmann 1999). Conservative Baden-Württemberg adopted this practice in 1956, but no other state did so for several decades. In Schleswig-Holstein, following a political scandal (the *Barschel Affäre*) that reduced citizen faith in government, the left-wing Land government decided to revise the state constitution to include more transparency and direct democracy (Sampels 1998, 53; Wehling 1999, 105). Schleswig-Holstein's April 1990 constitution adopted provisions for local-level direct democracy similar to Baden-Württemberg's, although they were slightly more conducive to citizen initiatives (Wollmann 2001, 8, 11; Rehmet, Weber, and Pavlovic 1999, 122, 127). Despite the slightly liberalized form of direct democracy adopted by Schleswig-Holstein, in the first year the rules were in effect, there were only nine successful citizen initiatives in the state's one thousand localities (Wollmann 1999, 19), leading one proponent of direct democracy to lament that Baden-Württemberg was a "bad example" to have followed (Geitmann 2002, 167).

While rules for local-level plebiscites were quite restrictive and not often in place in western Germany, they had been embraced by both sides of the political spectrum. In May 1990, the East German Volkskammer passed a *Kommunalverfassung,* or constitution setting up local government structures in the country. Given easterners' pro-plebiscite attitudes, it did not come as a surprise that the constitution allowed local-level direct democratic procedures. However, the constitution's rules for local-level referenda were modeled on those in Schleswig-Holstein and Baden-Württemberg (Wollmann 1996, 107; 2001, 6), making local-level referenda difficult in practice (Geitmann 1999, 238). These provisions were to remain in effect for eastern localities after unification, until otherwise changed by the five new Landtage.

Given that MdL in these new legislatures were disciplined members of western political parties, the institutional approach would expect little variance in the local-level direct democratic procedures chosen because there was little partisan strife about these instruments in the west and because the law passed down from the Volkskammer was consistent with the western consensus. In contrast, because western parties disagreed about the use of referenda at the national level and had created different forms of direct democracy at the state level, it seems likely that the Land-level use of plebiscites would also become a partisan political issue in eastern Germany.

Empirical Evidence: Direct Democracy and the New Eastern State Constitutions

The following section empirically investigates easterners' choices regarding local- and state-level direct democracy procedures. When the five new Länder joined the Federal Republic, their parliaments had to create new state constitutions that could, but did not have to, include provisions for direct democracy both at the local and state level. I find that, in keeping with deputies' pro-plebiscite attitudes, all state parliaments did adopt both local- and state-level direct democracy procedures. However, the specifics of the state-level procedures chosen were determined by western-style partisan politics.

Local-Level Direct Democratic Procedures Chosen by
the Eastern Länder

At the local level, all five of the new Länder adopted variations of the plebiscitary procedures first used in Baden-Württemberg. In fact, by 1998 all states in Germany except Berlin revised their constitutions to allow for this form of local-level direct democracy (Rehmet, Weber, and Pavlovic 1999).[7] As one observer noted, "If one would like to characterize the new laws governing localities in one sentence, one can speak of a certain convergence on the tenants of the southern German [institutions] with a Baden-Württembergian imprint" (Wehling 1999, 92). This form of local-level direct democracy was adopted "over all usual partisan boundaries and all differences in political traditions and mentalities: in 'red' Brandenburg and in 'black' Sachsen, in the old Hanseatic cities as in . . . [newly created] Niedersachsen, in Schleswig-Holstein in the north, just as in Rheinland-Pfalz in southwestern Germany" (Jung 1999, 108–9).[8]

At times the eastern Länder varied from the western model and actually made Bürgerbegehren more difficult to pass; for example, Sachsen and Sachsen-Anhalt required a signature quota of 15% of eligible voters rather than the 10% required in Schleswig-Holstein and Baden-Württemberg, and Thüringen's quota was the highest in the Federal Republic at 20% (Rehmet, Weber, and Pavlovic 1999, 122). In any case, while they chose to include direct democracy at the local level, the eastern Länder chose the very restrictive western form, leading one pro–direct democracy advocate to question whether the incorporation of these elements was not a "triumphal procession," as commonly claimed, but an "epidemic" (Jung 1999, 104).

Because the use of referenda at this level of government was not a hotly disputed partisan-political issue in Germany by the 1990s, however, it is difficult to discern whether its unquestioned adoption in the eastern state constitutions was a product of easterners' pro-plebiscite attitudes or of western parties' agreement on this issue. Many observers attribute it to both (Sampels 1998; Wehling 1999, 105; Wollmann 2001).

State-Level Direct Democratic Procedures Chosen by the Eastern Länder

At the state level, however, direct democracy procedures were more controversial, allowing us to better disentangle the influence of political attitudes and institutions. In keeping with easterners' pro-plebiscitary attitudes, all eastern states adopted some form of state-level direct democracy—in contrast to some western states at the time, including Berlin, Hamburg, and Niedersachsen. Furthermore, parliamentary transcripts reveal cross-party consensus that *some* form of direct democracy procedures indeed needed to be included in the constitution. The new Länder adopted some of the more liberal provisions used by western states, making direct democratic initiatives somewhat easier to achieve. (See table 4.2.) For example, in all states but Brandenburg, signatures for a Volksbegehren were allowed to be collected outside of a public office, simplifying citizen initiatives' tasks. These legal provisions were more conducive to referenda than any western states' but Bremen, which also allowed signature collection outside public offices. Similarly, all eastern states allowed longer time limits to collect signatures than any western state but Schleswig-Holstein. There was widespread consensus over these stipulations in all eastern Landtage, underscoring the broad support plebiscitary elements enjoyed among eastern MdL.

Despite their selection of some liberal western provisions for direct democracy, however, all eastern states chose a variation of the multistep referendum procedure used in western Germany. In fact, in many respects the new eastern constitutions did not differ much from those in the west. For example, all eastern states but Sachsen created a strict quorum of eligible voters needed to approve a referendum for it to be binding, a requirement similar to most western states. All eastern Länder adopted a rule banning referenda that have to do with the distribution of funds in the public budget and the pay of public officials.[9] This requirement effectively rules out most popular initiatives in practice. In addition, if a Volksbegehren is successful in eastern Germany and a Volksentscheid is actually held, the threshold needed for the latter to

Table 4.2 Eastern state laws regarding direct democracy

State (Year adopted direct democracy)	Referendum required for constitutional change?	Can referendum be used to change constitution?	% of voters who must sign to approve Volksbegehren	How long to collect signatures?	Where can signatures be collected?	Requirements for a Volksentscheid to pass
Brandenburg (1992)	No (but used to adopt new constitution)	Yes, if 50% of eligible voters turn out and 2/3 approve	4%	4 months	Public office	25% of eligible voters must approve
Mecklenburg-Vorpommern (1994)	No (but used to adopt new constitution)	Yes, if 50% of eligible voters turn out and 2/3 approve	10%	No limit	Either inside or outside of public office	33% of eligible voters must approve
Sachsen (1992)	No	Yes, if 50% of eligible voters approve	12%	8 months	Anywhere	No quorum
Sachsen-Anhalt (1992)	No	Yes, if 50% of eligible voters turn out and 2/3 approve	11%	6 months	Anywhere	25% of eligible voters must approve if no counter-proposal by Landtag
Thüringen (1994)	No (But used to adopt new constitution)	Yes, if 50% of eligible voters approve	14%	4 months	Anywhere	33% of eligible voters must approve

Note: Shaded aspects are the state laws most conducive to direct democracy
Source: Mehr Demokratie e.V. (2003a).

pass is, with the exception of Sachsen, similar to all western states. Sachsen, like its partner state Bayern and the western state of Hessen, has no required voter turnout for a referendum to be approved; a simple majority of those who turn out allows a measure to pass. The other eastern states, like all the other western states, adopted more stringent requirements. Brandenburg and Sachsen-Anhalt require at least 25% of eligible voters to support a referendum for it to pass, while Mecklenburg-Vorpommern and Thüringen have even higher thresholds—33% of eligible voters in these states must vote for a referendum in order for it to be adopted.[10] These procedures were likely to make it difficult for citizen initiatives to reach the ballot, in contrast to rules more conducive to referenda such as those used in Switzerland or U.S. states such as California.

Moreover, some of the provisions in the new Länder constitutions are actually *more* restrictive than in western Germany. No eastern state required constitutional amendments to be approved through a referendum, a less liberal rule than is in place in western Bayern, Hessen, and (later) Nordrhein-Westfalen. Similarly, while all eastern Länder did allow referenda to be used to change their constitutions, in contrast to western Hessen and the Saarland, all eastern states adopted the same high quotas on the percentage of eligible voters needed to make such changes.

While the above elements were not the source of considerable political contention in the east, other direct democratic constitutional provisions split the new MdL. The two issues which were most politically salient when drafting the new states' constitutions had to do with, first, the percentage of eligible voters' signatures needed for a Volksbegehren and, second, whether the new constitutions should be adopted by a popular vote in addition to a two-thirds majority in the Landtage.[11] In these debates, eastern MdL's positions on direct democracy fell strictly along partisan lines—partisan lines parallel to those at the national level. The Christian Democrats and FDP were the most reluctant to encourage citizen participation, whereas the Social Democrats and, even more so, the Greens and the PDS were much stronger supporters of direct democracy. In other words, even as early as the drafting of eastern constitutions, the party state shaped political outcomes in the new Länder. As the most thorough study (Klages and Paulus 1996) of the drafting of the eastern constitutions' plebiscitary elements concluded:

The role of political parties changed significantly in the course of the drafting of the constitutions. In the first phase of constitutional discussions they only played a minimal role. Since parties at this time were just being formed . . . they could not play a decisive role. . . . A party-political direction to the constitutional debates in the summer of 1990 could not yet be detected; this began only with the state parliament elections and with the begin of parliamentary work in late October 1990. (181)

[T]he constitutional discussion was increasingly shaped by party-political positions and controversies.(182)

The Fraktionen were the main actors in the parliamentary processes of drafting constitutions and they decisively shaped the discussion. Despite a general desire for consensus and a willingness to find compromises, the drafting of the new constitutions was determined by party-political controversies. (183)

On balance, then, while eastern MdL's pro-plebiscite attitudes did exert some influence over the drafting of direct democratic elements in the new state constitutions—all five new Länder did adopt some form of direct democracy—the form which plebiscitary procedures assumed was determined by partisan politics. From the start of the constitutional debates in the state parliaments, all Fraktionen adopted clear stances on the issues surrounding direct democracy—partisan stances that were consistent across states and generally in accordance with parties' previously outlined federal-level positions.

Partisan Debates over Direct Democracy at the Land Level

The Christian Democrats in all eastern Länder—just as at the national level—had the most limited interpretation of what direct democracy should involve. The CDU in Sachsen-Anhalt initially did not want to include *any* direct democratic elements in their constitution (Klages and Paulus 1996, 253). Elsewhere, CDU caucuses did not initially favor having constitutions adopted by referenda, and they endorsed high percentages of voter signatures for a Volksbegehren. They justified their positions with two main lines of argument. First, the CDU maintained, if the threshold for signatures was set too low, policies could be decided by activist or emotional minorities over the will of the majority; keeping decision making in the hands of the state parliaments would ensure that popularly elected majorities had the final say and would limit the ability of fringe groups to influence policy. They were especially worried that excess use of referenda would tire voters and drive down turnout, leaving only extremists to vote and pass referenda. Second, Christian Democrats argued that because referenda simplified complex issues into yes/no decisions, they should be avoided if at all possible; instead, the Landtage should take up issues raised by citizens. In floor debates across the new states, CDU parliamentarians consistently represented this party line:

> Ladies and Gentlemen: democracy requires active citizens. Only if there is a lively exchange between the population and state institutions can this constitution help contribute to the rebuilding of our state. However, this doesn't at the same time imply for me the orientation towards direct democracy and a retreat from representative democracy. Even the Basic Law, based on the bad experiences with the Weimar Constitution, practices extreme restraint on this front. . . . Here in Thüringen a majority of us have decided to favor representative democracy. . . . Only [the Landtag] is in my opinion in a position to find solutions to ever more difficult and complex problems and tasks. . . . This is exactly what plebiscitary elements cannot accomplish, however. There the most difficult tasks are reduced to yes/no questions. (TH-01-94, 7170)

> We know the PDS has the most members of all parties in Brandenburg. . . . We would like to ask that you, Ladies and Gentlemen from the PDS, take the smaller parties into consideration. . . . I'm thinking in particular of our very respected Social Democratic friends, who only have a proud 6,500 members in Brandenburg [but the majority in parliament]. Ladies and Gentlemen: if we only need 10,000 signatures to get a referendum, then it would be absolutely necessary that most of the Social Democratic members would have to get at least their spouse to sign a petition. You should really think about this seriously. If [all the PDS needs is 10,000 signatures] . . . then they could avoid having to make political decisions by relying on the [majority]

Social Democratic Party and instead . . . could mobilize their youth-
ful tomato- and egg-throwing party members. (BB-01-18, 1391–92)

The complexity of society requires effective public control, so that we
have neither rule by an uncontrollable technocracy nor the dema-
gogic misuse of uninformed, and therefore manipulable, majorities
by organized and informed minorities. It must be clear to everyone
why we are advocating the protection of parliamentary democracy.
(SX-01-46, 3063)

In three of the five new states, the Christian Democrats formed coalition governments with the FDP, and in the case of Sachsen they governed alone. The Free Democrats were less vocal in their opinions of
direct democracy, suggesting either that it was not a priority for the
party or that, as at the national level, the party was split. In the four
CDU-dominated states, however, they consistently supported the Christian Democratic position.[12] In Brandenburg the FDP served in a coalition government with the Greens and the SPD. While they went along
with the latter's positions on direct democracy, the Brandenburg FDP
clearly held a position closer to the Christian Democrats':

We spent a long time discussing the stance toward plebiscites in the
draft constitution. Here the draft constitution really exploits in a very
comprehensive way the possibilities for direct democracy. In our
opinion, it pushes the limits of what is possible. . . . Democratic elections, esteemed colleagues, are the broadest form of citizens' interest
articulation. . . . We should not lose the responsibility for political
agenda-setting. Especially now in this time of so-called tele-cracy or
media-cracy there is always the danger that needed technically correct decisions will be superceded through moods, through emotions,
and through exaggerated portrayals by the interests of single groups
or local organizations. The signature requirements in the draft of
the constitution lie on the low end in comparison to other constitutions. We at least succeeded, through the three-phase model for plebiscites, [in ensuring] that there's always the possibility that the
parliament can step in. . . . We certainly can't rely too much on plebiscites. A plebiscite demands a yes or no decision from citizens and is
therefore only in a limited degree able to secure a technically correct

hearing and discussion. That's why it is good and proper that we have foreseen in the constitution the possibility that the parliament can always insert itself. (BB-01-45, 3220–21)

The other three parties represented in eastern legislatures—the Social Democrats, the Greens, and the Party of Democratic Socialism— pushed for more direct democracy in the new eastern state constitutions. The SPD in all eastern states rejected Christian Democrats' claims that direct democracy would lead to radical decisions made by fringe minorities, in part because they recognized the restrictive nature of the form of direct democracy that they had chosen:

> Colleagues from the CDU . . . it is absurd to assume that [Brandenburg's] signature requirement of 20,000 will strengthen the far right or the fringe. What will strengthen the far right—or any radical group for that matter—is if they have no possibilities of political participation. . . . If 20,000 people start a Volksinitiative, it's just the first of three steps. The second step is then the Volksbegehren where already 80,000 signatures are needed. And to decide on a feared constitutional change like "Foreigners Out!" one doesn't just need a simple majority of voters but rather two thirds. Whoever knows the constitution can't follow your line of argumentation. . . . I'm not worried that here [in Brandenburg] a herd of political unrest will be created by political minorities. (BB-01-45, 3215–16)

Parallel to the SPD's division over direct democracy at the national level, on the one hand, the party championed direct democracy at the state level, but, on the other, it implemented a form of direct democracy unlikely to be widely utilizable (Klages and Paulus 1996, 245). The Social Democrats also felt secure in advocating this form of direct democracy because they disagreed with CDU members that including generous provisions for direct democracy would weaken the strength of state legislatures:

> In addition, Ladies and Gentlemen, I don't see plebiscites as in any way weakening parliamentary democracy. In contrast, . . . even in places where clearly lower quotas have been allowed, it's absolutely the case that plebiscites are rarely held. A modern state constitution

could have easily set its sights on a [signature] quota of 5–10%. (TH-01-94, 7167)

. . . a healing influence over parliamentary routine can emanate from the instrument of direct democracy. (BB-01-45, 3232)

There is no reason to fear a weakening of representative democracy through the use of referenda. It's rather the case that this has a stabilizing effect, since disappointed voters receive a different possibility to articulate their protest. (MVP-01-53, 2711)

The lack of the direct form of democracy after 1945 is owed to the conditions of the time. Today, after forty-five years of democratic history in western Germany and the autumn 1989 peaceful revolution in eastern Germany, it can only be taken as a sign of a mature political culture to meet the demands [of citizens] to participate in political decisions. We trust the democratic competency (*Demokratiefähigkeit*) of our citizens. (TH-01-28, 1713)

The CDU and SPD Fraktionen also disagreed over the issue of what percentage of eligible voters should be required to sign a petition requesting a Volksbegehren and whether a popular vote should be required for the new state constitutions to be valid:

The Thüringen constitution contains direct democratic elements and that is good. It also contains, in our opinion, too high signature requirements, and that is not good. . . . In the opinion of the SPD Fraktion this is the most significant shortcoming of the entire constitution. . . . When the SPD votes for the constitution, we'll do this under the given political conditions; with the given majority [in parliament] and with the corresponding political room for maneuver, no better result seemed to be possible. (TH-01-94, 7167–68)

It is particularly important for us [the SPD Fraktion] that the elements of Volksinitiative, Volksbegehren, and Volksentscheid were included in the [Sachsen-Anhalt] constitution, including the possibility for the people to change the constitution. Ladies and Gentlemen! Despite a degree of satisfaction with what we've accomplished, we must also regretfully note that we failed to get through an array of demands: The constitution will not be approved by a popular vote. And . . . the [signature] quotas are still too high. (SA-01-35, 30–31)

The final two parties, the Greens and the PDS, were the strongest supporters of direct democratic elements for the new state constitutions, just as they were at the national level. While both parties reluctantly accepted the three-tiered system for referenda described above, they went far beyond this in proposing novel elements not found in western Germany. In Sachsen the Greens proposed an upper house to the legislature, one that would be made up of a citizen Roundtable (SX-01-46, 3060–61); the Greens and the PDS in Thüringen had similar demands (TH-01-28-07, 1711). In Sachsen, the PDS favored adding a constitutional clause allowing the Landtag to be disbanded via referendum (SX-01-46, 3060). Finally, in Sachsen-Anhalt, the Greens advocated state financing of citizen initiatives along the lines of public campaign financing for parties (Klages and Paulus 1996, 216). None of these small parties' suggestions were adopted, however.

The Greens' and the PDS' strong support of direct democracy led them to be very critical of the western model being emulated in the eastern Länder; they condemned in the strongest terms the high thresholds for citizen signatures, the ban on referenda dealing with fiscal issues, and the lack of referenda to approve the constitutions in two eastern states:

A PDS deputy in Thüringen stated, "While the citizens are considered sovereign constitution-givers in constitutional theory, this remains constitutional fiction because in Bürgeranträge and Volksbegehren there are topics about which citizens are not even allowed to speak: for example, the state budget. . . . The sovereign is in your eyes too dumb. But that's simply its right. . . . Furthermore, just to be certain, there are strange thresholds set for direct democratic procedures . . . for a Volksbegehren 14% of eligible voters are needed—and that in four months. The sixty-four-thousand-dollar question: how is that possible? The answer is simple: it's not supposed to be possible. That is your political will. . . . All you want is the appearance of the possibility of direct democracy, but not its actual practicability" (TH-01-94, 7164).

In Sachsen-Anhalt, a PDS member claimed, "while Volksinitiativen, Volksbegehren, and Volksentscheide are included as forms of direct democracy, they are consciously limited, if not made impossible, through the thresholds set in the constitution" (SA-01-35, 26–27).

A PDS member in Sachsen argued, "[W]e consider it a joke of history that the Sachsen people, with all their experiences in bringing down the GDR, are not allowed to give themselves their own constitution per referendum" (SX-01-46, 3032). He continued by criticizing his state's high signature quotas, claiming, "these are, based on the experiences of the western states and other western democracies with a long [direct democratic] tradition like Switzerland, almost insurmountable hurdles. This creates . . . a constitutional farce. . . . The people in Sachsen cannot get the impression before the constitution is even passed that in the state of Sachsen there is a gap between the written constitution and constitutional reality—[this is] just like what they had to bear for most of their lives to date" (SX-01-46, 3035).

In Mecklenburg-Vorpommern the PDS stated, "We've named our critical objections to the constitution, and we still adhere to these criticisms. . . . [A]s much as we greet the inclusion of the Volksinitiative, Volksbegehren, and Volksentscheid procedures, from our perspective, the threshold of 140,000 signatures for a Volksbegehren is, just as we said before, decisively too high. Similarly, we are critical that the procedure of a Volksinitiative remains mostly in the realm of representative democracy because initiatives against the wishes of the Landtag are not possible according to this draft constitution" (MVP-01-78, 4455).

A Green in Sachsen argued, "Although it's true that [the constitution] contains elements of direct democracy the thresholds are too high, much too high! . . . [A]n important element of direct democracy is missing: the adoption of the constitution by the people, by the people as sovereign" (SX-01-46, 3037).

In the Mecklenburg-Vorpommern constitutional commission, representatives from the Greens and citizen movements fought to reduce the threshold of signatures for a Volksbegehren from 200,000 to 140,000 (MVP-01-78, 4445).

In Sachsen-Anhalt the Greens posited, "Ladies and Gentlemen: it has to do with aligning the ends with the means. We are not prepared to reach a certain end while using means . . . that deviate from this end. I want to use the example of the participation of citizens in voting on the constitution as an example. . . . The blatant and deep mistrust of citizens is one of the main reasons why we are speaking out against this constitution" (SA-01-35, 15–16).

Government Partisanship and Direct Democratic Procedures Chosen in the Eastern Länder

Although the newly elected MdL claimed to favor consensual, nonpartisan decision making, eastern Fraktionen clearly advocated specific policy stances akin to western parties'. As a result, partisan disagreements emerged shortly after the Landtage came into being. Nonetheless, it was not possible even for majority Fraktionen to pass constitutions without help from other parliamentary party groups because all five new states followed the federal practice of requiring a two-thirds parliamentary majority to pass constitutional changes (Klages and Paulus 1996, 186–87). In Brandenburg, all parties except the CDU voted in favor of the constitution.[13] The other four states had more conservative majorities. In Mecklenburg-Vorpommern and Sachsen-Anhalt, the PDS opposed the constitutions and all other parties were in favor.[14] Finally, in Sachsen and Thüringen, both the PDS and the Greens voted against the constitutions while they passed with the support of the CDU, FPD, and SPD.

Brandenburg was therefore unique among the new Länder, both in that the party least in favor of direct democracy (the CDU) was excluded from the coalition that passed the constitution and in that the party most in favor (the PDS) was included. As a result of this partisan composition, Brandenburg's was the most liberal of the eastern constitutions in terms of the two controversial provisions. While the signature collecting process for Volksbegehren was made easier in the new eastern states, the number of signatures required was—with the exception of Brandenburg—not significantly lower than in western Germany. Brandenburg required the lowest percentage of eligible voters to support a Volksbegehren of anywhere in the Federal Republic—4%. The other eastern states' thresholds ranged from 10% to 14%, and western states' prior to unification from 5% to 20%. Also in Brandenburg the new constitution was put to voters in a one-time constitutional referendum in addition to being approved by a two-thirds majority in the Landtag. Putting the constitutions to a popular vote was a key demand of the PDS and Greens, and to a lesser degree the SPD. Finally, Brandenburg was the only eastern Land to include a constitutional clause allowing the Landtag to be disbanded via referendum (Klages and Paulus 1996, 149).

Elsewhere in the east, the votes of the direct democracy–skeptic CDU were necessary to pass constitutions, while the pro-plebiscite PDS and, in some Länder, the Greens were excluded from winning coalitions. As a result, the thresholds of eligible voters needed for a Volksbegehren in these states remained higher than in Brandenburg. In Sachsen and Sachsen-Anhalt, as preferred by the CDU, the new constitutions were not put to a popular vote. The SPD in Thüringen convinced the CDU to consent to a one-time constitutional referendum in exchange for their support of the constitution; the latter was needed to obtain the necessary two-thirds majority.[15] In Mecklenburg-Vorpommern the constitution was also put to a popular vote. This came about despite the partisanship of the Landtag because a special constitutional commission was used to draft the constitution. This body contained not only members of the Landtag and the Justice Minister (in an advisory capacity) but also voting members who were representatives of the citizen movement, the Greens (who were not represented in the parliament), and other civil society groups (Landtag Mecklenburg-Vorpommern 2000, 925). The FDP ultimately convinced its CDU coalition partner to adopt the commission's recommendation that a plebiscite be used to adopt the new constitution.

Summary

Thus from the very beginning of the eastern Landtage we see the influence of the party state. While it is true that easterners' pro–direct democracy attitudes led all states to adopt some form of direct democracy somewhat more citizen-friendly than previous western state constitutions, none of the eastern Länder departed radically from the restrictive western model even though they were not legally required to adopt it.

Instead, constitutional debates were conducted along partisan lines parallel to those at the national level. Because a two-thirds majority was required to pass the new constitutions, the form of direct democracy chosen in each eastern state does not perfectly correlate with the partisan majorities in the Landtage but rather represents a compromise between the largest parties. However, in Brandenburg the constitution was passed without the support of the CDU and contained the most liberal provisions in terms of controversial issues, suggesting the Social Democrats', Greens', and PDS's influence there.

An Alternative Hypothesis

Despite the previously outlined electoral and other incentives that MdL have for such partisan behavior, their positions may have instead been shaped solely by the practical need to rely on western experts. As illustrated in earlier chapters, the new parliamentarians in eastern states were not lawyers or constitutional scholars and were strongly reliant on outside advisors including their parties' constitutional experts from the west. Furthermore, they were under intense pressure to draft their constitutions relatively quickly. Two observers of the process noted, "although the western German experts tried to restrain themselves from advocating their party's constitutional agenda, and instead concentrate on the unique aspects of the eastern states, often western German constitutional debates were brought to eastern German constitutional committees and continued there" (Klages and Paulus 1996, 185). When asked in 2001 why his state had chosen certain direct democracy provisions when drafting its constitution, a Green member of the Brandenburg legislature recalled that they had looked at a number of western German constitutions and had seen "similar wording in all of them" so they just decided to copy what had been adopted elsewhere. Thus it is likely that easterners were limited in their ability to act on their attitudes because they lacked the expertise and the time to create political institutions closer, for example, to the Swiss or U.S. models and instead relied on the western advisors sent to aid in the drafting of their constitutions.

However, it is significant that eastern MdL, especially those from the CDU, FDP, and SPD, chose to follow advice from their western counterparts rather than adopt draft provisions suggested by the western Greens or other pro-plebiscitary organizations who also offered direct democracy models more conducive to plebiscites. For example, the western citizens' group Initiative DEmokratie Entwickeln (IDEE) had prepared a model constitution, containing more generous direct democracy provisions than those in place in the west, that eastern MdL could have implemented (Sampels 1998, 53). In terms of local direct democracy, a citizens' group in Bayern put forth a model much more conducive to plebiscites than Baden-Württemberg's constitution; these rules were ultimately adopted in Bayern and could have been implemented in the eastern Länder as well (Rehmet, Weber, and Pavlovic 1999, 128–29). These plans were closer to MdL's ideal points than the proposals put forth by the referenda-skeptic western branches of their parties, and MdL clearly had attitudinal preferences for nonpartisan decision making. Recall the Christian Democrat quoted in chapter 3 who argued, "waging political warfare against a law whose only deficiency is that it comes from the opposition is macabre" (BB-01-18-03, 1368). Nonetheless, when it came time to consider proposals put forth by the Greens, the PDS, and citizen groups, the eastern CDU, FDP, and SPD Fraktionen rejected them in favor of the models proposed by the western branches of their own parties.

Furthermore, while inexperience and time pressure may explain why eastern Landtage initially adopted restrictive referenda rules, these factors cannot explain why eastern MdL did not subsequently alter these rules. All eastern constitutions may be amended, so eastern MdL have been free for over a decade to change their states' rules governing direct democracy as they gained not only time and expertise but also experienced first hand the dampening effect their constitutions had on citizen participation. One scholar summed up this effect, "The experience . . . to date shows the want of direct democratic forms of participation in the new states" (Paulus 1999, 202). Despite the high hurdles for citizen initiatives, the subsequent section shows that eastern MdL did not choose to alter their states' direct democratic procedures in the intervening decade. Indeed eastern Landtag majorities have routinely opposed calls for greater direct democracy in their states. Furthermore, as in western states, the governing majorities have been generally unsupportive of the direct democratic initiatives put forth for their consideration.

The Use of Land-Level Direct Democracy in Practice

After the eastern Länder passed their constitutions, the three western states that did not have provisions for state-level direct democracy adopted new rules allowing such plebiscites. (See table 4.3.) Like the eastern states, Niedersachsen, Berlin, and Hamburg adopted provisions that were toward the more citizen-friendly end of the spectrum. In 2002 Nordrhein-Westfalen allowed its constitution to be changed via referenda and reduced the percentage of eligible voters' signatures needed for a Volksbegehren from 20% to 8% (Mehr Demokratie e.V. 2003b, 5–6; 2003a). Since more and more states adopted Land-level direct democratic procedures in the 1990s, these channels were used with greater frequency than any time since the founding of the Federal Republic. Between World War II and 2001, a total of 131 direct democracy procedures were initiated at the Land level; 105 of these initiatives occurred since 1992 (Mehr Demokratie 2002, 3). Forty-seven of these were pursued in eastern states. Of the eastern initiatives, two-thirds were either attempts to increase direct democracy at the Land level or calls on the state to become more involved in the economy. This configuration again allows us to compare the influence on MdL's behavior of both political attitudes and values and the institutional incentives created by the party state. In this section I present empirical evidence from the Länder that supports the view that MdL's initial attitudinal support for direct democracy and economic equality did not translate into across-the-board support for citizen initiatives presented to the Landtage between 1990 and 2002.

Eastern Germans' Economic Values

Just as Germans' political attitudes and values have been extensively studied in the wake of unification, so too have their economic beliefs. Easterners' previously mentioned support for a democratic-socialist model of democracy, rather than a liberal-libertarian one, is characteristic of these beliefs: when asked whether social justice was a necessary component of democracy, 58% of easterners and only 36% of westerners agreed (Fuchs 1997, 98). Furthermore, the democratic-socialist model views the goal of public policy not only to ensure individual liberties, as does the liberal-libertarian model, but also to ensure a just division of societal resources among citizens.

In this literature, researchers also draw a distinction between a market or social market economic culture, and a socialist or planned economic culture (Roller 1994, Rohrschneider 1999). The former includes

Table 4.3 Western states adopting direct democracy after unification

State (Year adopted direct democracy)	Referendum required for constitutional change?	Can referendum be used to change constitution?	% of voters who must sign to approve Volksbegehren	How long to collect signatures?	Where can signatures be collected?	Requirements for a Volksentscheid to pass
Niedersachsen (1993)	No	Yes, if 50% of eligible voters approve	10%	12 months	Anywhere	25% of eligible voters must approve
Berlin (1995)	No	No	10%	2 months	Public office	33% of eligible voters must approve
Hamburg (1996)	No	Yes, if 50% of eligible voters turn out and 2/3 approve	5%	14 days	Either inside or outside of public office	20% of eligible voters must approve

Note: Shaded aspects are the state laws most conducive to direct democracy.
Source: Mehr Demokratie e.V. (2003a).

attitudinal support for private enterprise and property, economic competition, a relatively laissez-faire government orientation, the right to
earn unlimited profit, individual self-reliance and achievement, differ-
ential rewards for different levels of achievement, and the desirability of
inequality in earnings as a motivating factor. Individuals with socialist
economic values hold the opposite beliefs and have a particularly strong
preference for (a) equality of economic outcomes and (b) a strong role
for the government in ensuring these outcomes. Opinion surveys at
both the mass and elite levels in eastern and western Germany have consistently found that eastern Germans hold socialist economic values
whereas their western counterparts are much more strongly in favor of
market values.[16]

Evidence for these differences at the mass level is widespread and
consistent throughout the 1990s (Roller 1994; "Stolz aufs eigene Leben"
1995; Halter 1996; Roller 1997; Pollack and Pickel 1998; Rohrschneider 1999; Delhey 1999). For example, when forced to choose
between equality or freedom as a political goal, 53% of easterners favored equality compared to only 27% of westerners (Fuchs 1997, 102).
Similarly, when asked what role the government should play in a range
of policies, particularly ones oriented toward reducing income differentials among citizens, easterners are much more strongly in favor of
government action than their western counterparts. While partisan differences in support for the market economy do exist among eastern
voters, even CDU and FDP voters in the new states are less in favor of a
market economy than western SPD and Green voters (Rohrschneider
1999, 185). Eastern Germans are more likely to reject the notion that
income differentials are a necessary incentive for personal achievement
and to argue that the gap between rich and poor in contemporary Germany is too large. While these values are shared by eastern Europeans
across the board (Rohrschneider 1999, 195), eastern Germans stand
out even among eastern Europeans in terms of their support for economic equality (Delhey 1999, 6).

These attitudes are not limited to the eastern German mass public,
however. Rohrschneider's study of Berlin parliamentarians produced almost identical results. Not only did eastern elites express more support
for government intervention in the economy and less support for unlimited profit and large income differentials in closed-ended survey questions (Rohrschneider 1999, 169), they were also much more likely than

their western counterparts to elaborate on negative aspects of the market economy when asked open-ended questions about the pros and cons of the market economy model. While only 16.9% of western deputies interviewed volunteered a systematic disadvantage of capitalism in 1992, 59.5% of easterners did so. (See figure 4.2.) Moreover, these differences existed across eastern and western branches of the same political party; while in Berlin parties of the right were more supportive of the market economy model than parties of the left, in all party families western respondents were more supportive of a market economy than their eastern colleagues. In fact, eastern CDU and FDP deputies' views of a market economy were closer to western SPD members' views than to members of the western branches of their own parties (Rohrschneider 1999, 184).

Given these attitudinal differences, combined with easterners' preference for direct democracy and westerners' faith in representative democracy, it would seem that if eastern MdL's attitudes did influence their political behavior, they would be more likely than westerners to support citizen initiatives in general, and ones designed to obtain direct democracy and social equality in particular—regardless of their party affiliation.

Majority and Opposition Fraktionen and Citizen Initiatives

In western German parliaments, however, opposition party groups tend to support direct democratic initiatives, whereas governing Fraktionen prefer to keep decision making in their own hands (Mehr Demokratie e.V. 2003b, 2; Klages and Paulus 1996, 28). Because Germany's party state allows the majority Fraktion (or coalition) in the Landtag considerable power to shape public policy, these MdL have little incentive to cede political decision-making power to the public, especially in ways that might limit their ability to distribute scarce resources. As a result, members of majority parties or coalitions have not been very supportive of Volksinitiativen, Volksbegehren, and Volksentscheide in the western Länder.

In contrast, German opposition Fraktionen are severely curtailed in their ability to shape policy because the majority's party-line voting allows the latter to dominate decision making. For opposition party

Figure 4.2   Berlin state parliamentarians' support for a market economy, 1992

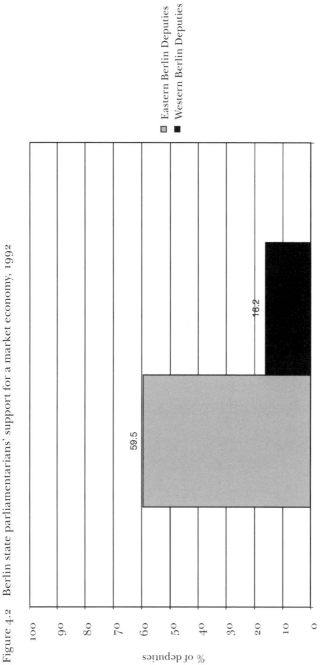

% of deputies mentioning a systemic disadvantage when asked to evaluate
the social market economy in 1992

Source: Rohrschneider (1999, 171).

groups, direct democratic initiatives offer a way to skirt the parliamentary majority and influence policy by turning directly to voters. Furthermore, opposition Fraktionen can highlight the majority's unwillingness to support popular calls for more direct democracy and economic equality in the hopes of winning supporters in the next election. In western Nordrhein-Westfalen and the Saarland, for example, opposition parties led campaigns to include greater direct democracy at the local level (Wehling 1999, 92–93).

Given these institutional incentives, there seems little reason to expect a different outcome in the five new Landtage than in western state parliaments. Eastern MdL from majority Fraktionen seem unlikely to support direct democratic initiatives, whereas eastern members of opposition party groups seem likely to embrace them. This should be especially true in the 1990s as the eastern states were confronted with tight fiscal constraints. While eastern MdL in majority party groups may have normatively favored greater government involvement in the economy, the fiscal realities they confronted within Germany's federal system would seem likely to reduce their ability to act on these attitudes.

Empirical Evidence: State Parliaments' Reactions to Citizen Initiatives

Of the forty-seven citizen initiatives put forth in the eastern Länder between 1990 and 2002, more than half (twenty-six) called for greater state involvement in the economy, and another five called for the promotion of direct democracy. (See table 4.4 for a complete list.) These citizen efforts were not met with across-the-board enthusiasm in the eastern Landtage, however, suggesting support for the institutionalist hypothesis. The following section traces the five eastern Landtage's reactions to citizen initiatives between 1990 and 2002.

Just as the constitutional rules governing direct democracy in the eastern states were similar to those in place in western states, so too were the results of these restrictive procedures. (See table 4.5.) During the period examined, a single decade, each eastern state has seen an average of 10.75 attempts at gathering signatures for a Volksinitiative, the first step in the three-step process toward a referenda.[17] This is higher than the overall German average of 8.9 attempts over the whole five decades since the founding of the Federal Republic. The enthusiasm with which eastern citizens have embraced direct democratic initiatives likely

Table 4.4   Topics of citizen initiatives in eastern states, 1990–2002

- Promoting a greater role for the state in . . .
  - Spending on preschool, schools, and youth (7)
  - Improving public transportation and infrastructure in underserved areas (5)
  - Spending on higher education, job creation, and job training (4)
  - Keeping rents/utility prices affordable (4)
  - Including social rights in the constitution (2)
  - Improving public health care (2)
  - Improving benefits to asylum seekers (1)
  - Preserving community savings banks (1)
- Increasing direct democracy (5)
- Changing county boundaries (5)
- Environment (4)
- Educational issues not involving spending (4)
- Other (3)

Note: Number of initiatives in each category appears in parentheses.
Source: Archiv/Datenbank Mehr Demokratie e.V. (2003).

reflects the mass pro-plebiscite sentiment in the new Länder. In both parts of Germany, however, these Volksinitiative have not been well-received by the Landtage. When asked to consider citizen proposals put forth in Volksinitiative, eastern parliaments turned down 78.6% of them.[18] This is slightly lower than the 83.3% rejection rate attempts across all states. Nonetheless, although eastern parliamentarians claim to support citizens' right to put forth initiatives, in practice they have turned down three of every four citizen requests. This pattern continues throughout the decade following unification and is true of political majorities both on the left and on the right side of the political spectrum.

Organizers of these initiatives have also not had much success in taking their causes to the next level in the direct democratic process, the Volksbegehren. Given the high threshold of signatures required and the logistical impediments to collecting these signatures, the results are not unexpected. Across Germany since the founding of the Federal Republic, two thirds of all attempts at Volksbegehren have failed to gather enough signatures, and the eastern figure as of 2004 stood at 34%. Furthermore, 27.6% of easterners' initial attempts at gathering signatures were abandoned by organizers, likely because of their slim chance of success. Finally, 13% of eastern Volksbegehren attempts were disqualified by the courts because they interfered with the parliament's exclusive control of the state budget.

Table 4.5 Eastern states' actual experiences with direct democracy, 1992–2002

State	Volksinitiative	Volksbegehren	Volksentscheid
Brandenburg	19 attempts 2 accepted by Landtag 2 meet with partial success in Landtag 1 in progress as of 2002	8 received too few signatures 5 were abandoned 1 legally disqualified 3 ongoing in 2002 2 adopted by Landtag before signature stage	None
Mecklenburg-Vorpommern	14 attempts: 5 accepted by Landtag	2 received too few signatures 6 were abandoned 1 legally disqualified 5 adopted by Landtag before signature stage	None
Sachsen	9 attempts: 0 accepted by Landtag 1 in progress as of 2002	3 received too few signatures 2 were abandoned 2 legally disqualified 1 ongoing in 2002 1 received enough signatures	1 held and passed Landtag did not implement result
Sachsen-Anhalt	1 attempt: not accepted by Landtag	Received too few signatures	None
Thüringen	NA: Thüringen does not have this step	2 fail to meet signature requirement 2 receive enough signatures but legally disqualified	None
Eastern German Average, 1990–2002	10.75 attempts: 78.0% rejected by Landtage	5.4 attempts 34.0% failed to meet signature requirements 27.6% abandoned	0.2
German Average, 1945–2002	8.9 attempts: 83.3% rejected by Landtag *	2.6 attempts 66.6% failed to meet signature requirements*	0.8 (Excluding Bayern: 0.4)**

Note: Table includes only citizen-initiated direct democracy procedures and excludes constitutional referenda or referenda on changes to state boundaries.

Source: Archiv/Datenbank Mehr Demokratie e.V. . (2003).

* Mehr Demokratie, eV. (2002, 5–6).

** Mehr Demokratie, e.V. (2002, 18).

Only three Volksbegehren actually received enough valid signatures to go on to the third step, a Volksentscheid or referenda. Of these, only one plebiscite was actually held as of 2004; in 2001 voters in Sachsen approved a measure halting the creation of a state-level bank and preserving autonomous local savings banks. In the other two cases, the initiatives were found unconstitutional and no plebiscites were held. This is similar to the low average rate since the founding of the Federal Republic. For all of Germany, less than one plebiscite on average per state has ever taken place.

Thus, while eastern MdL entered state legislatures in 1990 strongly in favor of direct democracy, and while they made some liberalizing adjustments to western German rules governing plebiscites, the institutions they created ultimately have not proved to be more conducive to referenda than their western counterparts' rules. In instances where the Landtage have had discretion in terms of how they dealt with citizen initiatives, they have not proven especially receptive, even when the proposals have been consistent with socialist economic values. For example, an enormously popular citizen initiative in Brandenburg, entitled "For Our Children," called for both overturning state budget cuts to preschools and for the right to a space in a publicly funded preschool for all children in the state. This demand for universal and affordable preschool harkened back to the GDR era when all citizens enjoyed such services, and is typical of the state involvement in the economy eastern Germans routinely support in attitudinal surveys. "For Our Children" received 147,000 signatures—well above the required 20,000 for a Volksinitiative. Rather than rejecting the popular initiative outright, the SPD/CDU coalition in the Landtag challenged it in court, arguing that because the measure would have required a one-quarter of one percent change to the state budget, it violated the constitutional clause banning referenda dealing with public spending (Mehr Demokratie e.V. 2002, 7, 15). The governing Fraktionen won their court case, meaning that a Volksbegehren, and likely a Volksinitiative, were ruled out as well. Similarly, the SPD minority government in Sachsen-Anhalt rejected a Volksinitiative there calling for a reduction in preschool fees (Interview CDU Sachsen-Anhalt) and the SPD/CDU dominated Landtag in Mecklenburg-Vorpommern rejected an initiative regarding equal access to preschools (Archiv/Datenbank Mehr Demokratie e.V. 2003).

In addition to regularly fighting measures like these, which called for a greater role for the state in caring for young children, Landtag majorities have also consistently rejected attempts at improving the conditions for direct democracy in the Länder. In Thüringen, the CDU executive challenged the constitutionality of a Volksbegehren entitled "More Democracy in Thüringen" that would have made Volksbegehren and Volksentscheide easier to realize (Mehr Demokratie e.V. 2002, 18). In Brandenburg, the SPD/CDU majority rejected two Volksinitiativen regarding direct democracy; the first called on the state government to work through the Bundesrat to obtain referenda at the national level, and the second called for lower signature thresholds for both Volksinitiative and plebiscites at the local level (Mehr Demokratie e.V. 2002, 14).

Finally, in Sachsen, the only state where a referendum actually took place, the CDU-majority Landtag actively worked against the plebiscite. First, the parliament refused to agree to a Volksinitiative requesting that local savings banks be preserved. Then when the organizers gathered 552,000 signatures—well above the 450,000 required ones—the CDU argued that not all signatures collected were properly registered and that only 449,466 were valid. The organizers subsequently won a court challenge allowing the signatures and consequently the referendum (Mehr Demokratie e.V. 2002, 16–17). It was held in October 2001, and voters overwhelmingly supported the measure. While the Landtag then withdrew the proposal to create a state bank, the CDU and SPD passed a bill in December 2002 creating a similar financial institution albeit with a different name, violating the spirit of the referendum (Mehr Demokratie e.V. 2003a, 7).

Thus not only did eastern Landtage initially create rules making direct democracy difficult in practice, they have also not altered these rules when their limiting influence has been made clear. Instead, parliamentary majorities have fought to keep decision-making power in their own hands rather than in the hands of the people. This has been the case even when citizens have demanded measures to achieve greater direct democracy or a greater economic role for the state, values which opinion polls show eastern MdL hold dear. This does not mean, however, that *all* eastern parliamentarians have actively worked to limit direct democracy or measures promoting social equality. Instead, just as in the west, plebiscitary procedures are strongly supported by Landtag opposition parties from all ends of the political spectrum. In both 2001 and 2002, four of the eighteen direct democratic processes underway in Germany were sponsored by opposition parties, while only one had the sponsorship of a governing party (the SPD's small Green coalition partner in Schleswig-Holstein); the other initiatives had nonpartisan sponsors. For example, the opposition PDS in Brandenburg was a cosponsor of a Volksinitiative regarding the fusion of two public television channels (Mehr Demokratie e.V. 2003a). In Mecklenburg-Vorpommern the Greens, who had never been elected to the Landtag, were the sole sponsor of a Volksinitiative promoting the use of trains and bicycles as means of transportation (Mehr Demokratie e.V. 2002, 16).

Most telling, in Sachsen the opposition SPD supported a Volksbegehren attempt to stop school closings and reduce class sizes (Mehr Demokratie e.V. 2003a). The opposition Social Democrats' vigorous support for greater government spending on schools in Sachsen stood in sharp contrast to the attitudes of SPD parliamentarians in states where the party was responsible for governing. As mentioned earlier, the Social Democrats in Brandenburg, Mecklenburg-Vorpommern, and Sachsen-Anhalt all worked against citizen initiatives for more spending on preschools. A member of the Sachsen-Anhalt SPD Fraktion argued that even though his state had the most generous preschool system in the Federal Republic, parents there were unhappy because they had to pay higher fees to support this system. He complained that getting enough signatures for a Volksinitiative to reduce parents' costs had been too easy, stating "for every child there are at least six signatures—mom, dad, and two sets of grandparents." Furthermore, he argued, the initiative's demands were unrealistic because the financial burden it would have placed on local governments would have been too high. Similarly, a member of the governing Social Democratic caucus in Brandenburg stated in a personal interview, "The title of the petition was 'For Our Children'—this is deceptive. Who is going to be against our children?" He argued:

> We are in a state of financial emergency. While it is true that we are not poor—we have a nineteen billion deutsche mark budget—it is hard to spend on everything we'd like to. If we spend more on preschools, we'll have to spend less on the elderly. Children have really strong lobbyists—who wants to look like they're against kids? And older people don't have such a strong lobby. But they're both weak groups. It might be tempting to listen to the loudest group, but this isn't fair.

He then went on to point out, "The PDS, as an opposition party is sup-posed to do," has supported citizen initiatives to increase spending on preschools. "I don't damn them," he said, but they demand more social spending "everywhere. This is deceptive; their critiques of our budget aren't serious" because the state could never afford all they demand.

Even the Christian Democrats, the party initially most opposed to the use of direct democracy, has supported citizen initiatives as an op-position party. For example, beginning in 1998 the CDU in Mecklen-burg-Vorpommern attempted to start a Volksinitiative in support of road building in the eastern part of the state (Mehr Demokratie e.V. 2001). In Sachsen-Anhalt the CDU opposition tried to start a Volksini-tiative regarding reducing the state's school system from the current thirteen-year system to a twelve-year system, as well as one which would have reformed elementary/middle school education (Interview CDU Sachsen-Anhalt). All these attempts failed to gather enough signatures, but the fact that they were attempted by even the opposition Christian Democrats shows what an attractive instrument direct democracy proce-dures are to an opposition Fraktion. As a result of party-line legislative voting, the CDU can accomplish little policy-wise when it is in the oppo-sition. By supporting plebiscite attempts, however, it can critique the governing party or coalition, appeal to popular support for direct demo-cratic initiatives or public spending, and possibly influence public policy in a way that it could not on the floor of the parliament. Majority Frak-tionen faced different incentives and therefore tended to oppose citizen initiatives, despite individual MdL's support for direct democracy and their socialist economic values. These findings indicate that eastern parliamentarians' support for, or opposition to, citizen petitions is not simply based on opposition to the content of particular proposals; in-stead there is an overarching pattern of support for direct democratic initiatives among opposition Fraktionen and opposition to them among members of the parliamentary majority.

Implications

The findings here again point to the logic of Germany's party state, rather than the political attitudes and values of individual legislators, as being the main influence on legislator behavior and policy choice.

Although eastern MdL expressed a strong preference for direct democracy and socialist economic values, their place in Germany's established party state led them to accept partisan models of direct democracy instead of acting on their preference for apolitical decision making and plebiscites. Once these rules were established, majority Fraktionen, enjoying power to shape policy themselves, had little incentive to either change these rules or allow much citizen influence over political decision making.

These results suggest that direct democracy advocates' great hopes that unification would bring greater use of referenda to Germany have been disappointed. Just as with party discipline, as post-materialist values have risen in western Germany, calls for the use of referenda there have increased. In the aftermath of unification, all western states ultimately adopted some form of direct democracy into their constitutions, and the number of citizen initiatives in the country swelled. However, elite reactions to these popular demands have not mirrored this popular enthusiasm for direct democracy. Germany's restrictive multistep process toward plebiscites remains intact, and the Landtage across Germany generally have not embraced citizen demands. Used to the power they enjoy in strongly representative institutions, western German political elites have held fast to older institutional structures even as society has changed. These patterns have been adopted in the east as well. Again, the findings presented here underscore the ability of western political institutions to survive societal change.

Eastern German State Legislators, Political Tolerance, and Germany's Same-Sex Partnership Law

Chapters 2 and 3 showed that, in terms of legislators' career paths and their floor voting, the logic of Germany's parliamentary and electoral institutions have outweighed the antiparty attitudes that MdL brought with them to office. Chapter 4 argued that even in the early 1990s relatively disciplined party voting in the eastern Landtage had a substantive impact on the policies passed vis-à-vis direct democracy; subsequently, parliamentarians' reactions to referenda initiatives were determined by the majority or opposition status of their Fraktion more so than by their attitudes toward direct democracy. This chapter goes on to argue that partisan loyalties continue to outweigh additional attitudinal differences between eastern and western state parliamentarians, this time in terms of political tolerance.

Political tolerance, or the willingness to grant rights such as the freedom of expression to disliked groups, is a key component of a democratic political culture (Almond and Verba 1963; Inglehart 1990). Where people are unwilling to put up with groups that they oppose, democracy is unlikely to thrive for several reasons. First, democracy requires broad competition for political power and influence over policy. In a society where people are unwilling to see certain groups express themselves, such contestation will be absent or at least narrowed. Second, democracy requires a "loyal opposition," that is, the losers of an election have to accept the outcome and trust that the winners will abide by democratic rules and ultimately be willing to leave office if a subsequent election shows this to be the will of the citizenry. In a society where people are unwilling to extend political rights to those with whom they disagree, it is unlikely that electoral losers will accept their fate peacefully because the winners are unlikely to allow them the freedom to contest a future election. Disputes are more likely to be resolved through violence or dictatorial means. Third, democracies are predicated on the rule of law and the equal treatment of all citizens under the law. In a society where politically intolerant citizens are unwilling to extend basic rights and freedoms to individuals with whom they disagree, the prospect of legislation curbing unpopular minorities' rights arises.

Because of its importance, tolerance among both masses and elites in established democracies has long been studied.[1] The fall of communism and the introduction of public opinion surveys to eastern Europe brought political scientists an unprecedented opportunity to investigate the willingness of both post-communist mass publics and political elites to "put up with what they don't like" by extending rights to disliked groups. Most of these investigations found eastern Europeans, including eastern Germans, to have a low level of political tolerance, even when respondents generally professed support for democracy.

Given the importance of political tolerance for functioning democracy, these survey findings suggest potential problems with the consolidation of democracy in eastern Germany and eastern Europe. However, the hypothesis that low political tolerance will lead to undemocratic actions on the part of elected officials is drawn from opinion surveys and has rarely been tested on actual policy-making behavior.[2] As such, research to date raises, but fails to answer, the important question of whether eastern Germans' intolerant attitudes actually translate into policies that deny disliked groups crucial rights.

There is evidence from established democracies that a direct relationship between political tolerance and democratic public policy, assumed by those who document politically intolerant attitudes, may not always exist. The far more nuanced discussion of political tolerance in consolidated democracies offers several institutional reasons to expect that the low average level of political intolerance among post-communist citizens may not always translate directly into intolerant public policy. First, in representative democracies like Germany, policy is actually made by political elites, not mass publics. In established democracies, learning within democratic political institutions has been shown to shape the political tolerance of elected officials over time; elites are often more tolerant than ordinary citizens. However, rather than being homogeneously tolerant, elites within long-established democracies have exhibited a wide range of opinions, suggesting that eastern German parliamentarians too are far from uniformly intolerant. In long-term democracies, elite political tolerance is often closely related to ideology or party affiliation. Given the importance of political parties in Germany's party state and given easterners' proven willingness to join political parties, to vote with their party's Fraktion, and to support policies put forth by their national-level party organization, it is likely that government partisanship, rather than the eastern or western origin of deputies, will determine policy outcomes. Finally, in established as well as consolidating democracies, neither intolerant nor tolerant political elites are entirely free to act on their attitudes. Politicians' ability to do so may be enhanced or diminished by constitutional or other external political constraints—for example, federal or EU guidelines—that limit the policy options open to them. In other words, political institutions are a vital intervening variable between attitudes and public policy.

In this chapter I compare actual policies passed by eastern and western German Landtage to determine whether post-communist political intolerance translates into more and less tolerant policy outcomes in western and eastern German Länder, respectively. One reason why there have been so many cross-national comparisons of individuals' attitudes toward political tolerance, and so few cross-national comparisons of policy outcomes, is that there are few empirical instances in which elites with varying levels of tolerance are confronted with comparable policy problems and institutional constraints (see also Gibson 1998). The German case, however, provides a near experimental setting which meets these conditions. In 2001, the German federal government passed the Lebenspartnerschaftsgesetz (LPartG) or Life Partnership Law, which granted legal status to same-sex couples. In surveys about political tolerance, homosexuals were frequently mentioned as a disliked group by both mass and elite respondents in both eastern and western Europe. The Life Partnership Law is a classic example of extending legal protections to a disliked group, allowing gay couples the rights to, among other things, officially register their unions, take each other's names, and inherit from each other. The Landtage—populated by eastern and western deputies with correspondingly different degrees of political tolerance—were charged with implementing this federal legislation and were granted discretion over various aspects of the law. For example, states could choose to allow couples to celebrate their unions in the same public offices where heterosexual weddings are held; alternatively, Länder could relegate partnership registration to administrative offices, making it more of a legal technicality than a celebration. Drawing on parliamentary debates, analyses of state laws, and newspaper reports, I compare the ways in which eastern and western German states have implemented the Life Partnership Law. If eastern MdL's low average level of political tolerance has an impact on public policy, then the five eastern German states would have interpreted the law in a narrower, less tolerant manner than the ten western German states did. If Germany's political institutions matter, in contrast, implementation of the Life Partnership Law would have varied with the partisanship of the Landtage in both east and west.

As the institutional approach expects, I find that both eastern and western German state laws show a range of tolerance toward homosexuals; the partisanship of the governing coalition rather than experiences with communism best explains the degree of tolerance exhibited toward gays and lesbians. Furthermore, both highly tolerant and highly intolerant actors across Germany were constrained by political institutions in terms of how many rights they could extend to same-sex couples. These findings are important, not only for the debate about political tolerance, but also—as was the case with the previous chapters—because they contribute to a wider debate about the sources of legislator behavior. Again, I offer support for institutional, rather than sociological or attitudinal causes of parliamentarians' behavior. To develop this argument, I compare German elites' levels of political tolerance and discuss the constraints placed on both politically tolerant and politically intolerant MdL by Germany's political system. Then I empirically examine the partisan debate surrounding gay unions, compare the state-to-state implementation of Germany's same-sex-partner law, and investigate deputies' motivations for creating the laws that they did. I conclude by discussing the implications of my findings.

POLITICAL TOLERANCE AND THE PARTY STATE

Opinion Surveys and Political Tolerance

Most attitudinal surveys of eastern Europeans have found them to have a low level of political tolerance, even when respondents generally professed support for democracy (Gibson and Duch 1993; Gibson 1998; Hickey 2001). Furthermore, mass levels of tolerance in eastern Europe are lower than in established democracies (Gibson, Duch, and Tedin 1992; Gibson and Duch 1993; Gibson 1998; Rohrschneider 1999, 133–35). Robert Rohrschneider's *Learning Democracy* explains why these results also apply to the German case:

> Western citizens were exposed to a political process that encourages . . . the extension of democratic rights to a range of ideological groups. Eastern Germans, in contrast, lack this experience. . . . Although eastern Germans support general democratic rights, it is easier to understand why, for example, one should have the right to vote than to accept that one's ideological enemy should enjoy the same liberty. Consequently, I expect that eastern Germans are less willing than western Germans to extend systematically democratic rights to political opponents, because the former lacked the opportunity to develop democratic restraint. This expectation is also consistent with Dahl's observation that democratic transitions in the second half of the twentieth century typically involve, first, the evolution of 'majoritarian' rights (e.g. free elections or the right to demonstrate) and then the evolution of rules for minority protection. (1999, 109–10)

Other reasons given for this post-communist intolerance include Stalinist era indoctrination (Gibson and Duch 1993), the communist party's encouragement of citizens to show intolerance toward regime opponents (Gibson, Duch, and Tedin 1992; 340–41; Gibson 1998, 37), citizens' lack of opportunity to exercise tolerance for most of the twentieth century (Gibson, Duch, and Tedin 1993; Rohrschneider 1999), low levels of post-materialism in eastern Europe (Gibson and Duch 1993; Inglehart 1990), lower levels of overall support for democracy in eastern Europe than in established polyarchies (Gibson and Duch 1993), as well as current unstable economic and social conditions (Gibson 1999). Western Germans and Europeans, in contrast, have higher abstract support for democracy, higher levels of post-materialist values, decades of opportunity to practice political tolerance, no recent experience with dictatorship, and higher levels of economic and social stability. As a result, they have been found to be more politically tolerant on average than their eastern counterparts (Rohrschneider 1999; Gibson and Duch 1993, 313).

These results apply not only to the mass public across Europe and in Germany, but also to elites in Berlin's state parliament. Rohrschneider's survey (1999) of eastern and western Berlin state legislators' political tolerance found that eastern Berlin members of the *Abgeordnetenhaus* (as Berlin's state parliament is called) held less politically tolerant attitudes than their counterparts from the western half of the city. He predicts that these attitudinal differences will have a very real effect on public policy, arguing:

> Does it matter why MPs tolerate a group? I believe so. A control-based toleration of disliked groups depends on political expediency while a principle-based commitment to civil liberties does not. If, for example, public-opinion sentiments become more negative about a particular minority group, MPs who are driven by a control-based toleration of groups may then support curtailing groups' civil liberties. In contrast, if civil liberties are extended to . . . groups out of a commitment to democratic principles, political circumstances by definition should be less likely to lower one's willingness to tolerate a disliked group. (132–33)

In other words, MdL's politically intolerant attitudes are expected to shape their political behavior. Western Berlin deputies and western Landtage are hypothesized to be more likely to extend rights to disliked groups than are eastern Berlin deputies or eastern Landtage.

The Party State and Political Tolerance

None of the studies discussed above have examined actual policy outcomes in eastern Europe or eastern Germany to determine whether or not the above-mentioned intolerant attitudes have in practice translated into public policies that limit the rights of disliked groups in these regions.[3] Nor have any eastern/western European or German comparisons been undertaken in this regard. The few studies that have examined the link between political tolerance and policy outcomes in western democracies have not always found a direct relationship between the two. For example, during the Vietnam war, local officials' intolerance of antiwar protest did not lead to more repressive public policies (Gibson

1989), and local intolerance of the Ku Klux Klan in Texas did not lead to a denial of their right to march in Houston (Gibson 1987).

If political institutions are taken into account, a number of reasons emerge why intolerant attitudes may not translate into intolerant public policies. One reason why mass intolerance may not lead to repressive public policies in existing democracies is that policy is made not by the average citizen but by elected officials. Political elites have generally been found to be more tolerant than the mass public (Barnum and Sullivan 1989; Sullivan et al. 1993) and to make democratic political decisions even in the presence of mass intolerance (McClosky 1964; McClosky and Brill 1983). Indeed, in the German case, eastern MdL are more tolerant than the average eastern citizen (Rohrschneider 1999). Greater elite tolerance is often attributed to selection bias.[4] People from higher educational and status groups generally have encountered a greater variety of views in life and are more open to alternative viewpoints. Such individuals, rather than less-educated people of lower socioeconomic status, are usually selected to run for public office. As a result of these elite recruitment patterns, then, eastern MdL are more tolerant than their constituents.

Elites' heightened tolerance has also been attributed in part to learning that goes on once elected to public office (Sullivan et al. 1993). While working in the Landtage, MdL come into contact with a greater range of alternative viewpoints than ordinary citizens do, and are thereby forced by the realities of office both to make compromises and to take responsibility for the implications of their actions. Their public role continuously exposes them to "the functional equivalent of a civics and tolerance curriculum" that ordinary citizens do not receive (Sullivan et al. 1993, 72). Indeed, Rohrschneider found that some eastern Berlin legislators became more tolerant in the decade since the fall of the Wall (Rohrschneider 1999, 120).[5]

Despite the moderating effects of institutional learning, the literature on elites in established western democracies has found significant variance in tolerance among elected officials; some political elites are as intolerant as members of the mass public (Shamir 1991; Sniderman et al. 1991; Gibson 1998). Among other factors, ideology plays a role in accounting for this variance; in the American context, conservatives have been found to be less politically tolerant than liberals (McClosky and Brill 1983, chap. 7; Sullivan et al. 1993, 56). Parallel to the American case, Rohrschneider's survey found the Greens among the most politically tolerant Fraktionen and Christian Democrats among the least politically tolerant (Rohrschneider 1999, 124).

Moreover, the imperatives of a democratic political system require political elites to compete for voter support in order to remain in office. Especially in Germany's proportional representation electoral system and the resulting multiparty system, parties must compete with each other by offering distinctive platforms. Parties' leaders have incentives to put forward policies that run the gamut from highly tolerant to extremely intolerant; even if the majority of the mass public is intolerant, there are still votes to be won from the tolerant minority (or vice versa). Party discipline, moreover, can be used to get elites who are more or less tolerant than other members of their caucus to go along with fellow party members when policy is made. In Germany's parliamentary system the logic of coalition-making may give a small, political party disproportionate influence over policy even if that party has a more extreme level of political tolerance than other parties. Finally, because politicians are rarely if ever confronted with only one political issue at a time, policy outcomes may be shaped by electoral or coalitional calculations, logrolling, or other extraneous factors that have nothing to do with elite political tolerance (Shamir 1991, 1023). These institutional factors hold for both eastern and western Landtage.

Thus it is likely that rather than being monolithically intolerant, as the attitudinal approach suggests, or uniformly tolerant, as the institutional learning approach suggests, eastern MdL are likely to exhibit a range of tolerance which will manifest itself along party lines. To paraphrase Sniderman et al., then, policy outcomes across Germany are likely shaped not by the mere fact that easterners or westerners are in power, but instead by *which* easterners or westerners are in power (1991, 363).

While tolerance may vary along partisan lines, however, key political institutions may be instrumental in either mitigating or exacerbating the effects of elite political (in)tolerance. For example, the United States Constitution's Bill of Rights guarantees the right to free speech—a right that is enforced by an independent judiciary—and limits the options open to intolerant elites. Shamir argues that if a Bill of Rights had been in place in Israel, intolerant elites would not have had the ability to curb the rights of extremist groups there (1991, 1037–38). In Germany, the Basic Law not only provides citizens with such rights, the court has vigorously enforced them in the past. However, Germany's Basic Law permits the banning of antidemocratic or fascist political parties, constraining the policy options open to the most politically tolerant of elites. Also important for German politicians is the fact that they are European Union members and at times subject to constraints from Brussels. Similarly, MdL are in a subordinate location in the country's federal system and are subject to constraints imposed by the Bundesregierung in Berlin. Clearly, constitutions and laws can be changed, and national governments can go against the EU, but rather than seeking to change institutional constraints, state parliamentarians can usually be expected to frame policy debates in terms of existing institutions.

In sum, the preceding discussion argues that the lower average level of political tolerance in eastern Germany will not necessarily lead the eastern Landtage to pass more repressive public policies than western parliaments for two institutional reasons:

• Just as elites in established western democracies exhibit a range of political tolerance, however, so too will eastern MdL. Political tolerance will vary along party—rather than east-west—lines, as will policy outcomes.

• Institutional constraints, such as the Basic Law, judicial review, and European Union regulations, place both upper and lower bounds on all politicians seeking to implement (in)tolerant policies. As a result, elite attitudes will not always translate directly into policy outcomes.

These expectations are tested empirically in the subsequent section.

EMPIRICAL EVIDENCE: SAME-SEX PARTNERSHIP IMPLEMENTATION LAWS IN GERMANY

Like most of the work on political tolerance, Rohrschneider's above-mentioned conclusions were reached using the "least-liked-group" methodology (Sullivan, Pierson, and Marcus 1982); in other words, parliamentarians were asked first which societal group they liked the least and then whether they would grant this group certain rights, such as the right to demonstrate or teach in schools. While eastern and western Berlin MdL hold very different political attitudes and values on the whole, they exhibited remarkable agreement when it came to naming

Table 5.1   Berlin state parliamentarians' least-liked groups

Easterners' least-liked groups (1995)	Westerners' least-liked groups (1992)
1. Fascists / right-wing groups	1. Fascists / right-wing groups
2. Communists	2. Communists / Stalinists
3. Pro-life and pro-choice groups	3. Expellee organizations (Vertriebenenverbände)
4. Expellee organizations (Vertriebenenverbände)	4. Pro-life and pro-choice groups /feminists
5. Homosexuals	5. Homosexuals

Note: Ranks calculated by totaling the percent of respondents listing these as either their first or second least-liked group.

Source: Rohrschneider (1999, 112–13).

disliked groups. (See table 5.1.) The vast majority of parliamentarians from both sides of Berlin identified fascists as their least-liked group, followed by communists. Based on Germany's disastrous experiences with fascism during the Third Reich, state representatives' dislike of fascists is perhaps unsurprising. In fact, all Germans at the mass level—in both east and west—are particularly unwilling to extend rights to fascists (Rohrschneider 1999), and western Germans are the most intolerant of fascists of all citizens in western Europe (Gibson, Duch, and Tedin 1992, 338). Similarly, the negative experiences of the GDR era and the Cold War likely explain many elites' dislike of communists. Berlin elites' third and fourth most commonly disliked groups included pro-choice and pro-life advocates as well as expellee organizations (Vertriebenen- verbände).[6] Finally, the fifth most commonly disliked group by Berlin elites was homosexuals (Rohrschneider 1999, 112–13).

For the purposes of studying the relationship between tolerance and policy outcomes, however, four of these five groups pose some difficulties. In the decade since unification there were no instances in which all of the Länder were charged with making decisions regarding the denial or granting of rights to fascists, pro- and anti-abortion groups, or expellee organizations. A similar difficulty arises when it comes to communists. While the questions of lustration regarding ex-members of the GDR regime and treatment of the successor to the communist party, the Party of Democratic Socialism (PDS), have arisen in all states in eastern

Germany, western states have not had to address these questions, making an east-west comparison difficult. In studies limited to the eastern Landtage, partisan variation—similar to that in the case at hand—can be observed in the debates over the issue of whether to allow individuals who had worked for the hated East German secret police, the *Stasi*, the right to be employed in the public sector following unification. Leftist majorities proved somewhat more willing to extend rights to this disliked group than conservative governments did (Sa'adah 1998, 217–20). A. James McAdams' book *Judging the Past in Unified Germany* compares two eastern states' handling of the lustration issue:

> In some cases, the principle determinant of how a given employee was treated appears to have been the politics of the federal state in which he or she happened to reside. In politically conservative Saxony, a CDU-governed Land . . . any evidence of involvement with the [*Stasi*] seems to have constituted sufficient grounds for disqualification from government service. Under these conditions, even *Stasi* drivers, cooks, and janitors were all subject to dismissal from their jobs, regardless of the nature or intensity of their previous commitments. In comparison with Saxony's handling of the [*Stasi*] issue, [Social Democratic] Brandenburg was a picture of moderation and restraint. . . . The state's civil service law was not only less intrusive into past activities than those of more conservative eastern Länder, but the disqualification rate for some categories of state employees was noticeably lower as well. (2001, 75–76)

However, while it is possible to gather eastern-only data or anecdotal east-west comparisons about the relationship between elite political tolerance and public policy towards communists, fascists, pro- and anti-choice groups, and expellee organizations, no systematic comparison is possible across the German Länder.[7]

In contrast to these top four most frequently disliked groups, the fifth one, homosexuals, was a group about which all German Landtage *did* have to determine specific policies in the period since unification. In 2001 all sixteen German states were required to develop policies for implementing federal legislation which established legally binding same-sex partnerships. This provides an excellent case with which to test the relationship between tolerance and policy outcomes.

Before the same-sex partnership law was passed, German public policy had long denied rights and freedoms to homosexuals. The 1871 Reich penal code included paragraph 175 which stated, "An unnatural sex act committed between persons of male sex . . . is punishable by imprisonment; the loss of civil rights might also be imposed." This paragraph was expanded by the Nazis to include even harsher penalties. When the Federal Republic and the German Democratic Republic were founded after World War II, Paragraph 175 remained in their penal codes until 1968, when it was struck down in the GDR, and 1969, when it was revised to allow homosexual relations among men over the age of 21 in the FRG. Only in 1994 was Paragraph 175 removed entirely from the united Germany's penal code and the age of consent lowered to 16, the same as for heterosexual relations.

Despite East Germany's elimination of Paragraph 175 in the 1960s, homosexuality remained a taboo in the GDR. Official recognition of the existence of gays in East Germany began only with the state-sanctioned film "Coming Out," which debuted November 9, 1989—the day the Berlin Wall fell.[8] Across eastern Europe, citizens had little official exposure to homosexuality, and after the fall of communism gays and lesbians were deemed a disliked group by both mass and elite respondents to surveys about political tolerance (Gibson, Duch, and Tedin 1992, 339; Rohrschneider 1999, 113; see also Motte-Shermann and Zyber 2002). Gay life in West Germany was much more open than in East Germany, at least in large cities. Nonetheless, western Germans are more likely than their eastern counterparts to belong to the Catholic or Lutheran churches (Conradt 2001, 57–58) and may hold religious objections to homosexuality. Indeed, political intolerance of gays and lesbians is prevalent among elites (Hayes and Moran-Ellis 1995) and mass publics (Yang 1997) in established democracies. Mass public opinion in united Germany clearly reflected these patterns of political intolerance toward gays and lesbians. The World Values Survey found that more than half of both western and eastern German citizens opposed giving homosexuals the right to be school teachers (cited in Rohrschneider 1999, 118). In 1999, half of eastern Germans and 56% of western Germans did not support extending same-sex couples the right to marry ("Keine Mehrheit" 1999).

Many political elites shared the mass public's antigay attitudes, and the causes of their homophobia came through in plenary debates about their Länder's Life Partnership Implementation Laws. There were MdL in Germany's five new states who clearly disliked homosexuals. Some justified their opposition with Marxist thought. A Brandenburg MdL quoted Friedrich Engels' reference to homosexuals as unnatural pedophiles who threatened to take over the political system if given the chance (BB-03-40, 2592). Other easterners gave religious reasons for opposing same-sex unions, arguing that same-sex marriage "does not correspond to . . . the Christian understanding of marriage" (MVP-03-60, 3915). Such dislike of homosexuals and same-sex unions was definitely not confined to eastern Germany, however. Some westerners used the Christian tradition to justify their opposition to gays and lesbians. For example, one member of the CSU in Bayern argued,

> Ladies and Gentlemen! I want to tell you why I am in principle opposed to [the Life Partnership] law. It has something to do with the fact that I am a Christian. I don't want to teach Sunday school classes to you here. But the Holy Scriptures contain very clear instructions about what we are discussing today. Mrs. Stahl [a Green MdL], making a mockery of a quote by Willy Brandt, says what belongs together is coming together here. In response I say to you it's exactly what doesn't belong together that's coming together. Fully unnatural life partnerships are being legalized. (BY-14-74, 5345)

Although eastern and western German parliamentarians' classification of homosexuals as a disliked group may have had different *causes,* table 5.1 indicates that this group is ranked a disliked group by both western and eastern MdL. Further, I am primarily concerned about the *effects* of this dislike. The literature on political intolerance in post-communist eastern Europe suggests that easterners are more likely to deny democratic rights to disliked groups such as homosexuals, while westerners will be more politically tolerant and extend such rights *despite* their dislike of homosexuals. The institutionalist perspective outlined above, in contrast, expects that the rights received by homosexuals across Germany will vary along partisan lines—regardless of east/west differences in political tolerance. Below I trace the political debate surrounding same-sex partnerships and then compare eastern and western states' implementation of the federal law.

The National-Level Debate

The issue of legal protections for same-sex partnerships was first put forth by the western Greens in a parliamentary motion proposed prior to German unification in 1990; this motion was not passed by the conservative government at the time (Bundesverfassungsgericht 2002). In 1993 the German Supreme Court rejected a lawsuit filed by gay couples requesting a state-sanctioned marriage; the suit, however, raised awareness of the ways in which homosexual couples were discriminated against under existing German law (Bundesverfassungsgericht 1993). The next year, the European Parliament urged member states to avoid discrimination of gays and lesbians in their legal codes and called on the European Commission to work for gay marriage or marriage-like arrangements (Bundesverfassungsgericht 2002). In the coming years, the Greens began to call for same-sex marriages, and the liberal Free Democrats proposed an end to discrimination of gays and lesbians. Neither party, however, was in a political position to implement these demands: the Greens were in the opposition, and the FDP's senior coalition partner strongly opposed same-sex unions. The situation changed in 1998 when the Greens entered into a governing coalition with the Social Democratic Party. At the insistence of the Greens, in particular, Volker Beck, who was a gay rights activist before being elected to the Bundestag, the coalition agreement pledged to carry out the wishes of the European Parliament, not only by ending discrimination against gays and lesbians, but also by promoting their equal treatment under the law through the establishment of state-sanctioned partnerships with binding rights and benefits.

The coalition did little to act on this promise during its first year and a half in office, choosing to focus on other issues instead. This delay was likely caused in part by the fact that the Social Democratic Party was quite divided on the issue of gay marriage. While the issue appealed to its younger post-materialist constituents, it found little resonance with the party's traditional union wing, and some party leaders felt that taking up same-sex partnerships would hurt the party's midterm election chances ("Nichts für Wahlen" 2001). Furthermore, the SPD's cabinet members disagreed on the issue as well. While Gerhard Schroeder, like the Greens, favored a same-sex partnership that would "include the same rights and responsibilities as [heterosexual] marriage," both Justice Minister Herta Däubler-Gmelin and Interior Minister Otto Schily favored a more limited partnership. Däubler-Gmelin pointed out that Article 6, Paragraph 1 of the Basic Law states that "marriage and family are under the special protection of law." She worried that if gay couples were given exactly the same legal protections as heterosexual couples, the law would be found unconstitutional since traditional marriage would no longer be "special" ("Alles Liebe" 2000). Schily worried about the costs of extending Germany's social safety net to same-sex partners and feared the law might be used as a way for needy foreigners to enter into pseudo-partnerships and gain access to Germany's welfare state ("Schily kritisiert Gesetz zur Homo-Ehe" 2000).

As the SPD debated details of same-sex partnerships, the Greens became more insistent on drafting a law which would offer maximum benefits to gays and lesbians. The party had had to compromise on its campaign promises for an immediate end to the use of nuclear energy and the adoption of dual citizenship. Gay marriage was "the last bastion" of their platform and party leaders vowed to defend it vigorously ("Alles Liebe" 2000). As a result of this strong stance, the coalition submitted a draft law to the Bundestag in July 2000 creating a "registered life partnership" (eingetragene Lebenspartnerschaft) which gave gay couples virtually all rights that married couples enjoy except the right to adopt children and the right of the surviving spouse to collect Social Security benefits. In addition, the SPD refused to overturn laws giving only (heterosexually) married women access to sperm banks. The SPD vetoed these latter benefits, as well as identical tax advantages to married couples, arguing that this would help marriage retain its constitutionally required "special" status. Table 5.2 lists the benefits that were included in the draft law; in order to implement these changes, over one hundred other German laws needed to be altered.

After the text of the draft law was released and discussed in parliamentary committees, all the opposition parties expressed their objections to it. The Christian Democrats and their Bavarian counterparts, the Christian Social Union, attacked the law on several fronts. Some members of the party opposed same-sex partnerships on moral grounds, echoing both the Catholic and Protestant churches' strong opposition.[9] The head of the CSU, Thomas Goppel, called the law "societally unacceptable" warning that it would "hollow out the most significant foundations of our society." In a classic display of political intolerance, he argued that because a majority of Germans were opposed to such partnerships, gay couples should not be granted legal rights ("Kirchen

Table 5.2 Provisions of the Life Partnership Law (LPartG) and the amended law

Rights extended in the Life Partnership Law	Rights included in the amendment
• The right to a "registered life partnership" that would be recorded by the state in much the same way as a heterosexual marriage; family members of the couples would have the same legal relationships as family members of wedded couples (father-in-law, sister-in-law, etc.) • The right to choose a common name • The right to inherit • The right to hospital visitations and to make medical decisions for an ill partner • The right to be included on a partner's health insurance at no additional cost • The right for a foreign partner to travel to and remain in Germany • The right not to testify against a partner in a court of law • The right to make everyday decisions regarding a child the couple is raising jointly (*kleines Sorgerecht*) • The right of a surviving partner to take over a lease or a mortgage after the death of a partner • The responsibility to support a dependent partner financially and divide up joint assets if a partnership breaks up • The right to some tax advantages	• The right to the same tax relief as enjoyed by married couples • The right of partners of public employees to the same benefits as heterosexual spouses • The responsibility to include partner income when welfare benefits are calculated • The right to seal the life partnership in the state Registry Office in the same way heterosexual unions are held

Source: Gesetz über die Eingetragene Lebenspartnerschaft (2001) and the Lebenspartnerschafts-ergänzungsgesetz (2001).

wehren" 2000). Other members of the two parties used constitutional grounds to justify their opposition to extending rights to homosexuals. CSU legal expert Norbert Geis, a vocal opponent of same-sex partnerships warned that the draft law was "almost one hundred percent a carbon copy of" heterosexual marriage and complained, "the SPD only wants to hide what its real goal is: the special constitutional protections of marriage should be abolished" (quoted in Leersch 2000). The CDU/CSU vowed to vote against the law both in the Bundestag, where they were in the minority, and in the Bundesrat, where they enjoyed a majority. Furthermore, they threatened to take any law that passed to the German Supreme Court. The CDU remained divided on how far their party should go to mobilize grassroots opposition to the law: party leader Angela Merkel (from the east) favored promoting a letter-writing campaign while Hessian governor Roland Koch (from the west) opposed such populist measures and ultimately prevailed ("Umstrittene Homo-Ehe" 2000).

The opposition Free Democrats also objected to the draft law, albeit not as vehemently. The liberals drafted more narrow legislation to avoid what they considered violations of the Basic Law's Article 6. Rather than establishing state-sponsored partnerships that could compete with constitutionally protected heterosexual marriage, the FDP preferred that couples be allowed to go to a notary public and make their own legal agreements regulating as many aspects of their partnership as they could; for example drawing up their own wills, prenuptial agreements, and drafting health care powers of attorney. The liberals only wanted changes to laws for cases beyond individuals' control, such as mandating that partners did not have to testify against one another in court (Fuhrer 2000). The Free Democrats did not speak out as vocally against the law as the Christian Democrats, nor did they try to mobilize grassroots opposition. In fact, they even showed some willingness to negotiate with the Greens and the SPD on details of the law. Nevertheless they ultimately decided to vote against it in the Bundestag and Bundesrat, citing constitutionality issues.

The final party represented at the national level was the Party of Democratic Socialism, made up primarily of eastern Germans. As the literature on political intolerance in eastern Europe would predict, they too opposed the Life Partnership Law. However, their opposition was not due to objections to extending rights to a disliked group. Instead, the PDS opposed the law because it didn't go far enough in granting gay couples equal rights. In a speech on the floor of the Bundestag, PDS representative Christina Schenk criticized, "The Greens promised their gay and lesbian constituents a legal institution . . . that would bring them the same rights and responsibilities as married couples and that would abolish discrimination. For reasons of justice, we could never have withheld our approval of such a legal institution. . . . What resulted, however, was a law that marks homosexuals as second class couples . . .

with only reduced rights" (Bundestag 14–131, 12619). Because the law failed to grant same-sex couples the right to adopt, to receive their partner's social security benefits, and to enjoy the same tax advantages, the PDS vowed to abstain when a vote was taken on the law.

In addition to these federal debates, leaders of the Catholic and Protestant churches had vociferously opposed life partnerships in the strongest terms, while gay activists celebrated them in celebrity-filled media spectacles (Iken 2001). The German press also paid considerable attention to the same-sex marriage issue. The *Frankfurter Allgemeine Zeitung*, Germany's daily newspaper of record, published 159 articles on the topic between 2000 and 2002, while the major weekly news magazines, *Spiegel*, *Stern*, and *Focus*, devoted 104 articles to gay marriage in the same period.[10]

Over the summer of 2000, it became clear to the governing parties that while they could pass the draft partnership law in the Bundestag, it would never be approved in the Bundesrat. In the German parliamentary system, however, only legislation that directly involves the Länder needs to be voted on by the Bundesrat; all other bills only require the approval of the Bundestag. As a result, the SPD and Greens decided to break the law into two separate pieces of legislation. The first bill, the Lebenspartnerschaftsgesetz or Life Partnership Law, contained all of the components in the left-hand column of table 5.2, none of which required the approval of the Bundesrat. The second bill, the Amendment to the Life Partnership Law, included the first three items in the right-hand column of table 5.2. These provisos, regarding state taxation, benefits for Land-level government employees, and welfare payments made by states, required direct action on the part of individual Länder and thus approval of the Bundesrat. The final item in the right-hand column of table 5.2, the right to enter into a partnership at public Registry Offices, proved to be problematic for the government. On the one hand, because individual states have jurisdiction over Registry Offices, any law mandating that partnerships be entered into at a Registry Office would require approval of the Bundesrat. On the other hand, if a Life Partnership Law were ever to be implemented, *some* authority had to be responsible for uniting couples. Ultimately the coalition used the following wording in the Life Partnership Law: partnerships were to be entered into at "the responsible government agency" (*zuständige Behörde*), beginning August 1, 2001. This phrase did not require any specific action on the part of the Länder so the Bundesrat's approval was not required. Instead, each Land would be allowed to decide for itself which agency was responsible for the registration of life partnerships.

On November 10, 2000, as expected, both the Life Partnership Law and the Amendment Law were passed by the Bundestag with the votes of the Greens and SPD. The CDU and FDP voted against both measures and the PDS abstained. The Amendment Law was then sent to the Bundesrat where the CDU/FDP majority rejected it on December 1, 2000. Usually, when the two chambers cannot agree on legislation, a joint committee of both houses is formed to work out a compromise. A joint committee was indeed formed in February 2001, but Christian Democrats refused to attend committee meetings, meaning that no progress could be made toward the Amendment Law's passage.

As promised, Christian Democrats began to challenge the Life Partnership Law's constitutionality immediately after its passage. Three states governed by Christian Democratic majorities—the eastern states of Sachsen and Thüringen and the western state Bayern—filed suit with the German Supreme Court on two grounds. First, they charged that the breaking up of the law into parts with the express purpose of avoiding the Bundesrat was illegal, and, second, they maintained, the legislation violated Article 6 of the Basic Law. Sachsen and Bayern also filed for a preliminary injunction (*Eilantrag*), asking the court to suspend implementation of the law until a verdict was reached. The request for a preliminary injunction was rejected by the court on July 18, 2001, and the partnership law went into effect as scheduled. The Supreme Court declared the law constitutional on July 17, 2002, arguing that same-sex partnerships did not threaten the constitutionally mandated "special protection" of marriage since only gay couples who were ineligible for marriage could take advantage of them. Dividing the law into two parts in order to avoid the Bundesrat was not considered unconstitutional either. As a result, the law remained in effect.

Before turning to a discussion of how this law was implemented at the state level in eastern and western Germany, I will make several observations about the passage of the partnership law at the national level and how it relates to the hypotheses outlined in the first section of this chapter. Because close to 80% of the Federal Republic's population is from western Germany, and because westerners dominate most federal-level positions, the majority of the voices in the above debate were western

Germans'. There is not enough evidence at the national level to generalize about eastern elites compared to their western counterparts. Clearly, however, as the findings from other established democracies predict, there was a broad range in the level of political tolerance on the part of western actors—mostly along party lines. While some Christian Democrats expressed extreme reluctance to extend rights to a disliked group, Greens and some Social Democrats fought hard to grant homosexuals the same treatment that heterosexuals enjoyed. The few eastern voices heard in the debate were similarly varied. While Angela Merkel (CDU) wanted to whip up popular resistance to extending rights to a disliked group, the communist-successor party, the PDS, would settle for nothing less than a full extension of these rights. What seems to have been important was not whether eastern or western elites had influence at the national level, but to which party these elites belonged.

Political institutions like Article 6 of the Basic Law and the rules governing the competencies of the Bundestag and Bundesrat clearly delineated upper and lower bounds for political tolerance. Politically tolerant actors from both eastern and western Germany still had to respect the constitution's demand to give marriage special protection and the Bundesrat's power to veto legislation. Similarly, politically intolerant actors from both parts of the country were still subject to EU rulings and the power that the Greens wielded within a coalition government. While the majority of the population was not comfortable with gay unions, this small party was in a position, by virtue of Germany's proportional representation electoral system and its parliamentary system, to realize this key component of its electoral platform. As a result, even states governed by MdL vehemently opposed to extending rights to gays and lesbians were forced to implement the Life Partnership Law.

Variation in State-Level Policies

After the Life Partnership Law was passed, each German state had to decide which public agency would be responsible for registering life partnerships and how they should go about doing so. Twelve states did so by passing a Life Partnership Implementation Law (*Ausführungsgesetz*) in their state legislatures. In the hopes that the Supreme Court would ultimately strike down the federal law, four other states held off

on passing an implementation law and instead relied on temporary executive orders. These latter states exhibited less political tolerance than
the former because they extended rights to a disliked group on a less
permanent basis. The laws/executive orders varied on four fronts.

First, and most importantly, the states had to designate the public authority responsible for registering the partnerships. In order for heterosexual couples to marry in Germany, they must go to the Registry Office
(Standesamt) in their town; unlike in the United States, clergy members
are not permitted to conduct legally binding weddings. Registry Offices
usually have attractive chambers where weddings are held, complete
with music, flowers, and champagne toasts. Some large cities offer weddings outside of the Registry Office; bureaucrats from Berlin-Mitte, for
example, will marry couples atop the two-hundred-meter-tall TV tower,
at the zoo, or on a boat, tram, or convertible double-decker bus. For
small fees, married couples can also receive a marriage certificate
(Urkunde) suitable for framing and a Family Book (Familienbuch), an
expandable book that includes documentation of the couple's marriage,
their married name, and information about any children they may have;
deaths, divorces, and future children can be added later.

In order to extend the most possible rights to same-sex couples, states
could have allowed them to enter into life partnerships at Registry Offices. Not only would this option grant them the same opportunities as
heterosexual couples to celebrate their unions, but it also would be quite
convenient, as most communities have a Registry Office. Opponents of
the law argued that this option made same-sex partnership registrations
too much like a "normal" wedding. Some gay and lesbian organizations
feared that states controlled by the opposition would designate the San-
itation or Cemetery Departments as the government agency responsible
for registering life partnerships. While this did not materialize, many
states left the decision about the responsible agency up to local officials,
allowing conservative communities to deny gay couples access to the
Registry Office in favor of another department.[11] A more restrictive option sent gay couples to county- or regional-level offices. This meant that
these couples were excluded from the local Registry Office and instead
had to travel to the county seat to an office usually used for administrative matters like filing for conscientious objector status or for exemp-
tions from television tax and seat-belt laws.[12] One Land sent interested
couples even farther from home, requiring them to travel to the state

capital. A final option put even more symbolic distance between the state and partnerships by sending couples not to a public agency but to a notary public who would then forward the paperwork to the state.

Second, states had to decide whether to recognize the significance of a registered life partnership with a book akin to the Family Books established by heterosexual couples. The way to have extended the most possible rights to gay couples would have been to indeed give them Family Books; no state did this, however, perhaps out of deference to Article 6. Many states did extend the right to Life Partnership Books (Lebenspartnerschaftsbücher) to homosexual couples. Other than the name, there is no difference between the two types of books. A more restrictive option chosen by some states was to recognize the existences of registered partnerships in the couples' parents' Family Books—where children's heterosexual marriages are also recorded—but not to grant the couple the right to establish a book of their own. Finally, the fewest rights were given to same-sex couples when no information about life partnerships was allowed to be entered in any state-sponsored book.

Third, the Länder had to determine whether to offer couples the option to purchase a certificate commemorating their partnership (Lebenspartnerschaftsurkunde), just as married couples can buy a marriage certificate documenting their union. Again, the least restrictive option would be to offer both gay and straight couples the option of purchasing such a certificate. The most restrictive option would be to deny homosexuals this way of celebrating the registration of their partnership. One state found a way to semantically differentiate between a heterosexual marriage and a same-sex partnership by offering the latter couples a "certification" (Bescheinigung) documenting their partnership at twice the price of the marriage "certificate" (Urkunde).[13]

Finally, states had to set fees for registering partnerships. Generally in Germany traditional marriages cost thirty-three euros. To extend the most possible rights to gay couples was to also charge them thirty-three euros, or to legally mandate that life partnerships and marriages always cost the same amount. Other Länder, wishing to grant fewer rights to same-sex couples than to heterosexual pairs, charged homosexual couples two to three times as much to record their unions.

Tables 5.3 and 5.4 outline the stipulations of the Implementation Laws/Executive Orders passed in all sixteen of Germany's western and eastern states, respectively. In each table, the Länder are ordered in terms of the partisanship of their governing coalitions; the more socially

Table 5.3 Western states' implementation laws

State (Governing Coalition)	Law or Executive Order	Office Responsible	Partnership Book	Certificate	Cost
Hamburg (SPD/Green)	Law	Registry Office	Yes	Yes	Same as for married couples
Nordrhein-Westfalen (SPD/Green)	Law	Registry Office	Yes	Yes (7 euros)	33 euros
Schleswig-Holstein (SPD/Green)	Law	Registry Office	Yes	Yes (7 euros)	33 euros
Niedersachsen (SPD)	Law	Registry Office	Yes	Yes	Same as for married couples
Rheinland-Pfalz (SPD/FDP)	Law	County Office	Goes in parents'	"Certification" (14 euros)	65 euros
Bremen (SPD/CDU)	Law	Registry Office	Goes in parents'	Yes (7 euros)	75 euros
Hessen (CDU/FDP)	Law	Locality Decides	Goes in parents'	Yes (7 euros)	33 euros
Baden-Württemberg (CDU/FDP)	Executive Order (Law passed June 2002)	County Office	No	Yes (7 euros)	75 euros
Saarland (CDU)	Law	Locality Decides	Goes in parents'	Yes (7 euros)	75 euros
Bayern (CSU)	Executive Order (Law passed late October 2001)	Notary Public	Yes, but run by notaries, not state	Yes (Included in price but run by notaries, not state)	100 euros

Note: States are listed according to the governing coalition: the further down, the more socially conservative.

Note: The darker the shading, the fewer rights extended to same-sex couples.

Source: Länder Ausführungsgesetze. (Available from the Lesben- und Schwulenverband in Deutschland, www.lsvd.de.)

Table 5.4   Eastern states' and Berlin's implementation laws

State (Governing Coalition)	Law or Executive Order	Office Responsible	Partnership Book	Certificate	Cost
Berlin (SPD/PDS)	Law	Registry Office	Yes	Yes	Not specified
Mecklenburg-Vorpommern (SPD/PDS)	Law	Registry Office	Yes	Yes (7 euros)	33 euros
Sachsen-Anhalt (SPD)	Law	Registry Office	Yes	Yes (7 euros)	33 euros
Brandenburg (SPD/CDU)	Law	Locality Decides	Goes in parents'	No	Same as for married couples
Thüringen (CDU/FDP)	Executive Order (Law passed August 2002)	1 State Office (Law: County Office)	Goes in parents'	No	Not specified
Sachsen (CDU)	Executive Order	3 State Offices	No	No	Not specified

Note: States are listed according to the governing coalition: the further down, the more socially conservative.
Note: The darker the shading, the fewer rights extended to same-sex couples.
Source: Länder Ausführungsgesetze. (Available from the Lesben- und Schwulenverband in Deutschland, www.lsvd.de.)

conservative the coalition, the lower in the table the state is listed. The columns represent the provisions of the laws listed above; the fewer rights extended to gay couples, the darker the cells are. These tables offer stark visual testament to the influence of the party state's political institutions, rather than post-communist political intolerance, in shaping public policy in Germany. Attitudinal research documenting post-communist political intolerance implies that the eastern German states would offer fewer rights to same-sex couples than their western counterparts in the long-democratic western Länder. This is clearly not the case. Instead, in both parts of Germany the legal benefits granted to a disliked group varied considerably from state to state along partisan lines, as expected when political institutions are taken into account.

In most instances, parties represented the same positions at the state level that they did at the national level. Voting patterns were somewhat different in some cases, however. Rather than abstaining because the federal law did not go far enough, PDS members voted in favor of liberal Implementation Laws. In some Länder, individual Christian Democrats or caucuses merely abstained rather than voting against liberal laws. Finally, when in coalitions, some parties had to compromise in order to pass a law.

Left-wing coalitions showed the greatest willingness to extend rights to a disliked group. In all states—east and west—governed by the Social Democrats and either the Greens or the Party of Democratic Socialism, gay partners received the same benefits as heterosexual couples.[14] Same-sex couples were granted the right to enter into life partnerships at Registry Offices, they were offered Partnership Books and certificates, and the fees for all services were the same as for married couples. These states had worked together with the federal Ministry of the Interior on a model law that was by and large implemented in all of these Länder. Some of these states had also played key roles in the development of the federal Life Partnership Law. A year after the SPD/Green government took office at the national level and a year before the draft law went to the Bundestag, the SPD/Green coalition in the western state of Hamburg began offering gay couples what became known as a "Hamburg Marriage"—allowing couples to hold a ceremony and symbolically register their unions with the state (Iken 2001). When three states filed suit to stop implementation of the law passed by the Bundestag, the SPD minority government in the eastern state of Sachsen-Anhalt showed its support by being the first Land to draft a model implementation law

("Mit dem Segen" 2001). Its Social Minister had supported an earlier letter-writing campaign to encourage the federal government to pass a law in the first place (SA-03-46, 3345). Both Hamburg and its western neighbor Schleswig-Holstein filed amicus briefs with the Supreme Court arguing for the constitutionality of the Life Partnership Law (Bundes-verfassungsgerichtshof 2002).

In three other states the SPD formed coalitions with more conservative parties including the FDP and the CDU. There, in both east and west, the implementation laws were somewhat more restrictive. In the eastern state of Brandenburg the government decided to devolve the decision about which office should be responsible for same-sex partnerships to the local level, whereas in the western state of Rheinland-Pfalz county offices were designated the responsible authorities. In the western city-state of Bremen the SPD/CDU coalition designated the Registry Office as the responsible agency; the Christian Democrats may have acceded to the wishes of the Social Democrats because the local governments in that state (the cities of Bremen and Bremerhaven) had SPD/Green majorities that would have chosen the Registry Office anyway. None of these states allowed couples to start Family Books, although partnerships were to be recorded in their parents' books. Bremen awarded certificates while Rheinland-Pfalz allowed couples a "receipt" rather than a "certificate" costing fourteen rather than seven euros. The eastern state's law was more restrictive; no mention was made of granting couples a certificate at all. On the other hand, eastern Brandenburg's law mandated that partnerships cost the same as a heterosexual marriage while the western states charged twice as much.

Finally, in six states the conservative Christian Democrats and Christian Social Union governed alone or (in some western Länder) with the Free Democrats as a junior coalition partner. These Länder granted same-sex couples the fewest benefits. Given the fact that three of these states, western Bayern and eastern Sachsen and Thüringen, had challenged the constitutionality of the law and that the first two had filed for an injunction against its implementation, their reluctance to extend rights to gay couples is not surprising. These states and the western state of Baden-Württemberg did not initially pass any partnership laws and instead relied on temporary executive orders. Once the Supreme Court refused to grant a preliminary injunction, however, the two western states passed partnership laws,[15] and Thüringen drafted a law which was ultimately passed in September 2002, over a year after other life partnership laws went into effect. Sachsen continued to operate under an executive order, arguing that it would be premature to pass a state implementation law until the (very unlikely) event that the Amendment to the Life Partnership Law was passed by the Bundesrat (SX-03-57, 3966).

None of the CDU-dominated states ensured same-sex couples access to the Registry Offices. Two of the western states—the Saarland and Hessen—devolved the decision to the local governments. In Baden-Württemberg counties were designated the responsible authority. While Hessen charged couples only thirty-three euros to register a partnership, Saarland and Baden-Württemberg charged twice the price of a heterosexual wedding. These three Länder allowed couples to receive certificates, but none granted them their own Life Partnership Books, although in Hessen and the Saarland mention could be made of a partnership in the couples' parents' books.

In contrast, the three CDU-dominated states that had filed suit against the law completely ruled out Registry Office access. The eastern state of Sachsen issued an executive order designating the state's three regional administrations (*Regierungspräsidien*) the responsible agencies. These bureaucracies are mid-way between county government and state government and are where citizens go to, among other things, register a business or receive state aid after a fire or other disaster. As a result, same-sex partners wishing to register their partnerships must travel to one of three cities in the state to do so, whereas heterosexual couples have access to their local Registry Office. Sachsen's executive order has provisions for neither a certificate nor a Partnership Book nor a specific fee.

Thüringen also issued a temporary executive order until the Supreme Court decision was announced. It made all interested same-sex partners in the entire state travel to the city of Weimar to the state-level Administrative Department (*Verwaltungsamt*) to register their partnerships.[16] The law ultimately passed, like Rheinland-Pfalz's and Baden-Württemberg's, specifies that county governments should ultimately be responsible for registering partnerships. Neither the executive order nor the law had provisions for Partnership Books, certificates, or cost, although partnerships could be recorded in couples' parents' Family Books.

Finally, in what was considered by the German press to be the most restrictive policy of all, the western state of Bayern refused to use any

state agency to sanction partnerships, relegating them to notary publics. While homosexual couples in Bayern can start a Life Partnership
Book and receive a certificate, these are not public documents but ones
drawn up and administered by the Bavarian Chamber of Notaries. Furthermore, gay couples are charged three times what heterosexual couples must pay for similar services.[17]

Summary

The evidence from the state level clearly shows a range of willingness to
extend rights to a disliked group. However, there was no distinctive east-
west pattern to political intolerance; instead government partisanship
in both east and west predicts the degree to which rights were extended
to German gays and lesbians. Contrary to the attitudinal approach's expectations, many eastern German parliamentarians were indeed willing
to grant civil rights to a small group disliked by many citizens. Where
eastern Social Democrats and their PDS allies had a majority, they extended more rights to homosexuals than did Christian Democratic governments in either half of Germany. Thus partisanship, rather than pre-
1989 background, predicted the degree of tolerance shown in public
policy. Both kinds of coalitions were constrained by their subordinate
institutional position in Germany's federal system, however. Politically
tolerant state legislators complained that the Life Partnership Law did
not go far enough in extending rights to homosexuals but were not in a
position to change the laws implemented at the federal level. Similarly,
politically intolerant Land-level actors tried but failed to stop implementation of a national law of which they completely disapproved. They were
forced to accept the Supreme Court decision and to allow same-sex partnerships to be registered in their states.

AN ALTERNATIVE HYPOTHESIS

One possible objection to the conclusions above would be that the policy outcomes observed had nothing to do with political tolerance. It
could be that left-wing coalitions in eastern Germany extended rights to
same-sex partners not in spite of the fact that homosexuals were an unpopular group but because they, or their constituents, had positive feel-

ings toward this group. Eastern implementation laws extending rights to gays and lesbians would not be examples of political tolerance if such rights were granted only because politicians were favorably disposed to homosexuals. Similarly, restrictive laws in western states may not have represented political intolerance on the part of elites but merely the influence of Article 6 of the Basic Law.

In order to determine whether eastern and western German elites' (in)tolerance toward homosexuals played a role in policy making, I examined the reasons MdL gave for supporting particular implementation laws. To do so, I read the transcripts of Landtag plenary sessions from a sample of twelve states, paired according to location (east or west) and the partisanship of their governments.[18] I studied the debates held during the first and second readings of the Implementation Law as well as during discussion of other motions related to marriage and same-sex partnerships. In these debates, state-level parties echoed the positions taken by the national branch of their own party. Further, politicians who were from different Länder but from the same party used the same examples or arguments in their speeches to the floor, indicating cross-state cooperation among deputies.

Some MdL in both eastern and western Germany showed clear signs of political intolerance when they argued that legal protections for same-sex partnerships were not needed because only a small minority would receive these rights. One eastern member of a far right party in Sachsen-Anhalt reasoned:

> The Life Partnership Law . . . is supposed to establish necessary legal protections for a discriminated minority. At the same time there exists . . . in no way an urgent societal need. In terms of homosexuals, we're dealing with a very small statistical size, the estimates range between 2% and 2.8% of the male population and 1.4% of women. Most homosexuals don't even want to get married. As soon as partnerships even come about, they break up. In places that have had registered partnerships for a longer period of time, they've hardly been used. (SA-03-59, 4179)

An eastern Christian Democrat in Thüringen also argued against passing an implementation law after the executive order had gone into effect, stating "we've heard the numbers. Since [the executive order] there have been thirteen partnerships registered. Ladies and gentlemen, let's

not dramatize to the world that we here in Thüringen don't have any-
thing better to do than occupy ourselves with this problem" (TH-03-39,
4040). Similarly, a western Christian Democrat argued against his state's
SPD-backed Implementation Law:

> Almost all scientific studies about the stability and length of same-sex
> partnerships have found the same results . . . that such couples, at
> least the vast majority, shy away from long-term commitments. . . . In
> places where it is possible to have a state-sanctioned partnership, as
> for example in Denmark, same-sex couples just don't make use of this
> possibility as politicians had expected. There this option isn't taken
> advantage of for the aforementioned reasons. Given these aspects,
> the justified question remains: What's all this about? . . . It's about . . .
> promoting the demands of minorities. Those are the policies that
> you are implementing here. Moreover, in doing so [the governing co-
> alition is] arbitrarily treating fundamental, formative values which
> actually affect and hold together the structure of the entire society.
> Not only is this arbitrariness readily accepted, it is being elevated to
> law. As a result, . . . the lines within the discussion on values are be-
> coming more and more blurred. (NS-14-79, 7771)

He went on to warn that if all Germans did not hold the same values,
they would no longer be able to reach understandings which united all
those who are in favor of democracy. In other words, democracy in his
opinion would only work if small, disliked groups were excluded. A
member of the CSU in the western state of Bayern also appealed to majority rule, criticizing the Greens in his state, "I'd like to ask you, why
don't you pursue policies for majorities?" (BY-14-44, 3009). A CSU
member of the executive there concurred, "Today we are yet again experiencing the usual flow of parliamentary discussion. The Greens are
running around with the initiative of some minority" (BY-14-44, 3011).
Thus political intolerance was clearly a motivating factor for restrictive
implementation laws both in eastern *and* in western Germany.

While many members of the Greens, SPD, and PDS certainly had positive attitudes toward gays and lesbians, while homosexuals were an important constituency of these parties, and while politicians at times
justified their support for their law in terms of popular approval of life
partnerships, members of these parties in both eastern and western
Germany also made very clear arguments for political tolerance. Even in

post-communist eastern Germany, politicians stressed the importance of extending rights to very small or unpopular minorities. In both parts of the country, supporters of life partnerships stressed that a liberal implementation law was a critical step in ending discrimination of an often-disliked group. As one eastern Social Democrat put it, "In my opinion it is high time that we cease to legally discriminate against same-sex domestic partnerships in Germany. . . . The law that the governing coalition passed in February is . . . a significant step toward equal treatment of lesbians and gays in our society" (MVP-03-60, 3916). One member of the PDS agreed, "there is not a single reason to deny homosexual couples the right to marry. It is a basic principle of the rule of law to treat the same things in the same ways. And it is the same thing: here as there there is love and mutual responsibility is being taken" (SA-03-59, 4177). An eastern SPD deputy who criticized the "free states" of Bavaria, Thüringen, and Sachsen for challenging the law argued, "I think that a state ruled by free citizens should accord minorities their due recognition . . . especially when it—as you said—has to do with a very small statistical percentage" (SA-03-59, 4180). When the Christian Democrats in the eastern state of Thüringen argued that the law was not needed because there was little interest a Social Democrat responded, "You said 'there have only been thirteen registrations so far' . . . but what's at stake is that I have the right [to register a partnership], that I can" (TH-03-49, 4041).

As expected, western politicians also expressed political tolerance. For example a Green in the western state of Bayern argued, "But also even if it only has to do with a minority, it is important that the state sends a signal and makes it clear that with gays and lesbians it's . . . about people who have exactly the same rights that we also have" (BY-14-44, 3006). A Social Democrat in Bayern appealed to history as a justification for such political tolerance:

> Dear colleagues, when we talk about such a highly sensitive topic, we must think about the fact that up until recent times people with same-sex orientations were prosecuted in the criminal code. We must also remember that less than sixty years ago these people were stigmatized by pink triangles. Back then these human beings were brought to concentration camps where they suffered intensely. Today 10% of the population is not heterosexually inclined . . . and public policy must recognize this reality and shape political structures so that

minorities are not excluded. . . . For us it's all about the fact that legal frameworks must incorporate minorities. Our position is determined by the principle that a society can only be peaceful and just when people have equal rights. (BY-14-44, 3010)

This historical justification for political tolerance was found in eastern Germany as well. As an eastern Social Democratic deputy put it, "our history gives us a special obligation to reduce all forms of discrimination against people or groups of people" (MVP-03-60, 3918). Another SPD representative, this time in Thüringen, cited the repression of gays and lesbians not only under the Nazis but also under communism as historical justification for current tolerance: "The CDU and much of the Catholic church criticize the new law with inappropriate stridence. In doing so, the CDU forgets that it was the church of all groups in East Germany that sheltered minorities, including homosexuals, under its roof. With unification homosexuals also saw a chance to end discrimination and gain legal . . . recognition" (TH-03-32, 2371). These kinds of statements clearly support the above expectation that eastern Germans, like their western counterparts, exhibit a wide array of political tolerance toward homosexuals—a willingness to extend them rights that often fell along party lines.

The parliamentary transcripts show not only the presence of partisan variation in political tolerance across Germany, however, they also provide a wealth of evidence to support the view that political institutions constrained both tolerant and intolerant actors. In almost all states, just as at the federal level, the presence of constitutional constraints on political tolerance were clearly apparent.[19] On the one hand, opponents of the law almost always argued that the Partnership Law proposed by the federal government came too close to constitutionally protected same-sex marriage. Such arguments were common in both eastern and western Germany. As the following Christian Democrats put it:

I would like to yet again stress that, despite the rejection of so-called gay marriage, we are for tolerance and acceptance and most importantly respect for people who find lifetime happiness in such partnerships. . . . The CDU is prepared to . . . improve or create legal protections for same-sex partnerships. . . . What we reject is equating [them] with the marriage of a man and a woman. . . . [The law] trans-

fers all the regulations of the code law governing marriage to homosexual unions and only changes the label on it. (MVP-03-60, 3914)

Marriage and family enjoy special protection and promotion not only
in laws but also in the constitution, according to Article 6 of the Basic
Law and Article 17 of the Thüringen state constitution. . . . We aren't
discriminating against anyone who, for whatever reason, wants to live
differently than others; however, we find it highly problematic when
this [form of relationship] is equated with the constitutionally protected institutions of marriage and family. (TH-03-32, 2371)

The CDU caucus will vote against this draft Life Partnership Implementation Law. The main reason for our rejection is our justified fear
that this law at its core contradicts the basic principles of our constitution. (NS-03-79, 7769)

Both eastern and western proponents of tolerant implementation
laws also used overarching legal institutions to justify their policies,
claiming that they did not violate Article 6. As one member of the PDS
argued, "many people affected by the law have told me that this is not
gay marriage and will not be because of the way the law is put together—
even if the law hadn't been split up into two parts—because there is no
right to adoption, no complete equality [with heterosexual unions] in
terms of tax advantages, no complete right to custody of children; instead everything is in a weakened, minimized version" (MVP-03-60,
3917). Greens, Social Democrats, and PDS representatives often mentioned the EU's ruling as a justification for the legal appropriateness of
the law. For example, a Social Democrat from the eastern state of Brandenburg argued, "our opinion—the SPD's opinion—that life partnerships as well [as marriages] should be entered into in a dignified form
at the Registry Office is based on, among other things, Article 21 of the
EU Charter" (BB-03-39, 2516). Similarly, a PDS deputy in Mecklenburg-
Vorpommern claimed, "And I think we are not completely free in our
decision, either at the national level or here, because there is a reso-
lution, a decision of the European Parliament from February 8, 1999.
In it, the member states of the EU were requested to establish legal
regulations that allow same-sex pairs the same rights that result from
marriage" (MVP-03-60, 3917). Finally, in the eastern Länder of Brandenburg and Thüringen, proponents of the Registry Office argued that

these states' constitutional bans on discrimination against gays and lesbians meant that the government was obligated to send same-sex couples to the Registry Offices (BB-03-39, 2516; TH-03-49, 4037).

There was a clear recognition on the part of politically tolerant actors, however, that Article 6 placed an upper bound on the rights they could extend to gays and lesbians. The SPD in the eastern state of Sachsen-Anhalt chided, "On the part of the PDS there are criticisms that the law does not go far enough. If we would follow the PDS's notions, then we'd admittedly come up against the bounds of constitutionality and fail in Karlsruhe" [the seat of the German Supreme Court] (SA-03-57, 4055). Similarly, in western Schleswig-Holstein a Green representative lamented, "I see no reason not to open marriage to same-sex couples. . . . [But] this is not possible at this time" (SH-15-35, 2638).

Similarly, it was clear that even the most intolerant actors had to pass *some* kind of regulations in order to implement same-sex partnerships. As one eastern Minister argued, "We must—if for no other reason than out of respect for federal law—make an implementation procedure for our state. . . . I request that you undertake a brisk review of the legislation in committee so that, . . . as the national government has ordered, we can process requests to register partnerships in our state beginning on August 1 this year" (MVP-03-60, 3914).

As stated above, as of 2004 fifteen of Germany's sixteen Landtage had indeed passed such laws, and Sachsen's executive order allowed for couples to enter into life partnerships in that state as well. While no official statistics are yet kept of same-sex partnerships, one study found that over 3000 partnerships had been entered into in 2001 (Finger 2001), and another counted 9000 during the first calendar year the law had been in place (Koltermann 2002). Further, the press reports that same-sex partnerships have become a "normal" administrative procedure in Germany (Irle 2002; Koltermann 2002). Even the Christian Democrats vowed not to overturn the law were they to receive a majority at the federal level. In 2002, Chancellor-candidate Stoiber claimed it would be "absurd" to try, maintaining, "I certainly can't reverse the facts" (Graw 2002; "Auch Stoiber" 2002).

Implications

The case of the German Life Partnership Law contributes to the debates on political tolerance, political attitudes and values, and political institutions in a number of ways. The findings presented here enrich the literature on political tolerance because they are one of very few empirical investigations of the relationship between levels of tolerance and actual policy outcomes. The case of the German Life Partnership Law establishes a clear, but limited, connection between attitudes toward political tolerance and policy outcomes. In states where the governing parties were in favor of extending rights to gays and lesbians, implementation laws granted same-sex couples many more rights than in Länder where the governing parties opposed extending rights to a disliked group.

However, the findings here also show several ways in which political institutions are an important intervening variable between political tolerance and policy outcomes. First and foremost, they provided both a lower and an upper bound for the kinds of policies (in)tolerant majorities could pass. Politically tolerant elites could not extend as many rights to gays and lesbians as they would have liked because of Article 6 of the Basic Law. In contrast, those who would have preferred to grant gays and lesbians no right to legally sanctioned partnerships were forced to comply with the federal partnership law, which had in part been inspired by EU decisions. Furthermore, Germany's multiparty parliamentary system meant that a politically tolerant but very small party was able to exert great influence over the political agenda and larger, less tolerant parties.

The findings presented here suggest that today's political and legal institutions may limit the influence of post-communist elites' political intolerance on their contemporary actions in office elsewhere in eastern Europe. Of course, as mentioned in chapter 1, Germany is a special case among eastern European countries in that it received a constitution containing individual rights and an established judiciary to enforce them, in addition to massive financial and personnel support from western Germany. Nonetheless, there were other variables at work in the German case that may also limit the effects of elite political intolerance in eastern Europe.

New eastern European democracies are also multiparty parliamentary systems like Germany. It seems likely that politicians there will face the same incentives to attract diverse constituencies as parties in Germany did. Even if the average citizen is politically intolerant, there will be politically tolerant voters that some small parties will have an incentive to attract. Further, power is likely to reside in coalition governments; in Germany this resulted in a politically tolerant but very small party being able to exert great influence over the political agenda and larger, less tolerant parties. This outcome is clearly possible in other multiparty parliamentary systems as well.

Of course, it could also be the case that a small, highly *intolerant* political party may gain inordinate political leverage through these institutions. Another institutional variable observed in the German case, however, reduces the likelihood that such a party could translate its wishes into public policy. The European Union's call for recognizing same-sex partnerships exerted a strong influence on the creation of Germany's federal Life Partnership Law. Today eastern European elites are also subject to constitutional constraints ensuring individual rights. More importantly, however, the new EU members and prospective members are closely scrutinized by Brussels and other external monitoring organizations for compliance with EU accession criteria and human rights violations. These external constraints are likely to exert a significant brake on intolerant elites in the region.

Thus examining the actual influence of elite political (in)tolerance on public policy offers a more optimistic prognosis for democratization in post-communist eastern Europe than does the simple study of individual attitudes. Multiparty parliamentary institutions and external institutional constraints—particularly EU accession criteria—are likely to limit the policy influence of politically intolerant actors in post-communist countries. A recent Amnesty International report found that during the 1990s legislatures had revoked repressive laws against homosexuality and put new more tolerant legal protections into place in Bulgaria, Estonia, Latvia, Moldavia, Poland, Romania, Russia, and the Ukraine—despite widespread mass intolerance of homosexuals in the region (Motte-Sherman and Zyber 2002). The above hypothesis can also be tested in other eastern European cases involving areas where EU entry criteria require democratic rights to be extended to other disliked groups. Additionally, whether the laws passed in eastern Europe will actually be enforced, and what the relationship between (in)tolerant attitudes and policy implementation is, are questions that lie beyond the scope of this study, but certainly merit further scholarly attention.

The eastern German example also indicates that—just as in established democracies—post-communist political elites express a wide range of political tolerance. Some MdL saw no reason to extend rights to a small, disliked minority, whereas others vigorously defended the need for such rights in a democracy. In Germany's multiparty system some parties favored politically tolerant implementation laws to win over pro–gay and lesbian constituents, whereas others sought to attract intolerant constituents. Thus policy outcomes were not determined by whether eastern or western MdL were making decisions but by the partisanship of state governments. Parliamentary transcripts reveal that debates held in the eastern and western Landtage broke down on similar partisan lines, lines parallel to those at the national level.

United Germany's political institutions therefore have not only led eastern MdL to overcome their aversion to affiliating with, or voting with, a political party, they have also helped override the higher levels of political intolerance that easterners brought with them to state parliaments. The case of the Life Partnership Law—just as the case of direct democracy—shows easterners' increased involvement with political parties and their dependence on the latter for reelection have led them not only to toe a party line when voting in the legislature, but also to adopt substantive policies favored by their party at the national level and in western states. The next chapter turns to the broader implications of these findings.

chapter 6

How and Why the Party State Matters

This book began by summarizing the conventional wisdom on the differences between eastern and western German mass and elite political attitudes and values. While westerners have become less trusting of political parties in recent decades, easterners today are far more skeptical of political parties than their western counterparts are. This antiparty sentiment extends to the notions of both party discipline and representative democracy—easterners are less supportive of these practices than are their western counterparts. Instead, easterners more strongly support nonpartisan decision making and direct democracy. Eastern Germans are also more in favor than westerners of government intervention in the economy to ensure equality of socioeconomic outcomes among citizens. When asked whether they would be willing to extend democratic rights to disliked groups, easterners are less willing to do so than their western counterparts.

Given these oft-observed differences in Germans' political attitudes and values, this book has raised the question of whether or not they translated into differing elite political behavior and policy choices across Germany in the decade following unification. Chapter 2 asked whether eastern German state legislators' skepticism of political parties led them to shy away from party affiliation, inner-party office, other partisan elected office, and party-affiliated interest group membership. Chapter 3 investigated whether eastern parliamentarians' support for nonpartisan decision making caused them to resist party-line legislative voting. Chapter 4 probed whether eastern political elites' support for direct democracy and economic equality motivated them to write more referendum-friendly state constitutions than westerners and to more strongly support citizen initiatives, including those designed to increase government involvement in the economy or promote direct democracy. Chapter 5 explored whether eastern German state legislators' political intolerance caused them to limit the rights of a disliked societal group.

In all cases, the answer to these questions was no. Even as early as 1990 state legislators ran for office on party tickets and joined parliamentary party groups after being elected. As the 1990s progressed, eastern MdL increasingly assumed leadership positions within their party organizations, held other partisan political offices, and joined interest groups affiliated with their political parties—despite their initial distrust of political parties. Similarly, despite their original resistance to party discipline, eastern parliamentarians became even more disciplined than their western counterparts over the course of the decade. Because legislators voted along party lines, state-level public policy was determined by the governing party or coalition. As a result, policy choices throughout the decade could be predicted by the partisanship of the legislative majority; the same party families adopted similar stances across both eastern and western Germany—even in areas where easterners had quite different attitudes and values than their western counterparts.

For example, while all eastern state constitutions, in contrast to some western states', did include provisions for direct democracy, and while some requirements for obtaining a referendum were more citizen-friendly than in western states, the overall shape of constitutional debates regarding direct democracy in the eastern Länder fell along partisan lines parallel to those at the national level. Similarly, just as in western states, eastern opposition parties have embraced direct democracy initiatives aimed at achieving greater direct democracy and social equality, whereas parties in government have preferred to keep decision making in their own hands, despite their members' attitudinal support for both direct democracy and social equality. Finally, even in the area of political tolerance—extending rights to a disliked group—the partisanship of the legislative majority, rather than the east/west origin of state legislators, best predicts the degree to which German Länder extended controversial rights to gays and lesbians.

After a decade working in united Germany's parliamentary and electoral systems, then, there is very little that distinguishes eastern and western MdL and their actions in office. These results clearly support the view that political institutions shape legislators' political behavior more strongly than do their attitudes and values. The remainder of the conclusion will focus first on *how* the party state has influenced the individuals who work within it and, second, on *why* this matters both for German politics and for the discipline of political science.

THE MECHANISMS OF THE PARTY STATE

Eastern parliamentarians' political attitudes and values have been overridden by five main mechanisms embodied in Germany's parliamentary and electoral institutions. These include selection bias, career incentives for office-seeking politicians, competitive elections, a high degree of efficiency, and federalism. In this section, I elaborate upon each of these in turn.

Voting in the March 1990 East German elections, citizens showed an overwhelming preference for western German parties and their eastern branches rather than for the nonpartisan citizens groups which had brought down the SED regime. This preference held in the first Landtag elections during the fall of that year and continues to this day. The results of the 1990 elections made clear that office-seeking individuals not affiliated with a political party stand little chance of election in Germany. As a result, if an individual wishes to become an MdL, or if an incumbent MdL desires to retain her seat, she must run under a party banner rather than as nonpartisan independent.

At the heart of the German party state's ability to influence the MdL within it, lies the fact that parties serve as the selectorate in this political system. That is, parties—rather than, for example, voters in a primary—enjoy the power to choose candidates for direct mandates and to decide who is to be placed where on their electoral lists. As a result, parties have the power to make or break political careers in Germany. For office-seeking individuals, this fact must take precedence over acting on their attitudes and values, should the two collide. For starters, individuals aspiring to state-level political office in 1990 needed to overcome any suspicion they had about political parties and at least run using a party label. Those whose opposition to political parties was so strong that they did not affiliate with the Alliance 90, CDU, FDP, SPD, or PDS did not get elected in 1990. As the Landtage have become more partisan over time, the fact that a career as an MdL is a career as a party politician has become even more apparent to people considering entering state politics. Thus one of the mechanisms through which the party state exerts its influence is selection bias. Individuals whose suspicion of political parties was so strong that they did not run on a party ticket were excluded from the Landtage from the start, and they continue to be shut out. The number of people active in the nonpartisan East German citizen movements who withdrew from political life after German unification make this selection bias apparent.

Once elected to the Landtage, eastern MdL need to remain in the good graces of their party if they are to be reelected, again requiring them to put aside any suspicions they may have vis-à-vis political parties. Career incentives, therefore, are a second mechanism through which the party state overrides elites' skepticism of partisan politics.[1] Just as western legislators had before them, these ambitious individuals realized that, as explained in chapter 2, holding inner-party office, other partisan elected offices, and positions in party-affiliated interest groups are means that help them obtain a coveted slot on the party list or the party's nomination for a direct mandate. In addition, as outlined in chapter 3, they have come to understand that bucking their parliamentary party group on the floor of parliament is no way to obtain the party support needed to continue their careers, even if it means going against their preference for nonpartisan consensus.

The assumption of office-seeking individuals, common in rational choice literature, seems safe to make in the case of eastern German MdL. First, the legislators considered in this book have already shown office-seeking tendencies as they stood for election at least once. Second, however, the poor economic climate in eastern Germany means that there are limited job opportunities outside of the Landtag for many MdL, especially positions with salaries and benefits comparable to the ones offered by the state legislature. Unlike their western counterparts, many of whom are tenured civil servants guaranteed a position should they lose their public office, few eastern Germans have civil service backgrounds. Further, many of those first elected in 1990 have never been employed in a capitalist economy outside of their Landtag mandate and would have difficulties reentering the workforce.

These first two mechanisms are self-reinforcing. Because only individuals with partisan proclivities were elected to the eastern Landtage in the first place, and only those who followed the incentives for greater partisan involvement were reelected, the eastern state legislatures became filled with the beneficiaries of the party state. Veteran MdL now hold positions of leadership within their parties, hold or have held other partisan elected offices, and are tied to interest organizations affiliated with their political parties. They have earned the trust of their colleagues by voting with their parliamentary party group in Landtag plenary sessions as well as in committee meetings. Because they hold these prerequisites for direct mandates and safe positions on their parties' lists, and because they desire to remain in office, incumbent MdL have little incentive to change the way in which candidates are selected in their states. For example, whereas changing state electoral law to allow voters to select candidates in open primaries would be consistent with easterners' preference for nonpartisan citizen involvement in politics, it might lessen the chances of incumbent MdL being reselected. Thus, over the first decade in office, eastern German political elites have not significantly changed the institutions of the party state.

Similarly, western MdL have preserved the institutions of the party state even as mass attitudes in the western Länder have become more like easterners' in terms of distrust of political parties and party discipline. Thus the party state is an institutional equilibrium in both parts of Germany, unlikely to change even as German society does.

However, despite the career incentives embodied in Germany's political institutions, individuals do not have to be office-seeking themselves for the party state to have an effect. Routine, competitive elections are another mechanism through which the party state exerts its logic. Those individuals who manage to get elected to the Landtage but who refuse to toe their party's line on the floor of the parliament, who resist greater partisan involvement, or who decide that partisan politics are not for them, are unlikely to be selected by their party's direct mandate nomination or an auspicious spot on the party's electoral list.[2] Interviews with an eastern and a western deputy who had decided to leave their parliamentary party groups and become independents (fraktionslose MdL), showed they were aware they had committed political suicide and would not be returned to their Landtage after the subsequent election. Thus elections serve not only as a carrot for office-seeking politicians to become partisan politicians, but also as a stick to remove those who fail to comply with the logic of the party state.

Competitive elections additionally reinforced to eastern Fraktionen the importance of having a distinctive partisan record as either government or opposition. While members of parliamentary party groups may have preferred cross-party consensus to partisan politics, electoral losses for some parties in the early 1990s convinced them of the need for a clear-cut profile to attract voters. Voting en bloc in the Landtag, taking a unique policy position vis-à-vis other parties, and (when relevant) using their majority in the legislature to claim credit for passing laws favorable to their constituents or defending the interests of those ignored by the majority, were strategies that all eastern party groups ultimately adopted, just as western MdL had. Finally, despite the high average level of mass political intolerance in the new Länder, some parties sought to attract the small politically tolerant segment of the eastern German electorate, just as the Greens in western Germany had.

Competitive elections also shaped the willingness of majority and opposition parliamentary party groups to support referenda. Majority Fraktionen enjoy a monopoly over political decision making in their Landtag. Deputies in these parliamentary party groups, able to make choices they believed would be attractive to their constituents, had little incentive to give up this power to citizens in the form of referenda. Thus, despite their initial preference for direct democracy, MdL in governing caucuses kept decision making in their own hands whenever possible. Only deputies in opposition Fraktionen found acting on their preference for direct democracy to also improve their chances of increasing their vote share. Support for popular citizen initiatives denied by majority parties attracted disgruntled voters and, if successful, allowed the opposition a rare chance to influence policy.

The party state's efficiency is a fourth mechanism through which it has established itself in the new Länder. For example, voting along party lines makes parliamentary decision making far easier than would cobbling together new majorities for every vote taken. MdL elected in 1990 quickly experienced the inefficiency of low party discipline as they sat on the floor of parliament late into the night, rehashing issues which had previously been agreed upon. Party voting also helps prevent cycling executives in Germany's parliamentary system. These efficiency incentives have been in place in parliaments from nineteenth-century England to post-communist central Europe and have led to disciplined voting across time and space.

Party organizations can be used not only to simplify individual deputies' voting decisions, but, in a federal system like Germany's, to help parliamentary party groups as a whole develop stances on a given political issue. Tasks such as drafting state constitutions and Life Partnership Implementation Laws confronted all of the political parties in all of the German Länder. Rather than starting from scratch in each Land on each issue, branches of the various parties coordinated across state lines. German parties enjoy considerable financial resources, including generous public funding, which in turn allows them to fund research assistants and research organizations, such as the CDU-backed Konrad Adenauer Stiftung or the SPD's Friedrich Ebert Stiftung, to help them develop public policies. Furthermore, those parties that hold relevant executive branch positions can draw on the expertise of the civil service to draft policy as well. Initially, this meant that eastern parliamentary party groups drew on proposals prepared using the expertise of their western counterparts, as happened in the drafting of the new states' constitutions. A decade later, however, eastern states were just as likely to serve as models for the west, as happened when the SPD in Sachsen-Anhalt drafted a model Life Partnership Implementation Law ultimately adopted throughout Germany in SPD/Green Länder.

This partisan cooperation across state lines provides MdL with ready-made expertise and positions to adopt on the wide range of issues with which they are routinely confronted. This type of cooperation was common in the party state prior to unification, and it is not surprising that busy MdL in the east have taken advantage of this efficient system. Parliamentary debates spanning the decade reveal not only similar policy proposals, but also similar language and examples used by speakers from the same parties from Land to Land. Because they are dependent on their parties to select them for the next election's ballot, MdL have strong incentives to draw on their own party's models rather than those of opposing parties. As a result, eastern MdL from different political parties promote widely different policies, although these deputies may have political values more in common with each other than with western members of their own party.

The fifth and final mechanism through which Germany's political systems shaped MdL's actions was federalism. The Länder's subordinate place in Germany's political system prevented legislators from consistently acting on their attitudes and values and instead constrained the options open to them. For example, while easterners preferred a high level of state involvement in the economy to achieve economic equality, Germany's system of fiscal federalism gave the Länder limited resources to spend and circumscribed their control over Germany's overall economic policy. As a result, even MdL in majority Fraktion were not always able to act on their socialist economic values. Similarly, the Landtage's subordinate position in the German federal system meant that politically intolerant actors were forced to extend at least some rights to a disliked group while highly politically tolerant MdL were unable to extend as many rights as they would have liked.

Thus, while western Germany sent extensive financial and personnel resources to the eastern Länder, and while these factors helped speed the adoption of the party state, they were not the cause of its adoption. The starkest testament to this fact is that the PDS, a solely eastern party with no western branch to advise it, behaves in the same way as the CDU, FDP, Greens, and SPD. Instead the formal institutions of the party state—including the Fraktionenparlament, the dual electoral system, and Germany's federal system—brought selection bias, career incentives, competitive elections, a high degree of efficiency, and federalism to the new states, which combined to limit the ability of individual MdL to act on their political attitudes and values.

Why the Party State Matters

Clearly, a great change has occurred among state-level political elites in eastern Germany over the course of the past decade. Outsiders to politics, with little partisan political experience let alone experience in democratizing, administering, and marketizing an entire state, quickly became consummate party politicians. They mastered parliamentary procedure, built up legislative parties and, to a degree, parties outside of the legislature, drafted constitutions, and passed legislation equivalent to that which was developed over four decades in western Germany. All of this was done extremely quickly, against the backdrop of rapid economic and social change, not only for the populace as a whole but for legislators personally. Today eastern state parliamentarians are difficult to distinguish from their western counterparts in terms of their qualifications for, and actions in, parliament. On the surface, then, the transfer of the Federal Republic's parliamentary and electoral system to the eastern Länder seems to be an unmitigated success.

In terms of the consolidation of democracy in eastern Germany, however, parliamentarians' success at adopting the western model may be quite problematic. Eastern MdL overcame their skepticism of political parties, party discipline, representative democracy, and political tolerance as a result of institutional incentives that touched them personally. Becoming disciplined party politicians has secured them well-paid jobs with good benefits and simplified their work days. While they may be uncomfortable with social inequality or rights for disliked groups, political elites have also had their hands tied by actual budget constraints and federal/EU laws requiring particular rights for such a group. The mass public has not shared these experiences, however, as they are much further removed from the shaping effect of the Federal Republic's parliamentary, electoral, fiscal, and legal institutions.

As a result, the gap between eastern German elite behavior and mass attitudes has grown rather than shrunk in the decade since unification. While eastern parliamentarians have mastered the rules of Germany's party state and play by them ever more skillfully, the mass public continues to be skeptical of such actions. As eastern elites grew closer and closer to their political parties, eastern German citizens continued to have less confidence than westerners that these parties could solve what they perceived to be the pressing problems of the day (Rattinger 2000).

As eastern MdL cultivated ties to interest groups, eastern citizens— in contrast to westerners—felt *less* represented by union, environmental, and economic groups as the decade wore on (Thaidigsmann 2000, 248–49). While majority Fraktionen turned down requests made by citizen initiatives, including calls for greater direct democracy, eastern German citizens felt constrained in their ability to shape their own affairs. When asked whether they believed citizens have an influence over what goes on, 58% of easterners disagreed and reported feeling powerless (Noelle-Neumann and Köcher 2002, 696).

While incumbent eastern parliamentarians learned the realities of budget constraints and worked against citizen initiatives seeking greater economic equality, the percentage of the eastern public viewing the Federal Republic as a just society plummeted from 21.6% in 1994 to 6.9% in 1998 (Kunz 2000, 525). Support for Germany's economic system plunged from 77% in 1990 to only 21% in 2001 (Noelle-Neumann

and Köcher 2002, 627). Vocal opposition Fraktionen's support for populist initiatives likely contributed to citizens' feelings that the state could
and should do more to smooth capitalism's harsher edges.

In short, as eastern German political elites have adapted to the new
institutions, their constituents have remained, or even grown more,
alienated from these institutions. This alienation is reflected in eastern
Germans' overall assessment of their political system. When asked in
public opinion surveys whether they are satisfied with the form of democracy used in the Federal Republic—as distinct from support for the
abstract notion of democracy—eastern Germans tend to be very supportive of democracy in theory but far less satisfied with the Federal Republic's actual form of democracy. This gap is much larger than in
western Germany, and it did not diminish in the 1990s (Gabriel 2000).
However, as western public opinion has become less supportive of partisan politics and as western MdL have clung to the party state, support
for Germany's political institutions has fallen in the west as well. One
study found that 81% of western Germans and only 41% of eastern citizens agreed in 1990 that German political institutions were the best
possible form of government. By 2001 these figures had dropped to
75% in the west and only 32% in the east (Noelle-Neumann and Köcher
2002, 595).

The evidence presented here cannot establish a causal link between
MdL's political behavior and mass dissatisfaction with united Germany's
political system. Indeed, it is most likely that eastern German citizens'
opinions of their political system have multifaceted roots, many of which
may be economic in nature. Nonetheless, it also does not take much
imagination to see that eastern elites' convergence on the unpopular
western model has likely damaged eastern citizens' assessments of the
quality of their new democracy. Thus even in this successful case of institutional transfer at the elite level, the imposed democratic political
institutions have had a limited effect on the consolidation of democracy
at the mass level.

The argument that institutions rather than attitudes shape elite political behavior has implications for the academic study of German politics as well as for the consolidation of democracy in the former GDR. In
making the argument that eastern German political elites' initial attitudes and values exert a limited influence on their political behavior
and policy choices today, I provide an important follow-up to the extensive work that has previously been done on eastern and western German

elites' political attitudes and values. The impact of the much-cited gulf between these elites' opinions has been limited due to the institutions of the party state. Thus, as eastern Europeanists would predict, eastern German political elites are today more similar to than they are different from their western counterparts.

Similarly, much research has documented the weakness of eastern German parties in the electorate and the paucity of civil society in the new Länder. While these bottom-up approaches to the study of post-communist eastern Germany have provided scholars with rich empirical detail about party political and civic life among the mass public, this literature has paid much less attention to the effects that these trends have had on elite political decision making. Often, the weakness of parties and civil society outside the legislature are assumed to have an adverse effect on the functioning of democracy, but this relationship has not been extensively investigated. The findings presented here show that parliamentary life, at least, is not greatly impacted by the underdevelopment of public life in the new states. Ambitious politicians do get involved with parties and interest groups, even if the mass public has shied away from these forms of participation. Thus there seems to be an, albeit limited, process of top-down creation of civil society in eastern Germany.[3]

However, the gap between masses' and elites' engagement with parties and interest groups may in turn be fueling the previously observed mass dissatisfaction with political life in the Federal Republic. If most citizens do not join parties or interest groups, they will find it difficult to communicate their preferences to these organizations and, in turn, for parties and interest groups to work to realize these preferences in the realm of public policy. Instead, parties and voluntary associations may promote platforms developed at best by eastern political elites or, in national-level organizations, policies developed by the westerners who dominate these groups. As a result, eastern citizens may feel less than represented by parties and interest associations and decline to participate in them, perpetuating a vicious cycle. Future research is needed to better understand the degree to which elite convergence on the party state has contributed to mass dissatisfaction with democracy in eastern Germany. The continued study of mass political attitudes and values also merits further scholarly attention.

This book also has broader implications for the study of European and comparative politics. As mentioned in chapter 3, the findings here suggest an institutional, rather than attitudinal, motivation for legislators to practice party discipline. Further, as outlined in chapter 5, I contribute to the study of political tolerance by substantiating a limited link between political tolerance and public policy choice and by arguing that political institutions are an important intervening variable. In addition, the staying power of the party state in western Germany and its adoption in eastern Germany suggest that Aldrich's (1995) view of political parties as institutions useful to office-seeking politicians— even in times of grassroots party decline—is correct, at least in parliamentary and electoral systems like Germany's. Chapter 2 showed that because holding party office, other public office, or voluntary group membership is a valuable asset for an aspiring politician in Germany's electoral system, eastern parliamentarians have formed affiliations with these groups even as citizens have stayed away in large numbers. Chapters 3 and 4 found that although eastern and increasingly western German citizens call for greater direct democracy and nonpartisan decision making, the efficiency of party discipline and the advantages to majority Fraktionen of representative democracy exert a strong hold on MdL. Had no ready-made parties existed, another equilibrium may have been reached, but with a functioning party system, the party state's institutional logic was simply too strong for easterners to resist—and for westerners to abandon in the face of societal change.

This study is also one of very few that follow a post-communist parliament over time, rather than simply providing a snapshot at one point in its development. Another example of such a study is Smith and Remington's *The Politics of Institutional Choice* (2001), which follows the Russian Duma from 1989 to 1999. In contrast to the Russian case, which allowed these authors to examine why particular legislative institutions were chosen, MdL in the German case inherited a ready-made form of parliamentarism from the west. This study of the German Landtage therefore offers political scientists a detailed account about the ability of transferred institutions to shape political elites' behavior. In this sense, it is an important empirical treatment of the aftermath of what Douglass North (1990) called "discontinuous institutional change" to governmental structures. By discontinuous institutional change North meant "a radical change in the formal rules, usually as a result of conquest or revolution" (89). He expected that such changes would ultimately induce actors within the changed institutions to conform to the new institutional incentives, regardless of their initial attitudes and values.

The findings here offer nuanced support for North's hypothesis. In the German instance of discontinuous institutional change, formal institutional constraints did shape elites' political behavior, even in a situation where the imposed rules of the game were at odds with elite political attitudes. However, these new rules *were viewed as desirable and feasible to adopt by political actors.* The collapse of the GDR and its economic failure, especially visible when compared to the west's prosperity, initially gave western German political institutions enormous cachet. Further, some western political parties had existed in Weimar era eastern Germany, and all had strong name recognition among eastern voters due to the western German media's penetration into the GDR. These political parties moreover sought to establish eastern branches, and voters showed a preference for these parties. Thus not only were the formal rules of the party state transferred eastward, a functioning party system also accompanied them almost instantaneously.

Had the party system not been transferred so quickly and successfully, easterners may have developed alternatives to parties or had greater incentives to change the institutions being transferred, or these institutions may not have been able to function the way they did in western Germany. Clearly, the transfer of a fully functioning party system from one region to another is a rare—if not unique—event. Perhaps the closest equivalent is the reincorporation of the southern states into the United States following the Civil War. Given the single member district electoral system of the U.S. and the weak level of party discipline in Congress, however, northern and southern branches of the same party often took quite different positions on the issues of the day. Thus even in a quite similar case, institutional transfer was limited in its effects. This observation leads to a somewhat more tempered view than North's of the possibility of successful institutional transfer.

Can Germany's Party State be Transferred Elsewhere?

As a result, there is a need to be cautious about the generalizability of the German case. In an era where the United States is actively intervening to promote democracy abroad, the success of German democratization after World War II and 1989 is often held up as an example of why such attempts at transferring democratic institutions to nondemocracies are desirable. The findings here should make clear that very special—and difficult to recreate—circumstances lay behind the successful post-1989 transfer of the party state to eastern Germany. Although transferred institutions at odds with elite political attitudes and values won out in this case, it occurred in a context where the formal institutions of the party state *and* an established party system were transferred to citizens familiar with these political parties. While formal rules delineating parliamentary institutions and a dual electoral system may easily be copied into any country's constitution, an established party system usually cannot be imported. Further, while the Federal Republic's political institutions overrode elite attitudes and values, they have not done so at the mass level, contributing to a persistent gap between the governing and the governed. Finally, because this is a single-country study, it is not possible for me to determine the role played by uniquely "German" factors—such as national culture or the previous experience of the Weimar-era democracy—in the successful transfer of the party state. The effects of these variables can be teased out in future multicountry studies, a promising avenue for future research.

In short, this book has shown that political institutions can matter for elite political behavior, even institutions that have been imposed from the outside onto a society quite different from the one in which the institutions originated. Institutional mechanisms—including selection bias, career incentives, competitive elections, efficiency, and federalism—can be strong enough that political elites do not act on their political attitudes and values. Nonetheless, the institutions that were transferred in the German case—the party state *and* an established party system—will be difficult to transfer into other settings and even in Germany have had only a limited impact on the mass public. These factors limit the optimistic lessons that can be drawn from the German case and the degree to which it can be used as an example by those favoring imposing democratic political institutions onto nondemocracies elsewhere in the world.

List of Interviews

Interviewees cited in text by Fraktion and state; date of interview is provided for each interviewee.

ALLIANCE 90/GREENS

Brandenburg, Peter Schüler, former Fraktion member, July 5, 2001.
Niedersachsen, Brigitte Pothmer, whip, June 8, 2001.
Sachsen, Karl-Heinz Gerstenberg, former Fraktion head, June 22, 2001.
Schleswig-Holstein, Karl-Martin Hentschel, Fraktion head, May 31, 2001.

CHRISTIAN DEMOCRATIC UNION (CDU)

Brandenburg, Dirk Hohmayer, whip, July 4, 2001.
Mecklenburg-Vorpommern, Rainer Prachtl, former president of the Landtag, June 11, 2001.
Niedersachsen, Uwe Schünemann, whip, June 7, 2001.
Sachsen, Klaus Leroff, whip, June 18, 2001.
Sachsen-Anhalt, Jürgen Scharf, whip, June 24, 2001.
Schleswig-Holstein, Heinz Maurus, whip, May 28, 2001.

GERMAN PEOPLE'S UNION (DVU)

Brandenburg, Liane Hesselbarth, Fraktion head, July 10, 2001.
Brandenburg, Sigmar-Peter Schuldt, whip, July 10, 2001.
Sachsen-Anhalt, Veronika Brandt, whip, June 24, 2001.

Sachsen-Anhalt, Jörg Büchner, Fraktion member, June 24, 2001.
Sachsen-Anhalt, Rudi Czaja, Fraktion member, June 24, 2001.

Free Democrats (FDP)

Brandenburg, Siegfried Lietzmann, former Fraktion head, July 10,
   2001.
Mecklenburg-Vorpommern, Klaus Gollert, former Minister, June 12,
   2001.
Sachsen, Ludwig Martin Rade, former Fraktion head, June 19, 2001.
Schleswig-Holstein, Ekkehard Klug, whip, May 29, 2001.

Independents

Niedersachsen, Christian Schwarzenholz, formerly Green, now PDS,
   June 5, 2001.
Sachsen-Anhalt, Torsten Miksch, formerly DVU, June 26, 2001.

Party of Democratic Socialism (PDS)

Mecklenburg-Vorpommern, Arnold Schoenenburg, whip, June 14,
   2001.
Sachsen, Andre Hahn, whip, June 20, 2001.
Sachsen-Anhalt, Wulf Gallert, whip, June 24, 2001.

Social Democrats (SPD)

Berlin, Eveline Markel, whip, July 3, 2001.
Brandenburg, Wolfgang Klein, whip, July 4, 2001.
Mecklenburg-Vorpommern, Reinhard Dankert, whip, June 13, 2001.
Niedersachsen, Dieter Möhrmann, whip, June 6, 2001.
Sachsen, Barbara Ludwig, whip, June 18, 2001.
Sachsen-Anhalt, Jens Bullerjahn, whip, June 27, 2001.
Sachsen-Anhalt, Jürgen Kriesch, press secretary, June 27, 2001.
Schleswig-Holstein, Holger Astrup, whip, May 30, 2001.

Südschleswigsche Wählerverband (SSW)

Schleswig-Holstein, Lars Harms, Fraktion member, June 1, 2001.
Schleswig-Holstein, Anke Spoorendonk, Fraktion head, June 1, 2001.

Other

Jörg Mayer, Sachsen-Anhalt Ministry of Planning, Agriculture, and Environment, June 27, 2001.
Gunnar Saft, *Sächsische Zeitung*, reporter, June 21, 2001.
Michael Seidel, *Nordkurier Zeitung*, reporter, June 11, 2001.
Bodo Stade, *Kieler Nachrichten*, reporter, May 30, 2001.

How Interest Group Involvement, Party Offices, and Elected Offices were Measured

How Party Leadership Roles / Party Offices were Measured

The following were considered party offices:

- Heading the local or county party organization (*Kreis-, Orts-, or Stadt-vorsitzenderIn*)
- Heading the party at the state level (*Landesvorstand, General-sekretärIn*)
- Playing a role in the party's federal leadership
- Playing another leadership role at these levels, such as secretary, treasurer, or vice president (*StellvertreterIn*)
- Being an officer in youth, women's, gay, senior, etc., group within party (e.g., Junge Union, Frauen Union, etc.)
- Member of a party working group (*Arbeitskreis*) at regional, state, or federal level—for example on education, the environment, employment, etc.
- Playing a full-time administrative role at party headquarters (*Geschäftsführerin*)
- Founding the political party around the time of unification
- Leading a party organization during the GDR era

Simple membership in a party was not considered a leadership position.

How Other Public Office Was Measured

The following were coded as other public offices:

- Any elected office in the Federal Republic below the state level, including but not limited to local mayor (*BürgermeisterIn*), town council (*Gemeinderat*) member, county council (*Kreistag*) member, or, in Berlin, a citizen deputy with representation on local committees (*Bürgerdeputierter*)
- Holding a state-level political office while not a member of the *Landtag* (for example *MinisterIn or MinisterpräsidentIn*)
- Holding any elected office at the national or European level (such as member of the *Bundestag* or European Parliament)
- Holding what are today elected positions during GDR times (most frequent mention was mayor or town council member)
- Having a seat at a Roundtable during the transition period of 1989–90
- Serving as a *Regierungsbevollmächtigter* (member of the interim government charged with setting up the new states in eastern Germany in the first part of 1990).

I did not code serving as a politically appointed bureaucrat (e.g., *StaatssekretärIn*) or as a legislative aide to an elected official (*wissenschaftliche(r) MitarbeiterIn*) in this category, although many easterners did have this type of experience.

How Involvement with Voluntary Associations was Measured

In most states, MdL are legally required to report, "paid or voluntary functions as well as membership in professional, economic, or other interest groups or similar organizations at the state or federal level." Berlin and Mecklenburg-Vorpommern also include sub-state-level organizations, while Brandenburg only requires reporting involvement with meaningful state or federal organizations. Similarly, legislators must report whether they sit on the board of any parastatal organizations. I coded any kind of voluntary group activity, including membership, in this category. GDR-era membership in youth groups or unions was not counted, however, as these organizations were not necessarily voluntary.

Notes

1. Throughout this book I use the terms West and East Germany to refer to the Federal Republic of Germany and the German Democratic Republic prior to 1990. I use the terms western and eastern Germany to refer to the distinct regions of the country following unification.

2. For this reason, comparative literature on post-communist political institutions, such as parliaments, often excludes eastern Germany; for example see Remington (1994) and Olson and Norton (1996). See Welzel (2000) for an example of a contribution to a volume on eastern Europe that actually addresses eastern Germany, but contrasts it with other post-communist settings.

3. This assumption underlies most of the German-language social science literature dealing with unification. Such sources are too numerous to mention here, but are cited throughout the text. One English-language treatment of eastern German parliamentarians that shares these assumptions is Rohrschneider (1999).

4. This excludes the leadership of the communist successor party, the Party of Democratic Socialism (PDS), which only won seats in the new Länder, and whose Bundestag caucus was mainly composed of easterners.

5. Easterners are defined as people who spent their adult years in the GDR. Many of the remaining 4.4%, westerners elected to these legislatures, were born in the east and fled to the west after the division of Germany. City, town, and county officials are also primarily easterners.

6. The Berlin state legislature (the *Abgeordnetenhaus*) held elections in 1991, 1995, 1999, and 2001.

7. The only exception is the western state Baden-Württemberg, where all deputies are directly elected.

8. I refer to homosexuals as a disliked group based on the results of an opinion survey in which German state parliamentarians were asked to identify which groups they themselves disliked. Homosexuals were among the most frequently mentioned disliked groups; see chapter 5 for more details.

Chapter 2. BECOMING PARTY POLITICIANS:
EASTERN GERMAN STATE LEGISLATORS'
TIES TO POLITICAL PARTIES

1. Most scholarly work on eastern European political elites focuses mainly on what they were doing *prior* to the fall of communism or *during* the transition to democracy. Studies have investigated whether political elites held positions of political power before 1989, although there is controversy as to how involvement in the previous regime should be measured (see Kryshtanovskaya and White 1996; Lane and Ross 1997; Rivera 2000; and for the eastern German case, see Lock 1998). Newcomers to politics after 1989 are generally only characterized in terms of what they have *not* done: they were *not* members of the old regime, they were *not* members of the communist party, etc. (see contributions to Higley, Pakulski, and Wesolowski 1998). For notable exceptions, see Frentzel-Zagorska and Wasilewski (2000), whose work focuses on Poland, as well as contributions to Higley and Lengyel (2000) who focus on the early 1990s.

2. Patzelt's (1997) survey of eastern German parliamentarians covers only the first electoral period. In terms of the rest of eastern Europe, Higley and Lengyel (2000) focus on the early 1990s.

3. The only exception here is Baden-Württemberg where all MdL have direct mandates.

4. It is legal for nonpartisan candidates to run together on an electoral list, but such lists have been rare in practice.

5. See chapter 3 for more details.

6. I draw the terms "elite of breakthrough" and "elite of consolidation" from Frentzel-Zagorska and Wasilewski (2000).

7. While there is little state-to-state variance when the average service of legislators is compared across the eastern Länder, there is a close relationship between the number of years MdL have served and their partisan affiliation. In both halves of Germany, Christian and Social Democrats have served the longest, representing their parties' ability to consistently exceed the 5% threshold for state-level representation. The figure for the end of the third term excludes data from eastern Berlin due to the atypically short duration of the third electoral term there (Fall 1999–Summer 2001).

8. These figures are based on the percentages of MdL voluntarily reporting in the 1990 Handbooks having held party office (not simple membership) prior to 1989. Because reporting was voluntary, the actual number may be higher. Thank you to Gerhard Lehmbruch for this observation. See also Lock (1998).

9. While there were no victorious candidates who ran as independents, five MdL elected on the PDS ticket were not members of the party.

10. There is no legal requirement for MdL to report party leadership positions, so the actual number in both sides may be higher. Patzelt's 1997 written survey of state legislators found higher rates in both sides of the country.

11. Quintiles refer to the ranking of a candidate in relation to victorious candidates, not their position on the overall list. Because losing candidates are not required to submit biographical information about themselves to the Handbooks, there is unfortunately no consistent source of data about them available. Data excludes Berlin because its electoral system does not use state-level lists. There were no significant differences across western quintiles; approximately four-fifths of all legislators in each quintile held party office.

12. Difference of means between the top and bottom quintiles significant at t.05 level, one-tailed test.

13. Parliamentarians' level of experience with outside offices does not vary as radically across eastern states as does the percentage of legislators who are party leaders. Of those holding or having held other elected offices, 86% of legislators in Thüringen, 74% of Mecklenburgers, 71% of Brandenburgers, 67% of Sachsen legislators, 62% of eastern Berliners, and 61% of the MdL in Sachsen-Anhalt also held leadership positions in their parties.

14. Many critics of the DVU also argue that Frey makes a special effort to select political novices to run on his party ticket so that he may better dictate to them what to do when they are in office.

15. This difference of means significant at the t.025 level, two-tailed test (p = .0022). Even when DVU-list candidates—none of whom has ever held another public office—are removed, the differences remain (p = .0648). Similarly, candidates on western electoral lists are significantly less likely than western direct mandate candidates to have held an additional elected office (p = .027).

16. In this case, p = .0136. Western means were 64.8% and 57.5% respectively.

17. The vast financial resources that West Germany had to offer certainly also played a role in easterners' quick acceptance of western parties. Many voters likely initially chose these parties, rather than groups of eastern intellectuals, in the hope of uniting with western Germany and obtaining access to the deutsche mark.

18. Given that they were in a subordinate position in a federal system, they also could not change national-level institutions.

19. Patzelt and Schirmer (1996, 21) make a similar argument when comparing the speed of eastern deputies' adaptation to their new roles in the Landtage in comparison to the Bundestag. Because the latter's membership was mainly western Germans, eastern members of the Bundestag more rapidly adapted to their new roles, but the same adaptation process ultimately occurred in the Landtage as well.

20. See chapter 3 for more details on party discipline.

21. These deputies had represented other parties such as the Statt-Partei in local offices.

22. For a further testament to the advantages that partisan affiliations provide western politicians—even those most staunchly opposed to 1950s-style politics—consider the western German Greens. They initially prided themselves on alternative recruitment procedures, such as banning elected office holders from holding party office and imposing strict term limits on office-holding members. The Greens began to abandon these requirements as they continued to win elections (Interview Independent Niedersachsen).

Chapter 3. BECOMING DISCIPLINED:
EASTERN GERMAN STATE LEGISLATORS
AND PARTY DISCIPLINE

A preliminary, shorter version of this chapter appeared as "The Development of Party Discipline in New Parliaments: East German State Legislatures 1990–2000," *The Journal of Legislative Studies* 9, no. 4 (2001): 88–101.

1. For a review of sociological literature on party discipline, see Kam (2001) and Bowler, Farrell, and Katz (1999, 6–7).

2. For a review of the rational choice approach to legislative behavior see Kam (2001) and Bowler, Farrell, and Katz (1999, 9–13).

3. The evidence from elsewhere in eastern Europe shows that, in the early days of post-communist legislatures, parliamentary parties were relatively undisciplined. Where their electoral system included single member districts, many candidates for parliament eschewed a party label and ran as independents who therefore had no parliamentary party to join. Other legislators ran for office as part of ad hoc political groupings or, in response to parliamentary incentives, joined together with other independents to form parliamentary factions; often such groups had neither a cohesive agenda, nor the desire or ability to discipline their members (Remington and Smith 1995; Haspel 1998a, 190; 1998b, 179). Considerable "political tourism" was observed; legislators jumped from party group to party group or joined several caucuses simultaneously (Karasimeonov 1996, 55; Norton and Olson 1996, 235; Reschova and Syllova 1996, 100; Sobyanin 1994). Even candidates who were elected using a party label often had only weak ties to their party organization, or such organization was lacking, making it difficult for caucus leaders to hold their deputies to a party line (Norton and Olson 1996, 235; Remington 1998, 214–15). The weakness of parliamentary factions meant that members were not always obligated to follow a party line or were not usually punished if they defected from it (Remington and Smith 1995, 472–73; Sobyanin 1994, 191). As a result, legislators in the early days of many post-communist parliaments reported little consultation with their parliamentary faction before votes were taken (Agh 1996, 24; Colton 1994, 59) and even the most disciplined caucuses still contained members whose votes "diametrically diverged" from the rest of their faction (Sobyanin 1994, 194).

4. Berlin's parliament is excluded from the analysis here because it is made up of both the eastern and western MdL.

5. For an excellent exception see Smith and Remington (2001).

6. The only other work being done on this topic that I know of is a dissertation project by Susanne Könen at the University of Göttingen.

7. For the case of Brandenburg's caucuses see Sa'adah (1998, 210–12).

8. Baden-Württemberg is the only exception; there all MdL hold direct mandates. However, as is shown below, even these deputies have incentives to be disciplined.

9. See chapter 2 for the incentives for candidates to run on a party ticket.

10. Throughout I define "substantive" as whether or not an item should be added to the parliamentary agenda, which voting rule to use, whether or not to send something to committee, and whether or not to approve a bill, amendment, committee decision, or motion. Nonsubstantive votes would include in what order to discuss agenda items and whether or not to take a break, postpone a discussion, or add additional time to debate an issue.

11. This and subsequent citations to parliamentary transcripts take the following form: The letters correspond to state abbreviations as given in the List of Abbreviations and German Terms at the beginning of the book. The first number refers to the electoral period; for example, in eastern states, 01 refers to the period between the first free elections in 1990 and the second elections in 1994/5, 02 to the period between the second and third free elections, and so on. The second number refers to the legislative session number within the electoral period. The third number, where it appears, refers to the agenda item. For example, SA-01-22-10 refers to Landtag Sachsen-Anhalt's transcript of the plenary session held during the first electoral period, session number 22, agenda item 10. Where the material is available as a PDF document, page numbers have been added following the citation. All translations are my own.

12. All transcripts are available at www.parlamentsspiegel.de. Details about coding and a dataset with results are available from the author upon request.

13. Some candidates running on party labels were not actually party members, however.

14. In some parts of the west, the far right was represented by the Republicans; Schleswig-Holstein's legislature also includes the South-Schleswig Voters Union (SSW), a party representing the Danish minority there.

15. In the third electoral period the newly elected DVU caucus in Sachsen-Anhalt split into two, however.

16. These scores were calculated by taking the absolute value of the number of yeas minus the number of nays and abstentions divided by the total number of yeas, nays, and abstentions. Deputies not voting were excluded from the analysis because it was not always possible to determine whether they were willfully missing a vote, attending a simultaneously held committee meeting, visiting with constituents, ill, or (un)excused for another reason. Abstentions were counted as defections because interviews with whips indicated they are so interpreted.

17. Some of the governing coalitions' losses were not due to active dissent on the part of their members but rather their inability to keep enough members on the floor to win votes. See, for example, SA-01-24-05.

18. Interestingly, however, although eastern MdL claimed to favor consensus decision making, unanimous voting occurred less often in the eastern Landtage in 1991 than in the west. See below for more discussion.

19. This figure excludes the minority government in Sachsen-Anhalt. Because the executive did not enjoy a parliamentary majority, it saw only 56.1% of its laws pass in 1996 but none were rejected; the rest remained in committee.

20. The minority government in Sachsen-Anhalt's committee decisions met only a slightly different fate on the floor of the Landtag there; 97.9% of committee decisions were upheld and 0.8% were defeated. The remaining were returned for further discussion.

21. These figures exclude the minority government in Sachsen-Anhalt which was slightly less successful, passing 88.6% of its motions and 78.9% of its amendments, and seeing 4.5% of its motions rejected and 13.1% of its amendments fail.

22. This figure excludes proposals made by PDS, the party that tolerated a minority government in Sachsen-Anhalt. Its Fraktion proposed four laws (none of which passed), sixty-eight motions (60.3% passed), and thirty-six amendments (47.2% passed).

23. The eastern figure excludes the minority government in Sachsen-Anhalt whose success rate was slightly lower: 71.4% of its laws had been passed by December and all others remained in committee.

24. In the remaining case the majority decided no new law was actually necessary and instead ordered the executive to better enforce existing legislation.

25. The eastern figures do not include the minority government in Sachsen-Anhalt which had a lower success rate than other eastern governments. It was able to pass 75% of its motions and 72.2% of its amendments; 14.3% of the former and 1.1% of the latter failed while the rest remained in committee in December 2000.

26. These figures do not include Sachsen-Anhalt where the toleration PDS Fraktion proposed two laws (none of which emerged from committee before the end of the year), fifty-five motions (58.2% passed), and twelve amendments (41.7% passed).

27. The one exception to this in 1996 and 2000 was Sachsen-Anhalt where, due to the minority government, committees had a greater influence over legislation as votes from an opposition Fraktion are required to pass bills. See for example SA-02-39-03 or SA-02-47-21.

Chapter 4. BECOMING REPRESENTATIVES:
EASTERN GERMAN STATE LEGISLATORS,
DIRECT DEMOCRACY, AND ECONOMIC EQUALITY

1. Later sections of this chapter will discuss the economic components of these ideal types in more detail.

2. For a complete discussion of these negotiations, see Klages and Paulus (1996).

3. This procedure was first used after unification when citizens of Berlin and Brandenburg voted on a merger of their Länder.

4. In addition to the steps toward referendum described here, seven states have the possibility of a nonbinding form of citizen petition. This instrument has different names in different states, but all require that the Landtag discuss the topic of the petition, although the state parliament is not required to take any particular action. The states with this instrument, and their name for it, are as follows: Bürgerantrag (Bremen and Thüringen), Volksinitiative (Berlin, Niedersachsen, Nordrhein-Westfalen, Sachsen-Anhalt), and Volkspetition (Hamburg). These nonbinding procedures are not discussed here.

5. This total only includes citizen-initiated plebiscites and does not count the eight constitutionally mandated referenda held in Bayern and Hessen, where citizens must approve constitutional amendments made by the Landtag. These are excluded because such referenda were not held as a result of citizen pressure.

6. These procedures are termed Bürgerbegehren, or Bürgerentscheide. Direct democracy at the local level in Germany also involves the direct election—or recall—of mayors (*Bürgermeister*) and heads of county government (*Landräte*). The use of these practices parallels the experience of local-level referenda. Direct elections and recalls were initially adopted by two western states (Baden-Württemberg and Bayern), then by the Volkskammer and all five new Länder, and then in the 1990s by the remaining western states (Wollmann 2001).

7. For more on local-level direct democratic procedures in the city states, including Berlin, see Jung (1999, notes 17, 21) and Dressel (2002).

8. The one exception was Bayern; see below.

9. In 2002 the Sachsen Supreme Court ruled that this law was unconstitutional in Sachsen because it conflicted with the constitutional requirement that citizens be able to pass legislation through direct democracy procedures; this finding was in opposition to the position of the Landtag majority, however (Mehr Demokratie e.V. 2003b, 5).

10. Sachsen-Anhalt waives this 25% requirement if the Landtag has placed a counterproposal on the ballot.

11. Such a vote would not, however, be required for subsequent constitutional amendments.

12. Just as at the federal level, however, the FDP was not entirely opposed to the use of referenda. In Mecklenburg-Vorpommern the FDP favored holding a popular vote to approve the new constitution and was able to convince its Christian Democratic coalition partner to go along with this plan (MVP-01-78, 4453, 4457).

13. The CDU Fraktion split its vote on the constitution.

14. The Greens were not represented in Mecklenburg-Vorpommern's Landtag.

15. The SPD also managed to force some other concessions from the Christian Democrats in Sachsen and Sachsen-Anhalt, since the latter governments needed a two-thirds majority to pass constitutions. In Sachsen-Anhalt, the SPD

forced the CDU to overcome its initial opposition to direct democracy to include a multistep procedure for referenda in that state. In Sachsen, the CDU agreed to drop the quorum of eligible voters needed for a Volksentscheid to pass (Klages and Paulus 1996, 252).

16. There is considerable debate within this literature as to the origins of these attitudinal differences. Some scholars have argued that these results occur despite individuals' personal economic situation given their socialization in the GDR (Roller 1994), while others believe that pocketbook assessments condition—at least in part—easterners' support for economic equality (Rohrschneider 1999); still others argue that these differences result primarily from easterners' experiences as an economically disadvantaged group in united Germany (Pollack and Pickel 1998). I remain agnostic in this debate; what is of interest here is whether these differing values have had any impact on eastern MdL's support for citizen initiatives geared toward achieving greater economic equality.

17. Note that this figure excludes the state of Thüringen, which only has a two-step process towards plebiscites (Volksinitiative and Volksbegehren).

18. This figure rises to 80.4% when Volksbegehren in Thüringen are included.

Chapter 5.　Eastern German State Legislators,
Political Tolerance, and Germany's
Same-Sex Partnership Law

1. See Gibson (1998, note 4) for a thorough overview of this literature.

2. For notable exceptions see Gibson (1987; 1989) and Shamir (1991).

3. Gibson (1998), however, does offer some speculations based on indirect evidence.

4. See Sullivan et al. (1993) for a review of this literature.

5. Overall, however, while Rohrschneider concurs that institutional learning should take place—making eastern Berliners more politically tolerant over time—he concludes that "this is a long term process indeed" (1999, 137).

6. These groups represent ethnic Germans who were expelled from their homes when the borders of Germany contracted following World War II. Some western Berlin MdL also named feminists, not pro-choice groups, as a disliked group.

7. The anecdotal evidence available suggests that MdL in both east and west have condemned fascist and extreme right-wing activity in the strongest terms. When the far right German People's Union was elected to the state legislature in Schleswig-Holstein, members of the other parties shunned the DVU deputies at social events such as the Landtag Christmas party, and spent as little time as possible on the floor responding to any comments they made. Later, when the DVU won seats in two eastern state legislatures, Brandenburg and Sachsen-Anhalt, deputies from other parties responded exactly the same way.

8. For the most thorough account of gay life in the GDR, see Lemke (1991).

9. Edmund Stoiber, the governor of Bavaria and CDU/CSU candidate for Federal Chancellor in the 2002 elections, also criticized the law, arguing that providing social security, tax, and health benefits for same-sex partners would add further strain to Germany's already overburdened social market economy ("Ja, wir haben zu wenig Kinder" 2000).

10. Results were obtained by doing a full-text Lexis-Nexus search for the terms "*Homo-Ehe*" and "*Lebenspartnerschaft*." The time period 2000–2002 was chosen because it extends from the time between when the Life Partnership Law was introduced in the Bundestag to when the German supreme court ultimately declared the law constitutional.

11. By 2003, no systematic study had been done as to the most popular alternate departments designated by communities in such states. Anecdotal evidence from news reports mention the *Ordnungsämter* (usually responsible for providing foreigners with residence permits and citizenship) and Departments of Human Resources (*Personalämter*).

12. Some large German cities have status equivalent to counties, meaning that urban couples did not have to travel far from home.

13. The word for certificate (Urkunde) is used for marriages, births, and deaths as well as documenting prizes and awards. The word for certification (Bescheinigung) is also used by German government agencies, but usually to document administrative transactions rather than events of lifetime significance.

14. In two states—Mecklenburg-Vorpommern in the east and Nordrhein-Westfalen in the west—these laws were not passed in time to go into effect August 1, 2001. In the former state interested couples had to wait until October, and in the latter state regional administrations were temporarily responsible. These delays were not due to political foot-dragging as in Christian Democratic states, however, but rather due to the scheduling of state legislative sessions and summer vacation. The SPD/Green government in Nordrhein-Westfalen was quite embarrassed by the delay (Spoerr 2001).

15. The 5:3 court decision to allow the law to go into effect was (correctly) taken by Bayern and Baden-Württemberg as a sign that the court would ultimately approve the constitutionality of the partnership law.

16. Social Democrats and Greens charged that this office is housed in a building erected by the Nazis and used, among other things, to organize deportations of homosexuals to concentration camps—a contention repeated by the press (Wenzel 2002). The Christian Democratic government maintains that the building was not completed until after the war and thus was never used to plan deportations. For these charges and countercharges see the parliamentary debates TH-03-48 and TH-03-49.

17. Although Bayern's law goes the furthest to distance the state from same-sex partnerships, notaries are in practice quite convenient for couples. Notaries are available in every community and have proclaimed themselves willing to register partnerships at any location a couple chooses—even the Olympic

Stadium in Munich. As a result, same-sex partners now actually have more options open to them than do heterosexual couples dependent on the Registry Offices' services (Busch-Janser 2001).

18. The CDU/CSU single-party majority states included Bayern (west) as well as Sachsen and Thüringen (east); the CDU/SPD coalition states included Bremen (west) and Brandenburg (east); the SPD/PDS states included Berlin (east and west) and Mecklenburg-Vorpommern (east). I also read transcripts from the western state of Schleswig-Holstein, governed by the SPD and Greens; it had no eastern counterpart as the Greens were not represented in that part of the country. Furthermore, I personally observed Landtag debates of the law in both Sachsen and Sachsen-Anhalt during the summer of 2001.

19. While no Christian Democrats suggested that Article 6 needed to be changed to allow more rights for homosexual couples, some supporters of same-sex unions went as far as to argue that the Basic Law should be changed. A western Social Democrat claimed, "registered life partnerships are not a problem for our constitution; rather it is a problem with our constitution that people with other sexual orientations have been discriminated against to date" (SH-15-35, 2635). Similarly, an eastern Social Democrat reasoned, "From my perspective, for same-sex couples to become completely equal [to heterosexual couples] . . . marriage must be opened to same-sex life partners. In order to do this, the legal term 'marriage' must be redefined through a change of Article 6 of the Basic Law" (SA-03-46, 3344). See also MVP-03-60, 3917. Despite this rhetoric, no serious campaign was begun to change Article 6, and MdL worked within institutional constraints.

Chapter 6. How and Why the Party State Matters

1. Examining the decision-making patterns of amateur politicians in Germany brings these career incentives into sharp relief. In eastern Berlin's local assemblies, where deputies hold day jobs and receive only minor stipends, disciplined party voting is rare (Davidson-Schmich 2000).

2. The same holds true for the MdL who fail to recognize and act on these incentives for partisan behavior.

3. For another study of eastern Germany that comes to a similar conclusion, see Chessa (2004).

Reference List

Agh, Attila. 1996. Democratic parliamentarism in Hungary: The first parliament (1990–1994) and the entry of the second parliament. *The Journal of Legislative Studies* 2 (1): 16–39.

Aldrich, John. 1995. *Why Parties?* Chicago: University of Chicago Press.

Alle Parteien in Not: Zum Superwahltag fehlen Kandidaten. 1998. *Berliner Morgenpost* 8 August.

Alles Liebe, oder was? 2000. *Der Spiegel*, 17 July (29): 86.

Almond, Gabriel A., and Sidney Verba. 1963. *The Civic Culture*. Princeton, NJ: Princeton University Press.

Archiv/Datenbank Mehr Demokratie e.V. 2003. Personal e-mail from Frank Rehmet. 22 April.

Auch Stoiber setzt auf Ökosteuer und Homo-Ehe. 2002. *Der Spiegel*, 17 January, on-line edition.

Bach, Stanley. 1996. From Soviet to parliament in Ukraine: The Verkhovna Rada during 1992–94. *The Journal of Legislative Studies* 2 (1): 213–30.

Barnum, David G., and John L. Sullivan. 1989. Attitudinal tolerance and political freedom in Britain. *British Journal of Political Science* 19 (1): 136–46.

Baukloh, Anja C., Susanne Lippert, and Steven Pfaff. 2001. Was geschah mit den früheren Oppositionsgruppen der DDR? Transformation und Institutionalisierung politischer Bewegurgen in Ostdeutschland. In *Der Vereinigungsschock: Vergleichende Betrachtungen zehn Jahre danach,* ed. Wolfgang Schluchter and Peter Quint. Weilerswist: Velbrück Wissenschaft.

Benzler, Susanne. 1995. *Deutschland-Ost vor Ort*. Opladen: Leske + Budrich.

Bowler, Shaun, David M. Farrell, and Richard S. Katz. 1999. *Party Discipline and Parliamentary Government*. Columbus: The Ohio State University Press.

Bundesverfassungsgericht. 1993. *1BvR 640/93*. Karlsruhe, Germany.

Bundesverfassungsgericht. 2002. *Leitsätze zum Urteil des Ersten Senats vom 17 Juli 2002; 1 BvF 1/01, 1 BvF 2/01*. Karlsruhe, Germany.

Bürklin, Wilhelm. 1997a. Die Potsdamer Elitenstudie von 1995. In *Eliten in Deutschland*, ed. Wilhelm Bürklin and Hilke Rebenstorf. Opladen: Leske + Budrich.

————. 1997b. Einstellungen und Wertorientierungen ost- und westdeutscher Eliten 1995. In *Politische Orientierungen und Verhaltensweisen im vereinigten Deutschland*, ed. Oscar W. Gabriel. Opladen: Leske + Budrich.

Busch-Janser, Florian. 2001. "Homo-Heirat" auf dem Olympiaturm. *Die Welt*, 6 August, Bayern edition.

Chessa, Cecilia. 2004. State subsidies, institutional diffusion, and transnational civil society. *East European Politics and Societies* 18 (1): 70–109.

Colton, Timothy J. 1994. Professional engagement and role definition among post-Soviet legislators. In *Parliaments in Transition: The New Legislative Politics in the Former USSR and Eastern Europe*, ed. Thomas F. Remington. Boulder, CO: Westview Press.

Conradt, David P. 2001. *The German Polity*. 7th ed. White Plains, NY: Longman.

Cox, Gary. 1987. *The Efficient Secret*. Cambridge: Cambridge University Press.

Crawford, Beverly, and Arend Lijphart. 1995. Explaining political and economic change in post-communist eastern Europe. *Comparative Political Studies* 28 (2): 171–99.

Dalton, Russell. 2000. The decline of party identifications. In *Parties without Partisans: Political Change in Advanced Industrial Democracies*, ed. Russell J. Dalton and Martin P. Wattenberg. New York: Oxford University Press.

Dalton, Russell, and Martin P. Wattenberg. 2000. Unthinkable democracies: Political change in advanced industrial democracies. In *Parties without Partisans: Political Change in Advanced Industrial Democracies*. Edited by Russell J. Dalton and Martin P. Wattenberg. New York: Oxford University Press.

Dalton, Russell, Ian McAllister, and Martin P. Wattenberg. 2000. The consequences of partisan dealignment. In *Parties without Partisans: Political Change in Advanced Industrial Democracies*, ed. Russell J. Dalton and Martin P. Wattenberg. New York: Oxford University Press.

Das Böse aus Bonn. 1996. *Der Spiegel* (1): 30–35.

Davidson-Schmich, Louise K. 2000. Toeing the line: Institutional rules, historical legacies, and party discipline in Berlin. *German Politics and Society* 18 (2): 1–29.

Delhey, Jan. 1999. Inequality and attitudes: Postcommunism, western capitalism, and beyond. Working paper FS 111 99–403, Wissenschaftszentrum Berlin für Sozialforschung, Berlin.

Dressel, Andreas. 2002. Bürgerbegehren und Bürgerentscheid in den Hamburger Bezirken—eine Zwischenbilanz. In *Direkte Democratie: Forschung und Perspektiven*, ed. Theo Schiller and Volker Mittendorf. Wiesbaden: Westdeutscher Verlag.

Farrell, David M., and Paul Webb. 2000. Political parties as campaign organizations. In *Parties without Partisans: Political Change in Advanced Industrial Democracies*, ed. Russell J. Dalton and Martin P. Wattenberg. New York: Oxford University Press.

Finger, Peter. 2002. Registrierte Lebenspartnerschaften—Eine Umfrage bei Standesämtern. *Das Standesamt* 55 (3): 65–67.

Fish, M. Steven. 1995. The advent of multipartism in Russia: 1993–5. *Post-Soviet Affairs* 11 (4): 340–83.

Frentzel-Zagorska, Janina, and Jacek Wasilewski. 2000. *The Second Generation of Democratic Elites in Central and Eastern Europe*. Warsaw: Polish Academy of Sciences.

Fuchs, Dieter. 1997. Welche Demokratie wollen die Deutschen? Einstellungen zur Demokratie im vereinigten Deutschland. In *Politische Orientierungen und Verhaltensweisen im vereinigten Deutschland*, ed. Oscar W. Gabriel. Opladen: Leske + Budrich.

Fuchs, Dieter, E. Roller, and B. Wessels. 1997. Die Akzeptanz der Demokratie des vereinigten Deutschlands. *Aus Politik und Zeitgeschichte* B51: 3–12.

Fuhrer, Armin. 2000. Union und SPD streiten über Familienpolitik. *Die Welt*, 5 August.

Gabriel, Oscar W. 2000. Demokratische Einstellungen in einem Land ohne demokratische Traditionen? Die Unterstützung der Demokratie in den neuen Bundesländern im Ost-West-Vergleich. In *Wirklich ein Volk?*, ed. Jürgen Falter, Oscar W. Gabriel, and Hans Rattinger. Opladen: Leske + Budrich.

Gallagher, Michael, Michael Laver, and Peter Mair. 2001. *Representative Government in Modern Europe*. 3d ed. New York: McGraw Hill.

Geitmann, Roland. 1999. Der Siegeszug der kommunalen Direktdemokratie. In *Mehr direkte Demokratie wagen*, ed. Hermann K. Heußner and Otmar Jung. Munich: Olzog Verlag.

———. 2002. Beschnittene Anwendungsbereiche für Bürgerbegehren und -entscheid. In *Direkte Demokratie: Forschung und Perspektiven*, ed. Theo Schiller and Volker Mittendorf. Wiesbaden: Westdeutscher Verlag.

Gesetz über die Eingetragene Lebenspartnerschaft. 2001. *Bundesgesetzblatt* 1, no. 9 (22 February): 266.

Gesetzgebungs- und Beratungsdienst beim Niedersächsischen Landtag. 1999. Rechtsstellung fraktionsloser Abgeordneter, Document number 891/1377–814. Hannover, Germany. Duplicated.

Gibson, James L. 1987. Homosexuals and the Ku Klux Klan: A contextual analysis of political tolerance. *The Western Political Quarterly* 40:427–48.

———. 1989. The policy consequences of political intolerance: Political repression during the Vietnam war era. *The Journal of Politics* 51 (1): 13–35.

———. 1998. Putting up with fellow Russians: An analysis of political tolerance in the fledgling Russian democracy. *Political Research Quarterly* 51 (1): 37–68.

———. 1999. The long term and short term stability of political intolerance: Implications for Russian democratization. Paper presented at the 95th annual meeting of the American Political Science Association, 2–5 September, Atlanta.

Gibson, James L., and Raymond M. Duch. 1993. Political intolerance in the USSR: The distribution and etiology of mass opinion. *Comparative Political Studies* 26 (3): 286–329.

Gibson, James L., Raymond M. Duch, and Kent L. Tedin. 1992. Democratic values and the transformation of the Soviet Union. *The Journal of Politics* 54 (2): 329–71.

Grabow, Karsten. 2000. *Abschied von der Massenpartei.* Wiesbaden: Deutscher Universitäts-Verlag.

———. 2001a. The re-emergence of the cadre party? Organizational patterns of Christian and Social Democrats in Unified Germany. *Party Politics* 7 (1): 23–43.

———. 2001b. Conversation with author. Potsdam, Germany, June.

Graw, Andreas. 2002. Stoibers Kompromisse. *Die Welt,* 18 January.

Hager, Carol J. 1997. Building democracy in central Europe. Paper presented at the 29th annual conference of the Northeast Political Science Association, 13–15 November, Philadelphia.

———. 2002. Dilemmas of local self-governance: Individualism, participation, and community building in three central European towns. Paper presented at the 98th annual meeting of the American Political Science Association, 29 August–1 September, Boston.

Halter, Hans. 1996. Der Geschmack der Einheit. *Der Spiegel* (45): 64–70.

Hanson, Stephen. 2001. The end of ideology and the decline of Russian political parties. Paper presented at the 59th annual meeting of the Midwest Political Science Association, 19–22 April, Chicago.

Haspel, Moshe. 1998a. Committees in the Russian State Duma: Continuity and change in comparative perspective. *Journal of Legislative Studies* 4 (1): 188–205.

———. 1998b. Should party in parliament be weak or strong? The rules debate in the Russian State Duma. *Journal of Communist Studies and Transition Politics* 14 (1 & 2): 178–200.

Hayes, Bernadette C., and Jo Moran-Ellis. 1995. Party identification and attitudes towards homosexuals in Great Britain. *International Journal of Public Opinion Research* 7 (spring): 23–39.

Hickey, Michael. 2001. The effects of personality types on political tolerance: Evidence from the Russian transition. Paper presented at the 73d annual meeting of the Southern Political Science Association, 7–10 November, Atlanta.

Higley, John, and Gyorgy Lengyel. 2000. *Elites after State Socialism: Theories and Analysis.* Lanham, MD: Rowman & Littlefield.

Higley, John, Jan Pakulski, and Wlodzimierz Wesolowski. 1998. *Postcommunist Elites and Democracy in Eastern Europe.* New York: St. Martin's Press.

Hix, Simon, and Christopher Lord. 1997. *Political Parties in the European Union.* New York: St. Martin's Press.

Hoffmann-Lange, Ursula. 1998. Elite transformation and democratic consolidation in Germany after 1945 and 1989. In *Postcommunist Elites and Democracy in Eastern Europe,* ed. John Higley, Jan Pakulski, and Wlodzimierz Wesolowski. New York: St. Martin's Press.

Hoffmann-Lange, Ursula, Martina Gille, and Winfried Krüger. 1994. Jugend und Politik in Deutschland. In *Politische Kultur in Ost- und Westdeutschland,* ed. Oskar Niedermayer and Klaus von Beyme. Berlin: Akademie Verlag.

Iken, Matthias. 2001. Wer führt beim Walzer? *Die Welt,* 2 August.

Inglehart, Ronald. 1990. *Culture Shift.* Princeton, NJ: Princeton University Press.

Irle, Katja. 2002. Die Homo-Ehe ist Normalität in den Standesämtern. *Frankfurter Rundschau,* 9 April.

Ja, wir haben zu wenig Kinder. 2000. *Die Welt,* 9 August.

Ja zur gleichgeschlechtlichen Gemeinschaft. 2000. *Die Welt,* 7 October.

Jewell, Malcolm E. 1970. Attitudinal determinants of legislative behavior: The utility of role analysis. In *Legislatures in Developmental Perspective,* ed. Allan Kornberg and Lloyd D. Musolf. Durham, NC: Duke University Press.

Jung, Otmar. 1999. Siegeszug direktdemokratischer Institutionen als Ergänzung des repräsentativen Systems? Erfahrung der 90er Jahre. In *Demokratie vor neuen Herausforderungen,* ed. Hans Herbert von Arnim. Berlin: Duncker & Humblot.

Kaltefleiter, Werner. 1976. The recruitment market of the German elite. In *Elite Recruitment in Democratic Nations,* ed. Heinz Eulau and Moshe M. Czudnowski. New York: Sage.

Kam, Christopher. 2001. Institutional and sociological perspectives on backbench dissent and intra-party politics in Westminster parliamentary systems. Paper presented at the 73d annual meeting of the Southern Political Science Association, 7–11 November, Atlanta.

Katz, Richard S., and Peter Mair. 1995. What's different about post-communist party systems? *Party Politics* 1 (1): 5–28.

Karasimeonov, Georgi. 1996. The Legislature in Post-Communist Bulgaria. *The Journal of Legislative Studies* 2 (1): 40–59.

Keine Mehrheit für die Homo-Ehe. 1999. *Berliner Zeitung,* 6 May.

Kirchen wehren sich gegen geplante Homo-Ehe. 2000. *Die Welt,* 6 July.

Kirchheimer, Otto. 1990. The catch-all party. In *The West European Party System,* ed. Peter Mair. New York: Oxford University Press.

Klages, Andreas, and Petra Paulus. 1996. *Direkte Demokratie in Deutschland: Impulse aus der deutschen Einheit.* Marburg: Schüren.

Kolinsky, Eva. 1993. Concepts of party democracy in the east. In *Parties and Party Systems in the New Germany,* ed. Stephen Padgett. Aldershot: Dartmouth.

Koltermann, Ulrike. 2002. Kaum mehr als ein symbolischer Akt. *Stern,* 17 July.

Kopecky, Petr. 1995. Developing party organizations in east-central Europe: What type of party is likely to emerge? *Party Politics* 1 (4): 515–34.

Kryshtanovskaya, Olga, and Stephen White. 1996. From Soviet nomenklatura to Russian elite. *Europe-Asia Studies* 48 (5): 711–34.

Kunz, Volker. 2000. Einstellungen zu Wirtschaft und Gesellschaft in den alten und neuen Bundesländern. In *Wirklich ein Volk?,* ed. Jürgen Falter, Oscar W. Gabriel, and Hans Rattinger. Opladen: Leske + Budrich.

Landtag Mecklenburg-Vorpommern. 2000. *Erste Wahlperiode: Zur Arbeit des Landtages in der 1. Wahlperiode.* Schwerin: Drucksache Balewski GmbH.

Lane, David, and Cameron Ross. 1997. Russian political elites, 1991–5: Recruitment and renewal. *International Politics* 34 (2): 169–92.

Laver, Michael, and Kenneth A. Shepsle. 1999. How political parties emerged from the primeval slime: Party cohesion, party discipline, and the formation of governments. In *Party Discipline and Parliamentary Government*, ed. Shaun Bowler, David M. Farrell, and Richard S. Katz. Columbus: The Ohio State University Press.

Lebenspartnerschaftsergänzungsgesetz. 2001. Bundestags Druksache 14/4545. 8 November.

Leersch, Hans-Jürgen. 2000. Die Ehe im freien Fall. *Die Welt*, 6 July.

Lemke, Jürgen. 1991. *Gay Voices from East Germany*. Bloomington: Indiana University Press.

Linnemann, Rainer. 1994. *Die Parteien in den neuen Bundesländern*. New York: Waxmann Muenster.

Lock, Stefan. 1998. *Ostdeutsche Landtagsabgeordnete: 1990–1994*. Berlin: Verlag für Wissenschaft und Forschung.

Mair, Peter. 1996. *What Is Different about Post-communist Party Systems?* Studies in Public Policy 259. Glasgow: Centre for the Study of Public Policy, University of Strathclyde.

Malova, Darina, and Sana Sivakova. 1996. The national council of the Slovak Republic: Between democratic transition and national state building. *The Journal of Legislative Studies* 2 (1): 108–32.

Matsusaka, John G. 1995. Fiscal effects of the voter initiative: Evidence from the last 30 years. *The Journal of Political Economy* 103 (3): 587–623.

McAdams, A. James. 2001 Judging the Past in Unified Germany. Cambridge: Cambridge University Press.

McClosky, Herbert. 1964. Consensus and ideology in American politics. *American Political Science Review* 58 (2): 361–82.

McClosky, Herbert, and Alida Brill. 1983. *Dimensions of Tolerance: What Americans Believe about Civil Liberties*. New York: Sage.

Mehr Demokratie e.V. 2002. Volksbegehrens-Bericht 2001. January 15. Available at www.mehr-demokratie.de.

———. 2003a. Infocenter für Direkte Demokratie—Direkte Demokratie in den Bundesländern. Available at www.mehr-demokratie.de.

———. 2003b. Volksbegehrens-Bericht 2002. February. Available at www.mehr-demokratie.de.

Minkenberg, Michael. 1993. The Wall after the Wall: On the continuing division of Germany and the remaking of political culture. *Comparative Politics* 26 (1): 53–69.

Mit dem Segen der Länder. 2001. *Focus*, 19 March.

Motte-Sherman, Colin de la, and Kerstin Zyber. 2002. Osteuropa: Trotz neuer Gesetze kein Ende der alten Vorurteile. *ai Journal*, 1 June.

Naßmacher, Hiltrud. 1996. Die Rathausparteien. In *Intermediäre Strukturen in Ostdeutschland*, ed. Oskar Niedermayer. Opladen: Leske + Budrich.

Negrine, R. and S. Papathanassopoulos. 1996. The Americanization of political campaigns: A critique. *Harvard International Journal of Press/Politics* 1 (2): 45–62.

Neumann, Sigmund. 1990. The party of democratic integration. In *The West European Party System*, ed. Peter Mair. New York: Oxford University Press.

Nichts für Wahlen. 2001. *Focus,* 15 January, 13.

Noelle-Neumann, Elisabeth, and Renate Köcher, eds. 2002. *Allensbacher Jahrbuch der Demoskopie, 1998–2002.* Munich: K. G. Sauer.

North, Douglass C. 1990. *Institutions, Institutional Change, and Economic Performance.* New York: Cambridge University Press.

Norton, Philip, and David M. Olson. 1996. Parliaments in adolescence. *The Journal of Legislative Studies* 2 (1): 231–43.

Olivo, Christiane. 1999. The failure of the Greens in eastern Germany: The east-west cleavage in party politics. Paper presented at the 95th annual meeting of the American Political Science Association, 2–5 September, Atlanta.

Olk, Thomas. 1996. Wohlfahrtsverbände im Transformationsprozeß Ostdeutschlands. In *Sozialer Wandel und Akteure in Ostdeutschland*, ed. Raj Kollmorgen, Rolf Reißig, and Johannes Weiß. Opladen: Leske + Budrich.

Olson, David M., and Philip Norton, eds. 1996. *The New Parliaments of Central and Eastern Europe.* London: Frank Cass.

Osterland, Martin. 1994. Coping with democracy: The re-institution of local self-government in eastern Germany. *European Urban and Regional Studies* 1 (1): 5–18.

Padgett, Stephen. 2000. *Organizing Democracy in Eastern Germany.* Cambridge: Cambridge University Press.

Panebianco, Angelo. 1988. *Political Parties: Organization and Power.* Trans. Marc Silver. New York: Cambridge University Press.

Patzelt, Werner J. 1995. *Abgeordnete und Ihr Beruf.* Berlin: Akademie Verlag.

———. 1997. Ostdeutsche Parlamentarier in ihrer ersten Wahlperiode: Wandel und Angleichung. *Historical Social Research* 22 (3/4): 160–80.

———. 1998a. Ein latenter Verfassungskonflikt? *Politische Vierteljahresschrift* 39 (4): 725–57.

———. 1998b. Wider das Gerede vom "Fraktionszwang!" Funktionslogische Zusammenhänge, populäre Vermutungen, und die Sicht der Abgeordneten. *Zeitschrift für Parlamentsfragen* 2:323–47.

Patzelt, Werner J., and Roland Schirmer. 1996. Parlamentarismusgründung in den neuen Bundesländern. *Aus Politik und Zeitgeschichte* B27 (Juni): 20–28.

Paulus, Petra. 1999. Im Osten viel Neues? Direktdemokratische Bilanz der ostdeutschen Verfassungsgebung. In *Mehr direkte Demokratie wagen*, ed. Hermann K. Heußner and Otmar Jung. Munich: Olzog Verlag.

Pollack, Detlef, and Gert Pickel. 1998. Die ostdeutsche Identität—Erbe des DDR-Sozialismus oder Produkt der Wiedervereinigung? Die Einstellung der Ostdeutschen zu sozialer Ungleichheit und Demokratie. *Aus Politik und Zeitgeschichte* B41–42: 9–23.

Rattinger, Hans. 2000. Die Bürger und ihre Parteien. In *Wirklich ein Volk?*, ed. Jürgen Falter, Oscar W. Gabriel, and Hans Rattinger. Opladen: Leske + Budrich.

Rehmet, Frank, Tim Weber, and Dragan Pavlovic. 1999. Bürgerbegehren und Bürgerentscheide in Bayern, Hessen, und Schleswig-Holstein. In *Direkte Demokratie in Theorie und kommunaler Praxis*, ed. Theo Schiller. Frankfurt: Campus Verlag.

Remington, Thomas F. 1994. *Parliaments in Transition: The New Legislative Politics in the Former USSR and Eastern Europe*. Boulder, CO: Westview Press.

———. 1998. Political conflict and institutional design: Paths of party development in Russia. *Journal of Communist Studies and Transition Politics* 14 (1 & 2): 201–23.

Remington, Thomas F, and Steven S. Smith. 1995. The development of parliamentary parties in Russia. *Legislative Studies Quarterly* 20 (4): 457–89.

———. 1996. The early legislative process in the Russian Federal Assembly. *The Journal of Legislative Studies* 2 (1): 161–92.

Reschova, Janica, and Jindriska Syllova. 1996. The legislature of the Czech Republic. *The Journal of Legislative Studies* 2 (1): 82–107.

Rivera, Sharon Werning. 2000. Elites in post-communist Russia: A changing of the guard? *Europe-Asia Studies* 52 (3): 413–32.

Rohrschneider, Robert. 1994. Report from the laboratory: The influence of institutions on political elites' democratic values in Germany. *American Political Science Review* 88 (4): 927–41.

———. 1999. *Learning Democracy: Democratic and Economic Values in United Germany*. New York: Oxford University Press.

Roller, Edeltraud. 1994. Ideological basis of the market economy: Attitudes toward distribution principles and the role of government in western and eastern Germany. *European Sociological Review* 10 (2): 105–17.

———. 1997. Sozialpolitische Orientierungen nach der deutschen Vereinigung. In *Politische Orientierungen und Verhaltensweisen im vereinigten Deutschland*, ed. Oscar W. Gabriel. Opladen: Leske + Budrich.

Rose, Richard. 1995. Mobilizing demobilized voters in post-communist societies. *Party Politics* 1 (4): 549–63.

Rose, Richard, and William Mishler. 1997. Trust, distrust, and skepticism: Popular evaluations of civil and political institutions in post-communist societies. *The Journal of Politics* 59 (2): 418–51.

Rose, Richard, Wolfgang Zapf, Wolfgang Seifert, and Edward Page. 1993. *Germans in Comparative Perspective*. Studies in Public Policy 218. Glasgow: Centre for the Study of Public Policy, University of Strathclyde.

Rueschemeyer, Marilyn. 1998. The Social Democratic Party in eastern Germany: Political participation in the former GDR after unification. In *Participation and Democracy in East and West*, ed. Dietrich Rueschemeyer, Marilyn Rueschemeyer, and Björn Wittrock. Armonk, NY: M. E. Sharpe.

Sa'adah, Anne. 1998. *Germany's Second Chance*. Cambridge, MA: Harvard University Press.

Saalfeld, Thomas. 1997. Professionalization of parliamentary roles in Germany: An aggregate level analysis 1949–94. *The Journal of Legislative Studies* 3 (1): 32–54.

Sächsischer Landtag. 2001. *Volkshandbuch,* 2nd ed. Rheinbreitbach: Neuer Darmstädter Verlag.

Sampels, Guido. 1998. *Bürgerpartizipation in den neuen Länderverfassungen.* Berlin: Berlin Verlag.

Scarrow, Susan E. 2000. Parties without members: Party organization in a changing electoral environment. In *Parties without Partisans: Political Change in Advanced Industrial Democracies,* ed. Russell Dalton and Martin P. Wattenberg. New York: Oxford University Press.

Scherzer, Landolf. 2000. *Der Letzte.* Berlin: Aufbau Verlag.

Schily kritisiert Gesetz zur Homo-Ehe. 2000. *Die Welt,* 4 July.

Schindler, Peter. 1999. *Datenhandbuch zur Geschichte des deutschen Bundestages: 1949–1999.* Baden-Baden: Nomos Verlag.

Schlesinger, Joseph A. 1975. The primary goals of political parties: A clarification of positive theory. *American Political Science Review* 69 (3): 840–49.

Schüttemeyer, Suzanne S. 1994. Hierarchy and efficiency in the Bundestag: The German answer for institutionalizing parliament. In *Parliaments in the Modern World,* ed. G. W. Copeland and Samuel C. Patterson. Ann Arbor: University of Michigan Press.

Shamir, Michael. 1991. Political intolerance among masses and elites in Israel: A reevaluation of the elitist theory of democracy. *The Journal of Politics* 53 (4): 1018–43.

Sjöblom, Gunnar. 1983. Political change and political accountability: A propositional inventory of causes and effects. In *Western European Party Systems,* ed. Hans Daalder and Peter Mair. London: Sage.

Smith, Steven S., and Thomas F. Remington. 2001. *The Politics of Institutional Choice.* Princeton, NJ: Princeton University Press.

Sniderman, Paul M., Joseph F. Fletcher, Peter H. Russell, Philip E. Tetlock, and Brian J. Gaines. 1991. The fallacy of democratic elitism: Elite competition and commitment to civil liberties. *British Journal of Political Science* 21 (3): 349–70.

Sobyanin, Alexander. 1994. Political cleavages among the Russian deputies. In *Parliaments in Transition,* ed. Thomas F. Remington. Boulder, CO: Westview Press.

Sontheimer, Kurt. 1973. *The Government and Politics of West Germany.* New York: Praeger.

SPD: 550 Mitglieder, 400 Kandidaten. 1998. *Berliner Morgenpost,* 4 August.

Spoerr, Kathrin. 2001. In NRW können Homosexuelle erst ab Oktober heiraten. *Die Welt,* 24 July.

Stolz aufs eigene Leben. 1995. *Der Spiegel* (27): 40–52.

Sullivan, John L., James E. Pierson, and George E. Marcus. 1982. *Political Tolerance and American Democracy.* Chicago: University of Chicago Press.

Sullivan, John L., Pat Walsh, Michal Shamir, David G. Barnum, and James L. Gibson. 1993. Why politicians are more tolerant: Selective recruitment and socialization among political elites in Britain, Israel, New Zealand, and the United States. *British Journal of Political Science* 23 (1): 51–76.

Swanson, David, and Paolo Mancini, eds. 1996. *Politics, Media, and Modern Democracy: An International Study of Innovations in Electoral Campaigning and Their Consequences.* Westport, CT: Praeger.

Taagepera, Rein, and Matthew Soberg Shugart. 1989. *Seats and Votes.* New Haven, CT: Yale University Press.

Thaidigsmann, S. Isabell. 2000. Parteien und Verbände als Vertreter von Bürgerinteressen. In *Wirklich ein Volk?*, ed. Jürgen Falter, Oscar W. Gabriel, and Hans Rattinger. Opladen: Leske + Budrich.

Umstrittene Homo-Ehe. 2000. *Der Spiegel,* 31: 16.

Van Biezen, Ingrid. 2002. Patterns of party organization in new democracies: A comparative assessment of southern and east-central Europe. Paper presented at the 98th annual meeting of the American Political Science Association, 29 August–1 September, Boston.

————. 2003. *Political Parties in New Democracies: Party Organization in Southern and East-Central Europe.* New York: Palgrave Macmillan.

von Alemann, Ulrich. 1996. Die Vielfalt der Verbände. *Informationen zur politischen Bildung* 253: 17–21.

von Beyme, Klaus. 1986. The role of deputies in West Germany. In *Parliaments and Parliamentarians in Democratic Politics*, ed. Ezra N. Suleiman. New York: Holmes and Meier.

Wehling, Hans-Georg. 1999. Besonderheiten der Demokratie auf Gemeindeebene. In *Demokratie vor neuen Herausforderungen*, ed. Hans Herbert von Arnim. Berlin: Duncker & Humblot.

Weil, Frederick. 1993. The development of democratic attitudes in eastern and western Germany in a comparative perspective. *Research on Democracy and Society Democratization in Eastern and Western Europe.* Vol. 1 of *Research on Democracy and Society.* Greenwich, CT: JAI Press.

Welsh, Helga A. 1994. Parliamentary elites in times of political transition: The case of eastern Germany. *West European Politics* 19 (3): 507–25.

Welzel, Christian. 2000. East Germany: Elite change and democracy's "instant success." In *Elites after State Socialism*, ed. John Higley and György Lengyel. Lanham, MD: Rowman & Littlefield.

Wenzel, Jens. 2002. Homo-Ehe: Weniger Rechte und doch nicht diskriminiert? *Freies Wort,* 10 April.

Wessels, Bernhard. 1998. Social alliances and coalitions: The organizational underpinnings of democracy in Western Germany. In *Participation and Democracy in East and West*, ed. Dietrich Rueschemeyer, Marilyn Rueschemeyer, and Björn Wittrock. Armonk, NY: M. E. Sharpe.

West, Paul. 1989. America's latest export: Political consultants. *Campaigns and Elections* 10 (1): 15–20.

Wollmann, Hellmut. 1996. Institutionenbildung in Ostdeutschland: Neubau, Umbau, und "schöpferische Zerstörung." In *Politisches System*, ed. Max Kaase, Andreas Eisen, Oscar W. Gabriel, and Hellumt Wollmann. Opladen: Leske + Budrich.

————. 1999. Kommunalpolitik: Mehr (direkte) Demokratie wagen. *Aus Politik und Zeitgeschichte* B24–25: 13–22.

————. 2001. Direkte Demokratie in den ostdeutschen Kommunen—Regelungsschub und Anwendungspraxis. In *Zehn Jahre Verwaltungsaufbau Ost—eine Evaluation,* ed. Hans-Ulrich Derlien. Baden-Baden: Nomos.

————. 2003. Kommunale Referenden in den ostdeutschen Kommunen: Regelung, Anwendungspraxis, Bestimmungsfaktoren. In *Direkte Demokratie—Forschungsstand und Perspektiven,* ed. Theo Schiller and Volker Mittendorf. Opladen: Westdeutscher Verlag.

Wyman, Matthew, Stephen White, Bill Miller, and Paul Heywood. 1995. The place of "party" in post-communist eastern Europe. *Party Politics* 1 (4): 535–48.

Yang, Alan S. 1997. Trends: Attitudes towards homosexuality. *Public Opinion Quarterly* 61 (3): 477–507.

Yoder, Jennifer A. 1999. *From East Germans to Germans? The New Postcommunist Elites.* Durham, NC: Duke University Press.

Index

LOUISE K. DAVIDSON-SCHMICH

is assistant professor of political science at the University of Miami.